W9-BEJ-285

Summary of Contents

Build Your Own Web Server Using Linux and Apache

by Stuart Langridge

and Tony Steidler-Dennison

Build Your Own Web Server Using Linux and Apache

by Stuart Langridge and Tony Steidler-Dennison

Copyright © 2005 SitePoint Pty. Ltd.

Expert Reviewer: Stephen Pierzchala   **Editor**: Georgina Laidlaw
Managing Editor: Simon Mackie   **Index Editor**: Bill Johncocks
Technical Editor: Craig Anderson   **Cover Design**: Jess Mason
Technical Director: Kevin Yank   **Cover Layout**: Alex Walker
Printing History:
   First Edition: December 2005

Notice of Rights

Notice of Liability

Trademark Notice

Published by SitePoint Pty. Ltd.

424 Smith Street Collingwood
VIC Australia 3066.
Web: www.sitepoint.com
Email: business@sitepoint.com

ISBN 0–9572402–2–6
Printed and bound in the United States of America

About the Authors

Stuart Langridge has been a Linux user since 1997, and quite possibly is the only person in the world to have a BSc in Computer Science and Philosophy. He's also one-quarter of the team at LugRadio, the world's premiere Free and Open Source Software radio show. He's a keen advocate of Free Software across the board, for its ethics as much as its functionality, and thinks that you should be, too. When he's not fiddling about with computers, he's an information architect, the author of SitePoint's *DHTML Utopia: Modern Web Design Using JavaScript & DOM*, and drinker of decent beers.

Tony Steidler-Dennison is a Systems Engineer with Rockwell Collins, Inc., designing avionics and cabin data servers for commercial airliners. He's also the host of The Roadhouse Podcast, "the finest blues you've never heard."

About the Expert Reviewer

Stephen Pierzchala is currently the Senior Performance Analyst at Gomez, Inc.,[1] as well as the Chief Performance Evangelist for WebPerformance,[2] and the primary developer for the GrabPERF Performance Monitoring System.[3] He has actively worked with, supported and analyzed data from Internet technologies since 1994. A Canadian by birth (and inclination), he has been living in the United States since 1999. Stephen lives in Marlborough, Massachusetts with his wife, Samantha, and two sons, Cameron and Kinnear.

About The Technical Director

As Technical Director for SitePoint, Kevin Yank oversees all of its technical publications—books, articles, newsletters and blogs. He has written over 50 articles for SitePoint, but is best known for his book, *Build Your Own Database Driven Website Using PHP & MySQL*. Kevin lives in Melbourne, Australia, and enjoys performing improvised comedy theatre and flying light aircraft.

About SitePoint

SitePoint specializes in publishing fun, practical, and easy-to-understand content for Web professionals. Visit http://www.sitepoint.com/ to access our books, newsletters, articles and community forums.

---

[1] http://www.gomez.com/
[2] http://www.webperformance.org/
[3] http://www.grabperf.org/

To Niamh, who is going to know what this one is all about one day

—Stuart

For my girls, whom I seldom see when I'm cloistered away writing, and who have the utmost patience when I'm surly and behind my deadlines

—Tony

Table of Contents

Introduction

More organizations install Linux into their server rooms every day. The reasons for this vary, but those who make the switch to Linux often claim that its reliability, cost, choice, scalability, and the freedom it offers from vendor lock-in, are some of the reasons why they decided to switch. But, whatever your reasons for choosing Linux, as system administrator, you need to know what to do with these new servers.

This book gives you the knowledge you need to build, configure, and maintain servers running the LAMP (Linux, Apache, MySQL, and PHP) open source Web application platform.

In these pages, we'll show you how to build a Linux server, and help you decide which flavour of Linux best suits your situation. You'll learn how to set up Apache to serve Websites, use MySQL to store data, and employ PHP to build Web applications. You'll also discover how to secure your new LAMP server, and how best to access and control it both on site, and remotely.

Everything you'll need to build and maintain your Linux servers, and to deploy Web applications to them, is contained in these chapters. Enjoy!

Who Should Read This Book?

If you know what it's like to be a systems administrator, but don't know about Linux, this book is for you.

If you're currently thinking about introducing Linux to your firm on a trial basis—perhaps to run some Websites, or because your development team keep banging on at you to let them use Apache—this book will give you the grounding you need to successfully build Linux servers and keep them running.

You and your organization can enjoy the stability and ease-of-use of a free operating system and tools that are compliant with open standards. This book will show you how.

What's In This Book?

Chapter 1: *Building The Linux Environment*

We kick off by discussing what Linux is, and seeing how easy it is to set up a Linux server. I'll walk you through a review of the hardware you'll need before we choose which flavour of Linux we'll install. In making this decision, we'll explore the alternatives, and I'll provide a few tips on how to ensure you make the right decision. By the chapter's close, you'll have installed Linux successfully on your server.

Chapter 2: *Day-to-day Usage*

This chapter explains hot to run and manage your Linux server on a daily basis. In particular, we'll discuss the key differences between Linux and Windows systems. You'll finish up with a solid grounding in the essentials, including filesystems and layout.

Chapter 3: *The Command Line*

The command line is one of the most powerful aspects of Linux. While it's easy to use Linux's graphical tools—tools that allow us to achieve most of our goals—the command line gives us an extra level of control over our systems. In this chapter, we'll identify those extra capabilities, and discuss the command line's advantages over the GUI.

Chapter 4: *System Administration*

Linux system administrators must be comfortable with creating new users, and scheduling tasks to run unattended, as well as concepts like services and runlevels. In this chapter, we discuss the lot as we take a tour of the Linux system administrator's toolkit.

Chapter 5: *Building The Server*

It's time to turn our Linux server into a LAMP server as we install Apache, MySQL, and PHP. We'll explore some of the basics of Apache itself, including how it works, and how it fits into the Linux environment. Then, you'll see how to configure Apache on setup, how to set up secure (SSL/https) access for your Websites, and how to add MySQL and PHP to the mix.

Chapter 6: *Server Administration*

This chapter focuses on a selection of handy tools that will help you to configure your LAMP server and add new packages to it. In particular, we discuss Webmin, which facilitates the Web-based configuration of services, and yum, which helps with package installation.

Chapter 7: *Remote Administration*

Remote administration makes the job of the Linux system administrator much easier. In this chapter, we'll get a feel for working with SSH—the secure shell—which allows command line access to a server across the network, and VNC, which enables you to access your LAMP server's GUI remotely. We'll discuss which tools are best used in particular situations, and look at some of the extra functionality that SSH offers above and beyond its primary job as a command-line shell.

Chapter 8: *Occasional Administration*

"Occasional Administration" encompasses those system elements that you'll likely need to set up once, then tweak only occasionally. After an introduction to backup tools, we set up Web traffic reporting, which will help us understand the nature of the visits the server receives. We also take a close look at the log files that the system creates, and discuss how these can be used to track and manage server usage, identify errors, and more.

Chapter 9: *Server Security*

Security is a critical aspect of running any server, but it's particularly important for those that offer services over the Internet. In this chapter, we set up a firewall on our LAMP server, and install intrusion detection services as a means to identify remote cracking attempts. We'll also meet Tripwire, a security system that protects against malicious users compromising the server if they somehow manage to gain access.

Appendix A: *Command Line Reference*

As we step through the process of setting up your server, you'll be introduced to a number of powerful command line tools. This appendix lists the more useful tools, and some of the options that can be used to customize their behavior.

Appendix B: *Troubleshooting*

Our tour concludes with some troubleshooting and an FAQ section that provides answers to common questions about Linux, Apache, and the other tools you may have installed.

Linux and Distributions

If you're being very technical, Linux is just the operating system kernel: the bit at the very lowest level of your software that talks directly to the hardware. All the other programs—the graphical interface, the Apache Web server, MySQL, the menus at the top of the screen—they're all separate, open-source programs, coded by different teams of developers, and released at different times. It's possible to build your own Linux system out of these disparate parts, but it's a long and complicated job. Instead, various groups and companies have taken on the role of providing a Linux **distribution** (sometimes shortened to **distro**): they collect all the bits of software you need, make sure they all fit together correctly, and give them all to you in one go. There are many, many Linux distributions. Some have specialized purposes: the distributor has made sure that the distribution contains software suited to musicians, for example, or medical personnel, or security analysts, or that the distribution is designed to run directly from CD, or from a USB pen drive, or without a graphical interface. Most, though, are general: they're designed to cover all bases.

General-purpose Distributions

Some of the most popular general distributions are Debian, Canonical's Ubuntu Linux, Novell's SuSE Linux Desktop, Knoppix, Linspire, and Red Hat's Enterprise Linux and Fedora Core distributions. Some distributions contain proprietary software, and require a licence fee; others do not. Each has its merits, and each its proponents.

Debian has a very strong free-software ethos, and an excellent packaging system (apt) which has been emulated by most other distributions. Ubuntu Linux is derived from Debian, but places a much stronger focus on being a good desktop distribution. Novell's SuSE Linux has a commercial edge to it, mixing open-source and proprietary tools; Novell is a relatively new player in the Linux sphere, but SuSE Linux has been around for some time. Red Hat Enterprise Linux also has a commercial edge, and comes in flavors tailored to desktops and servers. Development of Red Hat Enterprise Linux is in part driven by the more community spirited Fedora Core. Linspire is heavily focused on home users; like SuSE, it mixes open-source tools with proprietary software, and is oriented towards being a desktop operating system. Knoppix is slightly unusual in that it is not designed to be installed and run; instead, it comes on, and runs entirely from, a so-called "Live CD." You can simply put the CD in and boot up to obtain all the benefits of a working Linux computer without losing or overwriting your existing system or files. It's perfect for testing out hardware, or getting familiar with the Linux environment without taking the ultimate plunge and installing the system from scratch.

Fedora Core

In this book, we'll be focusing on Fedora Core 4, from Red Hat. The Fedora distribution is very current, so you'll have all the latest tools at your disposal, and boasts a very wide portfolio of compatible software. Red Hat employs many notable open-source developers to work on distributions, and Fedora receives the benefits of this work, while still remaining open-source and community-maintained. Using Fedora, you can enjoy those benefits: you'll have the most robust, modern tools at your fingertips, while using the most popular Linux distribution available.

The Book's Website

Located at http://www.sitepoint.com/books/linux1/, the Website that supports this book will give you access to the following facilities.

The Code Archive

One of the more powerful aspects of Linux is the scriptable command line. This book includes some scripts to help you get started with shell scripting, which can be downloaded from the book's web site.

Updates and Errata

The Errata page on the book's Website has the latest information about known typographical and code errors, and updates necessitated by changes to technologies.

The SitePoint Forums

While I've made every attempt to anticipate any questions you may have, and answer them in this book, there is no way that *any* book could cover everything there is to know about establishing, running, and maintaining a Linux server. If you have a question about anything in this book, the best place to go for a quick answer is http://www.sitepoint.com/forums/—SitePoint's vibrant and knowledgeable community.

The SitePoint Newsletters

In addition to books like this one, SitePoint offers free email newsletters.

The SitePoint Tech Times covers the latest news, product releases, trends, tips, and techniques for all technical aspects of Web development. The long-running *SitePoint Tribune* is a biweekly digest of the business and money making aspects of the Web. Whether you're a freelance developer looking for tips to score that dream contract, or a marketing major striving to keep abreast of changes to the major search engines, this is the newsletter for you. *The SitePoint Design View* is a monthly compilation of the best in Web design. From new CSS layout methods to subtle PhotoShop techniques, SitePoint's chief designer shares his years of experience in its pages.

Browse the archives or sign up to any of SitePoint's free newsletters at http://www.sitepoint.com/newsletter/.

Your Feedback

If you can't find your answer through the forums, or you wish to contact me for any other reason, the best place to write is `books@sitepoint.com`. We have a well-manned email support system set up to track your inquiries, and if our support staff is unable to answer your question, they send it straight to me. Suggestions for improvement as well as notices of any mistakes you may find are especially welcome.

Acknowledgements

This book would not have been what it is without the SitePoint team, particularly Stephen, Craig, and Simon. A big round of applause also goes out to Ade, for coping in his typically composed and bald style with the bombardment of questions. Much thanks, bald man.

Inspiration is theirs; mistakes are mine alone.

1

Building The Linux Environment

Installing a Linux distribution can be both exhilarating and frustrating. My first two attempts at Linux installs—the first in 1996, the second in 1997—were unsuccessful. Installation routines and hardware support in Linux at the time were much less advanced than they are today; Red Hat was still at a relatively early stage in its evolution, Mandriva had yet to be created, and SuSE was just coming out from under the shadow of Slackware. After two failures, I simply decided that I wasn't going to be beaten by a Linux distribution. I set my machine up in a dual-boot configuration (including both Linux and Windows partitions) with the commitment to use Windows as little as possible. Within a year, the only reason Windows remained on the machine was my wife's lack of familiarity with Linux. Given that her computing needs were to surf the Web and read email, she, too, eventually made a smooth transition to Linux as the full-time computing platform.

We'll talk about the dual-boot option at length in this chapter. But first, it's important to undertake some preliminary research that will help you solve the issues you might experience during installation, whether you're using a pure Linux system, or a dual-boot configuration.

The Necessary Research

Few things are more frustrating than a lack of hardware support, especially when you've become used to the quick driver installs offered by Windows. In fact, Windows comes complete with a basic set of drivers that are intended to anticipate the hardware attached to your machine. Hardware manufacturers also release driver discs for devices such as video cards, network cards and scanners for Windows machines. Developing these drivers costs the hardware manufacturers a great deal of money, so for a long time it didn't make economic sense for hardware developers to supply drivers for Linux.

As Linux has gained market share within the server market, Linux driver development has improved markedly. Storage devices, RAID arrays, Ethernet cards—all have enjoyed increasing Linux driver development in the past few years.

In order to avoid the headache of missing drivers, it's important to do a little research before installing your Linux distribution. While it's unlikely that you'll have a problem with modern distributions, you'll still want to do the research just to avoid any hardware issues.

Most of the major distributions release **hardware compatibility lists**. These lists itemize the hardware that's known to work with the drivers included in the distributions. Red Hat/Fedora, Mandriva, and SuSE also provide hardware mailing lists for distributions from their Websites. These lists, though, tend to rely on users to help solve hardware compatibility issues after the fact, rather than providing information for users before an installation.

Additionally, there's an excellent compatibility list for Linux in general. It doesn't provide quite the degree of granularity you'll find in the manufacturer-specific lists, so it should be used as a fallback, rather than your primary source of information.

Hardware Compatibility Lists

Red Hat/Fedora

Red Hat's major product line is Red Hat Enterprise Linux (RHEL), which is mostly based on Red Hat's free software distribution, Fedora. Fedora is not actually maintained by Red Hat; it's maintained by the community of Fedora developers. However, Red Hat does a lot of work on Fedora, because that work flows into RHEL.

Red Hat's Hardware Catalog[1] doesn't extend beyond RHEL to the Fedora releases, which is something that you'll need to remember when looking to the Red Hat site for Fedora support. The list provides information on CPUs, video cards, SCSI controllers, IDE controllers, network cards, modems, and sound cards.

SuSE

SuSE offers two lists: the Express Search[2] and Extended Search.[3] The difference between the two is that the Extended Search offers fields beyond Vendor, Device, and Category. In practice, you're likely only to need the Express Search.

Mandriva Linux

The Mandriva Linux Hardware Compatibility Database[4] is a very comprehensive list of hardware that has been tested by the Mandriva Linux community.

General Linux

The Linux Hardware Compatibility HOWTO[5] is perhaps the most comprehensive of the high-level Linux links. It was begun in 1997 and is updated as often as twice annually. It provides information on all device types and all major manufacturers.

Aside from providing interesting and useful user forums, LinuxQuestions.org also provides an outstanding list of Linux-compatible hardware.[6] This is the most up-to-date of the high-level Linux lists, with updates appearing daily where applicable. While it's not as comprehensive as the HOWTO, the LinuxQuestions list is easily as important because of this timeliness.

Linux Compatible[7] provides both updated lists, and forums in which users can help other users resolve existing hardware issues.

---

[1] http://bugzilla.redhat.com/hwcert/
[2] http://hardwaredb.suse.de/searchForm.php?searchtype=simple&LANG=en_UK
[3] http://hardwaredb.suse.de/searchForm.php?searchtype=extended&LANG=en_UK
[4] http://www1.mandrivalinux.com/en/hardware.php3
[5] http://www.ibiblio.org/pub/Linux/docs/HOWTO/other-formats/html_single/Hardware-HOWTO.html
[6] http://www.linuxquestions.org/hcl/
[7] http://www.linuxcompatible.org/

Installing the Distribution

Once you have completed your preliminary hardware research, it's time to walk through the installation process. We'll take a look at both the graphical and text-based installers, the second of which can be useful when you're installing Linux on a machine with limited resources. Don't forget that, if your situation demands it, you can install Fedora Core on your server without a desktop. In any event, it's a good idea to read through the following sections before putting the installation CD into your computer.

The Dual-Boot Option

We've already mentioned the dual-boot option for your server: running both Windows and Linux on the system. As I've mentioned, this provides a great set of "technical training wheels" as you adjust to the new capabilities and options in your Linux server. The following installation instructions will work equally well with a dual-boot configuration. However, there are a few important points to keep in mind when choosing this option.

❑ If you're building your dual-boot server on a fresh box, be sure to install and configure Windows first. By default, Windows doesn't recognize any of the native Linux filesystems.[8] If Linux is installed first, the Windows boot loader will take over and load Windows; Linux will be there, but you won't be able to boot into it. A Linux installation will cooperate with Windows and allow you to boot into both.

❑ Linux provides a means to read the FAT32 (typically used by Windows 98 and ME) or NTFS (usually used by Windows NT, 2000, and XP) filesystems. In the case of FAT32, you'll also be able to write to the Windows partitions. If you're using an NTFS-based Windows installation, the files on the Windows partition will be read-only.

❑ If you're installing Linux on a system that already contains a Windows operating system, it may be useful to purchase a nondestructive partition management tool, such as Partition Magic.[9] This will allow you to move the partitions on your Windows system, creating room on the drive for the Linux installation, and preserving the data that already exists on the drive.

---

[8]There are third-party utilities that allow Windows to read the drives of a Linux installation on the same machine, though; see http://pro.mount-everything.com/ for one commercial example.
[9] http://www.symantec.com/partitionmagic/

With the exception of these important points, the process of installing a dual-boot system is the same as a single OS installation.

Graphical Installation

Some would argue that the real rise of Linux began with the advent of graphical installers. Prior to that time, installation was a "mouseless" affair, using the keyboard arrow keys and space bar. Red Hat—the distribution upon which Fedora is based—was a pioneer in graphical Linux installation routines. Since that time, the creators have continued to refine and improve upon the process, the result being a very clean and easy-to-follow installation procedure. As you'll see in the screen shots I'll present throughout the rest of this chapter, installing Fedora on your new server is nearly painless!

I've provided screen shots for nearly every step of the process. While the procedure is easy, there are a few steps that are particularly important to a successful install-ation. Hopefully, the abundance of screen shots in the following discussion will help you to more easily understand the installation process.

Obtaining Installation CDs

There are two main ways to obtain Fedora Core installation CDs: you can download the CDs from http://fedora.redhat.com/download/ and burn them yourself, or you can buy them.

The installation CDs are downloaded as a series of ISO images, named something like FC4-i386-disc1.iso (FC4 means Fedora Core 4, i386 means it's for Intel x86 processors, and disc1 means that it's the first CD). ISO images are direct copies of an entire CD, stored in a single file. Once you've downloaded the images, you'll need to burn each of them to a CD.[10] Most CD burning programs offer a menu option to burn an ISO image; a list of instructions for the use of various popular Windows CD burning tools[11] is also available online. If in doubt, the help files, or Websites, associated with your CD burning tool are likely to explain how to burn an ISO image onto a CD.[12]

---

[10]Alternatively, if you have a DVD burner, and the machine onto which you plan to install Fedora has a DVD drive, you can download the DVD image (instead of the CD images) and burn it to one DVD in the same way you'd burn a CD.

[11] http://iso.snoekonline.com/iso.htm

[12]If your CD burning program cannot burn ISO images, CDBurnerXP Pro [http://www.cdburnerxp.se/] is simple to use, and runs on all versions of Windows.

Buying Fedora on CD will cost you a little, but it's quicker and easier than downloading the images if you don't have a fast broadband connection (the four CD images total almost 2.5GB). You can buy Fedora Installation CDs from any number of vendors, most of whom will charge you little more than the cost of the blank CDs, plus postage and packing; the easiest way to find these vendors is to search the Web for "cheap Linux CDs" in your country, or ask a local Linux User Group. This may well be the best way to get hold of the CDs if this is your first time running Linux.

The Installation

To begin the installation, put the first installation CD in the CD-ROM drive and reboot the machine. If your machine is configured to boot from the CD-ROM, you'll see the screen shown in Figure 1.1 when the machine starts.

The initial installation offers several options. You can choose to install in graphical mode by hitting **Enter**, or in text mode by typing `linux text` at the `boot:` prompt. Either way, the first thing the installer will do is offer to check the installation media for you. This is a good way to determine if your installation CDs have been tampered with, or have become corrupted. The process will take a little while, but I'd recommend that you do run this test.

Like any operating system, Linux requires a minimal set of hardware drivers during the installation. After testing the installation media, you'll see lots of text scrolling down the screen—this is the initial hardware probing process in action. Red Hat helped pioneer the development of graphical Linux installers with **Anaconda**, Red Hat's installation program. It includes a highly accurate probing and testing mechanism that makes the rest of the installation routine quite painless.

Once all this media testing and hardware probing is done, you'll finally see the Welcome to Fedora Core screen. Click the Next button to get started.

Figure 1.1. The initial Fedora installation screen.

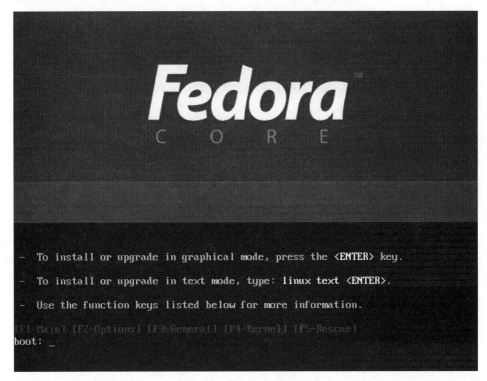

Selecting your Language

Figure 1.2. Choosing an installation language.

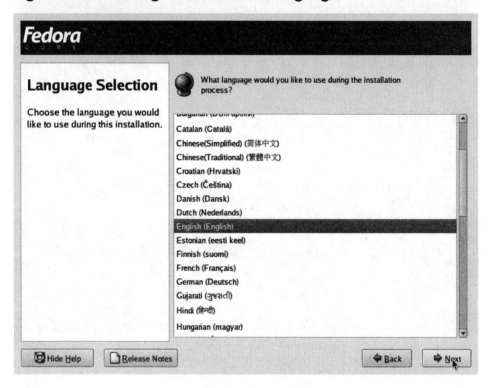

Fedora is truly an international operating system: the installation screens are available in more than 30 languages. Select your native tongue from the Language Selection screen shown in Figure 1.2 and click Next.

Figure 1.3. Choosing a keyboard layout.

The number of keyboard languages available to Fedora is similar to the number of languages available through the installation screens. Select the language of your keyboard from the screen shown in Figure 1.3.

Installation Types

Figure 1.4. Choosing an installation type.

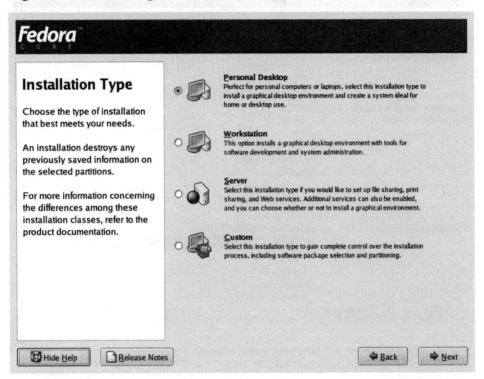

The Fedora installer offers three specialized installation types: Personal Desktop for home or office use, Workstation for development or system administration work, and Server for file, print and Web server use. There's also a Custom option if you'd like to take complete control over the way your system is configured. As we're setting up a Web server, select the Server option from the Installation Type screen shown in Figure 1.4, before clicking Next.

Disk Partitioning

The Fedora installer offers two partitioning methods—automatic and manual—as shown in Figure 1.5.

Figure 1.5. Selecting a partitioning method.

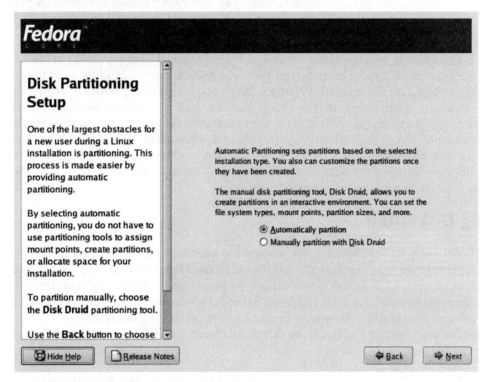

Automatic partitioning creates three partitions:

☐ The /boot partition is the home of the kernel: the program at the very heart of Linux. Fedora recommends a /boot partition of no less than 100MB, though you'll seldom need this much.

☐ The swap partition is used as a fallback for memory when all of the system memory is in use.

☐ The / partition contains everything that isn't on its own partition.

What, no Drive Letters?

Partitions in Linux appear differently than those in Windows. Linux partitions don't use the drive letter designations, such as C:, which you may already be used to. The primary partition on Linux is labeled / (you'll see how this fits into the overall partitioning layout later). Other common partitions on a system include /boot (contains the kernel and boot loader), /home (contains user-specific files), and /var (contains program configuration and variable data). These labels are called **mount points**, and we'll discuss them further in Chapter 4.

It's possible to organize your system so that it's spread over multiple partitions; for example, it's quite common to put /var (where data, including such things as MySQL databases and Websites, live) on a separate partition. However, automatic partitioning makes things simpler, and spreading your data across different partitions doesn't achieve very much. Some administrators strongly recommend it, but the Fedora rescue CD (also downloadable as an ISO image from the Fedora Website) will help you avoid most problems that might have been aided by splitting the data across different partitions in the past. Therefore, the default partitioning setup is usually sufficient.

Using Disk Druid

Fedora also offers **Disk Druid**, a graphical partitioning tool. If you'd prefer a scheme other than the default, you'll need to use Disk Druid during the installation process. Disk Druid presents both graphical and textual representations of the partition table on your machine. To select a partition, click on the graphical drive representation (shown in Figure 1.6), or on the textual representation. In either case, you can add, edit, or delete partitions by clicking on the appropriate tool bar buttons.

If the system onto which you're installing Linux has a previous installation of Windows (or some other operating system), you might want to manually delete the partition that contained Windows. Also, if you don't see any space marked as "Free" in the diagram at the top of the screen, you'll need to delete something to make room for Fedora. To do this, select the partition to delete, and click the Delete button.

Deleting Partitions

Once you delete a partition, there's no way to get back the data that was on it.[13] Delete with care!

---

[13]Well, there's no *easy* way. Advanced recovery tools do exist.

Figure 1.6. The Disk Druid partitioning tool.

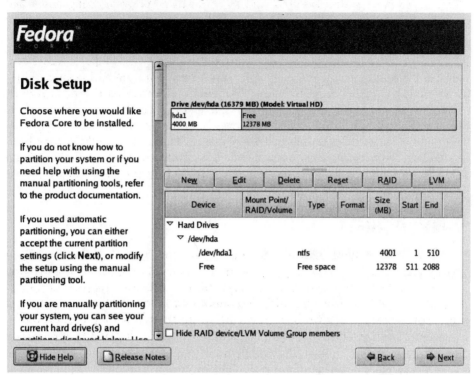

 Tip

Correcting an Accidental Deletion

If you accidentally mark a partition for deletion, or make some other mistake, you can set everything back to its original state by clicking the Reset button. The changes you make to the partitions won't actually take effect until later in the installation procedure.

Figure 1.7. Adding a partition.

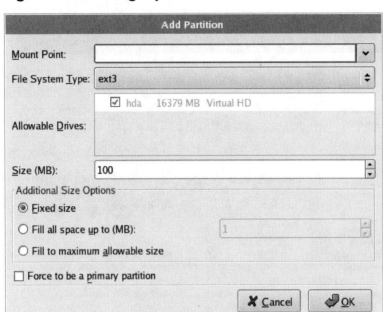

Click the New button to open the Add Partition dialog shown in Figure 1.7. From here, you can designate the mount point, the filesystem type, and the partition's size in megabytes. The window also offers further size options, including the ability to create a partition with all remaining space on the drive.

Selecting the Mount Point drop-down will display all common partition labels (mount points) available for your server, as shown in Figure 1.8; alternatively, you can enter the mount point label manually. Bear in mind that these are the most common mount points, and are familiar to all Linux system administrators. Creating a custom mount point might confuse other administrators of your server.

Once you've created a partition, you can edit it by selecting the partition, then clicking the Edit button, which will give you almost the same options as the Add Partition dialog.

Figure 1.8. Selecting a mount point.

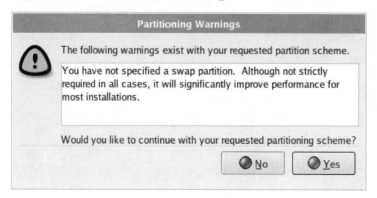

If you try to proceed past the Disk Setup screen without creating a swap partition, you'll receive the warning shown in Figure 1.9. A swap partition in Linux serves much the same purpose as virtual memory in Windows: when the system's memory becomes full, part of the data in memory is written to the swap partition, freeing up that memory space. When the data that was written to the swap partition is needed again, it is read back into memory. To create a swap partition, click the Add button and select swap as the File System Type.

Figure 1.9. The swap warning.

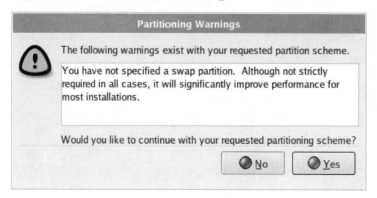

Tip

Swap Space

A good rule of thumb to use when creating swap space on your Linux machine is to create one and a half times the size of the machine's physical memory. For example, if you have 1GB of physical memory, create a 1.5GB swap partition.

The GRUB Boot Loader

If you have decided to go with a dual-boot install, you'll need to set up the GRUB boot loader. GRUB is a program that will let you select from a list of installed operating systems, then makes the computer start up the selected OS. As Figure 1.10 shows, it's pretty easy to set up. Note that you should set a boot loader password to prevent unauthorized users from gaining access to the kernel's startup parameters.

Figure 1.10. Configuring GRUB.

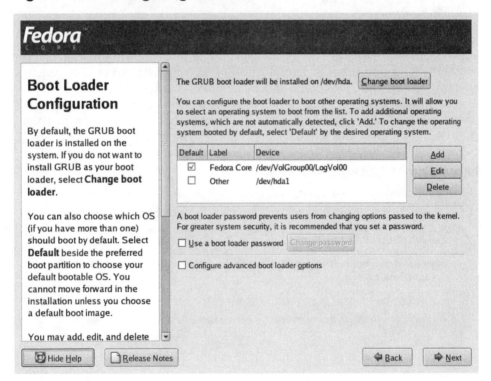

Networking

After you've set up all of your partitions, you'll be offered the networking options shown in Figure 1.11. Existing Ethernet cards within the machine will be denoted as eth*n*; if the machine has only one network card, it will be called eth0. The default configuration will be something like that displayed in Figure 1.11. The first network connection (usually eth0) will be made active, and will be automatically configured via DHCP.[14] If the machine is on an internal network, you'll probably be able to just leave this as the default. For a Web server that's connected directly to the Internet, you'll need to manually configure your static IP address and manually-configured gateway, DNS, and hostname. In this case, your ISP will be able to provide you with the IP address, gateway, and other details to use.

Figure 1.11. Configuring Fedora's networking options.

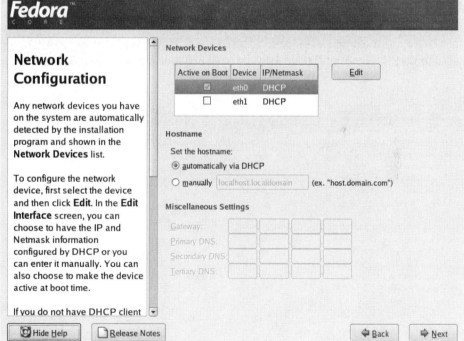

---

[14]Dynamic Host Configuration Protocol (DHCP) will be used to auto-detect your network settings to enable you to connect to the Internet, or to a private network.

Figure 1.12. Manually configuring the Ethernet interface.

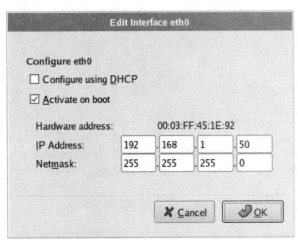

Clicking the Edit button in the Network Configuration screen will display the Edit Interface window shown in Figure 1.12. Here, you can make custom configuration adjustments such as giving the server a static IP address.

When the network device settings have been configured from the previous screen, you're free to configure the hostname, gateway and DNS settings. Figure 1.13 shows a network device configured primarily for internal use.

Figure 1.13. A manually configured network interface.

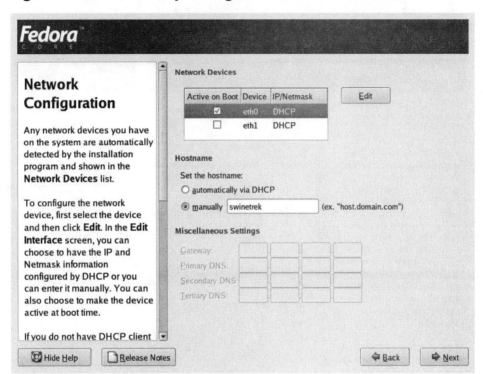

Network Security

Figure 1.14. Setting server security options.

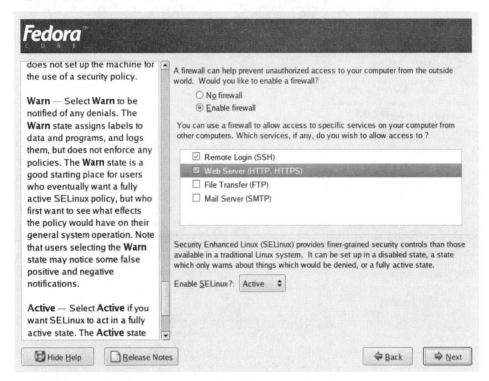

The Fedora Core distribution—and many of the other major distributions of Linux—strive to make configuring your network security as easy as possible. By default, Fedora turns on a firewall that blocks all traffic coming in from the network. To customize the firewall, simply select the services you want to run on this machine; alternatively, you can simply disable the firewall, which will leave the machine open and vulnerable to hacker attacks. You can also choose to enable Security Enhanced Linux (SELinux), which can help to minimize any damage caused if hackers gain control of parts of the system. Note that SELinux should not be considered an alternative to a firewall—neither the firewall, nor SELinux, makes your system completely secure, so it's best to enable them both. For our purposes, you should only allow Remote Login and Web Server traffic through the firewall, and set Enable SELinux? to Active, as illustrated in Figure 1.14. Chapter 9 covers security in more detail.

Telnet and FTP Security

Though they're shown as options in the Fedora security configuration screens, both telnet and FTP are widely recognized as insecure protocols. SSH is a much more secure option than telnet for accessing remote machines, as SFTP is a more secure option than FTP for transferring files. If an FTP capability is required, it's recommended that it be set up on a different server that's isolated as much as possible from the rest of the network.

Setting the Time Zone

Fedora offers two options for setting the time zone for your server. You can roll the mouse over the metropolitan area that's closest to you, or you can select from an exhaustive list of cities. In either case, the chosen city will be highlighted on the map, as shown in Figure 1.15.

Figure 1.15. Setting the time zone.

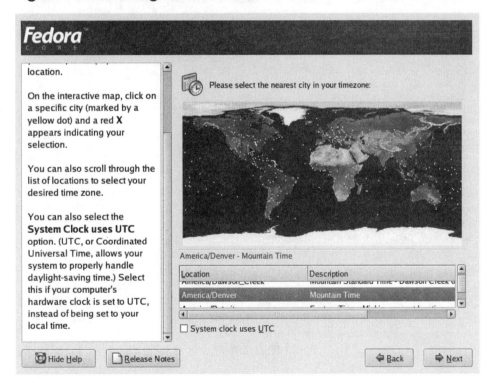

Setting up the Root User

All Linux systems have an administrative account, **root**. This account has access to everything on the computer; it's similar to the Administrator account in Windows systems. As the power of root in Linux is so broad, it's critical that you make accessing the root account as difficult as possible. Choose a secure password for the root account—one that consists of both upper- and lowercase letters, as well as numbers and special characters—and enter it into the fields as shown in Figure 1.16. I would recommend that you record your root password somewhere and keep it safe: if you forget the password, it becomes very difficult to gain access to your machine should things go wrong.

Figure 1.16. Setting the root password.

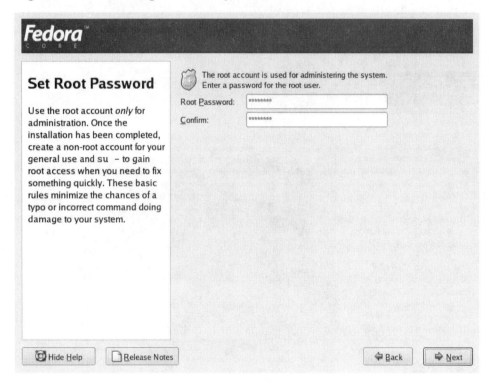

Installing Software Packages

Previously, when you were asked to select an installation type (you selected from personal desktop, workstation, server, or custom), your selection determined which software package groups would be made available for selection in this screen. For your server installation, you'll see the full range of server software offered as part of the Fedora distribution, with a few nice extras thrown in. Select each of the package groups you want to install by clicking the appropriate check boxes, as shown in Figure 1.17.

Figure 1.17. Selecting package groups.

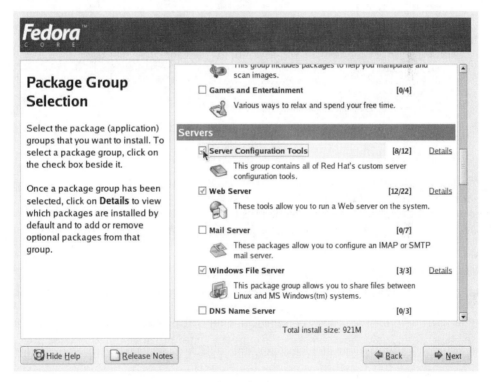

Figure 1.18. Refining the package selection.

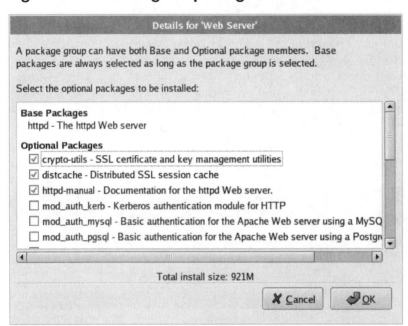

Each package group contains a number of packages; you can see a list of these (similar to the one shown in Figure 1.18) by clicking the Details link that appears when the package group is checked. This list is made up of base packages—packages that are required for this package group—and optional packages, which you can choose to install as your needs dictate.

Through a long process of refinement, the Red Hat distributions have come to provide a full range of packages that meet nearly any common computing need. While it's a good goal to keep a server installation to a minimum, you may find that there are some packages you just can't do without. If you're using Linux for the first time, it's perfectly okay to accept the defaults; it's easy to add packages later if you realize that something else is required, and the defaults are carefully chosen by the Fedora team to cover the needs of most people.

Of particular importance to your install are the GNOME Desktop Environment and the Server Configuration Tools, which provide a rich set of graphical tools for server configuration. The Server Configuration Tools provide the ability to configure Apache, mail servers, the boot loader, and other software critical to the configuration and operation of your server. Command line tools for accomplishing these tasks are, for the most part, provided in the core installation, but these can be complex and difficult to use. If you intend to administer your server using graphical tools, you'll need to pick and choose carefully from this section. Since you're setting up a LAMP (Linux, Apache, MySQL, and PHP) server, you should install the (Apache) Web Server, MySQL, and PHP at this point.

Aside from the Server Configuration Tools, Fedora provides a full range of server software, including the Apache Web server, IMAP and Postfix mail servers, Samba for sharing files with Windows machines, a DNS server, an FTP server, and others. Beware of the temptation to install too many things at this stage, though; it's easy to install additional packages later, as required, and the more services that are installed now, the more security work you'll need to do later on. It's better to install only the things that you know you need now, and to add new services later, as you discover a requirement for them.

Of particular interest to your installation will be the optional Web Server packages provided in the Fedora Core distribution. These include the PHP scripting language, tools for connecting to MySQL and PostgreSQL database servers from PHP, and a full range of other software for communicating with the Apache server. If you're building a server for a dynamic, database-driven Website, you'll choose the pieces you need to make that possible from this section. You're also going to require a database; if you don't have a dedicated database server, Fedora Core 4 ships with two database packages: MySQL and PostgreSQL. MySQL is the simpler and most widely used of the two, so we'll be focusing on it in this book.

PHP and MySQL: Further Reading

We'll cover the high-level details of installing PHP and MySQL in a later chapter. However, the fine details of utilizing those packages lie outside the scope of this book. If you're looking for a detailed reference for building a dynamic server with PHP and MySQL, check out Kevin Yank's *Build Your Own Database Driven Website Using PHP & MySQL*[15] (SitePoint, ISBN 0–9579218–1–0).

Other package groups in which you may be interested include the following:

❑ The Network Servers package group contains software for various network utility functions, such as DHCP and Kerberos.

---

[15] http://www.sitepoint.com/books/phpmysql1/

❑ The Development Tools package group provides the tools necessary to build packages from source code. It's a good idea to have these tools installed, though you may not immediately see how they'll be used.

❑ The Administration Tools package group provides a full set of tools developed by Red Hat for server administration and configuration. You should install all of these, as they'll help you configure your system in the way you choose. There are alternative, command line-based tools intended for experienced administrators, but the graphical tools are easier for those who aren't experienced in Linux system administration to use.

❑ The System Tools package group contains a variety of useful tools that allow you to monitor the traffic to your server, connect to VNC and Windows Terminal servers and much more.

As you can see, a huge number of packages are available as part of Fedora Core. The installation provides a full range of software tools for building, configuring, and administering your Web server. It's not uncommon for budget restraints to dictate that your Web server serve more than a single purpose; if you're under such restrictions, you'll find the Fedora tools even more useful.

More Information, Please

As you may have noticed throughout the above series of screens, Fedora provides further information on each of the sections via the Release Notes button beneath the left window pane. This pane further serves as a help screen, providing specific details for each selected install package. Much like the brief package descriptions in the package Details screen, this pane provides a great resource for learning about your Linux system as you're installing it. The help screens provide much more detail than the brief summaries.

"Installing, Please Wait..."

With the package selection completed, you've finished the heavy lifting in the installation of Fedora Linux. The remainder is to be completed by the installer itself: formatting the hard disk with the partitions you created, installing each of the packages you selected, and performing **dependency checking** for each of the packages.

The process of installing your server will expose you to the power of the **RPM Package Manager**[16] (RPM) system; RPM is a format that's used to distribute software for inclusion in Fedora Core, as well as other Linux distributions such as SuSE and Mandriva Linux. The installation of your server will occur as a series of RPM transactions, which check for dependencies and install each chosen or required piece of software.

Dependencies Demystified

Nearly all computer software is dependent upon other pieces of software. A simple and obvious example of this is that any software running on your new server is going to depend on Linux. This relationship is called a dependency. Dependencies are engendered by the philosophy of modular software design, or building big programs from other, smaller programs. RPM investigates and handles these dependencies, checking for the existence of dependent code and noting those pieces that might be missing.

Now it's time to make yourself a nice cup of coffee: the installation of your Fedora Linux system may take as long as 45 minutes, depending on the speed of your machine. You'll be asked a few times during the installation to insert additional CD-ROMs and, when the installation is complete, you'll be prompted to reboot the machine. Your new server will start by presenting a screen that displays information about the Linux distribution and kernel version.

Note that if you've set up a dual-boot system, a countdown will occur before the boot loader automatically starts the default operating system. The countdown time can be adjusted through the boot loader configuration. This could be important for a production Web server: should the system go down, you'll probably want the machine to return to the network as quickly as possible.

---

[16]RPM was originally an acronym for Red Hat Package Manager, but was officially changed to a recursive acronym when it came into wide use outside of Red Hat. Other examples of recursive acronyms are PHP (PHP Hypertext Preprocessor) and GNU (GNU's Not Unix).

Last Steps

Figure 1.19. The Setup Agent's Welcome screen.

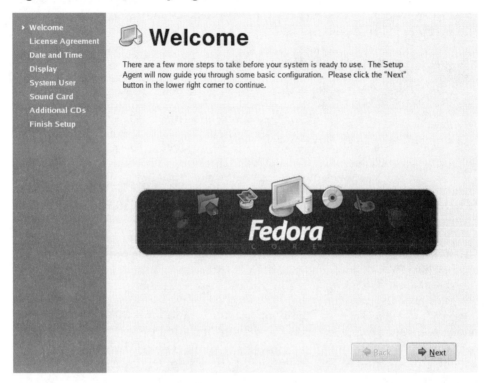

With the main installation completed, a few housekeeping items are all that remain to be done. Your Fedora server will walk through the process of loading drivers, then present you with the **Setup Agent**: a set of tools for configuring your system once it has been installed. The use of such tools has become a common approach among Linux distributions, with SuSE providing the YaST2 tool, and Mandriva utilizing SystemDrak. You'll be presented with the Setup Agent's welcome screen, shown in Figure 1.19, followed by the licence agreement. Once you've indicated that you agree to the license, you'll enter the configuration screens.

The Date and Time configuration screen provides two tabs: Date & Time and Network Time Protocol. The first tab allows you to confirm that the system clock is accurate. The second tab provides the ability to configure the Network Time Protocol (NTP) software, which can be used to synchronize your system's clock with an authoritative source. Selecting **Enable Network Time Protocol** in this screen, as illustrated in Figure 1.20, will enable the NTP daemon—a program that runs in the background, periodically checking your system time against the time returned by an NTP server. Several of these servers are listed in the Server drop-down.[17] If NTP is enabled and a server selected, the daemon will start, checking the selected server before moving on to the next Setup Agent screen.

Figure 1.20. The Network Time Protocol tab.

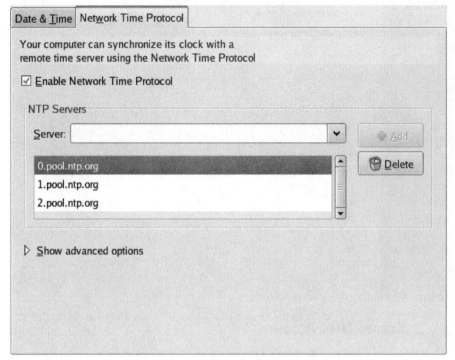

On the Display screen, you can select the type of monitor you're using, the resolution at which you'd like to work, and the color depth. If you can't find your monitor in the list, you can choose Generic CRT Display or Generic LCD Display.

The Setup Agent also provides a screen that allows us to configure an additional user. The user details include a Username, Full Name, and Password, as shown in

---

[17]A good NTP server is pool.ntp.org. This is actually a name shared by many servers, ensuring that it's always available.

Figure 1.21. If you decide to allow network logins, you can also select that option from this screen.

Figure 1.21. Setting up a system user.

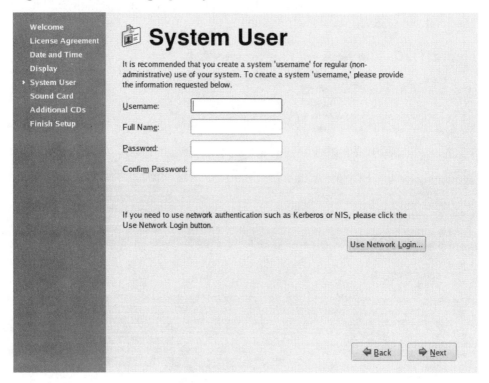

IMPORTANT

Create User Accounts

As with Windows, it's highly recommended that you create user accounts in addition to the main administration or root account. The root account is omnipotent; it has permissions to create, modify, and destroy any file on the system. Performing an action as root without careful forethought can have catastrophic consequences for your system. Nearly every Linux user can recount in detail the first (and likely only) time they rendered their system inoperable from the root account.

If the Fedora installer found a sound card on your system, you'll be asked to confirm its details. You'll also see a button with which to test it out, though, on a production Web server, this may not be necessary. There's also an Additional

Software screen, which you can use to install any extra software you might need. You can just skip this screen for now.

Congratulations, you've now set up a Linux Web server! The graphical installation provides new Linux users with a manageable set of tools to get the system up and running. However, there are cases in which the text mode installation is a quicker and more efficient means to the same end. Let's take a look at the text mode installer now.

Text Mode Installation

Using the text mode installer doesn't have to be an intimidating process: it provides all the tools available in the graphical installation, and follows the same general flow and logic, but it lacks a pretty interface. You shouldn't need to use the text-based installer unless your chosen LAMP server has less than 128MB of memory, and for the purposes of this book, the use of such a server is not recommended, as the graphical environment will run *very* slowly. Most administrators who install Linux on a machine with such little memory do not intend to use the graphical interface at all: they plan to control the machine from the command line. This is useful for experienced administrators, but it's not a good introduction to Linux if you're new to the operating system.

If you've chosen this path, you'll need to adjust to using the keyboard, rather than the mouse, to navigate through the text screens. Navigation is accomplished primarily with three keys: **Enter**, **Tab** and the space bar. **Enter** will confirm your choices, **Tab** will allow you to move between choices, and the space bar will allow you to select options within these choices.

Figure 1.22. Beginning installation in text mode.

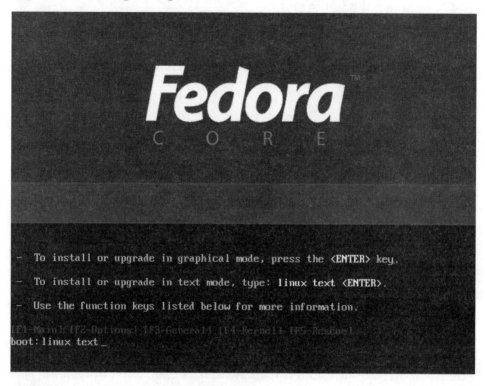

The text mode installation begins in a fashion similar to the graphical install. However, rather than simply pressing **Enter** to begin the installation, we type **linux text** at the prompt, as shown in Figure 1.22. The installation routine will load the initial set of drivers required for interaction with the monitor and keyboard, and offer to run a test of the installation media. It's recommended that you run this test to see if your installation CDs have been tampered with.

The Welcome to Fedora Core screen is a good place to get a feel for keyboard-based navigation. Hit **Tab** to move between selections, highlighting the current option. Hit **Enter** to select the current option. Select OK and hit **Enter**.

Figure 1.23. Language selection in text mode.

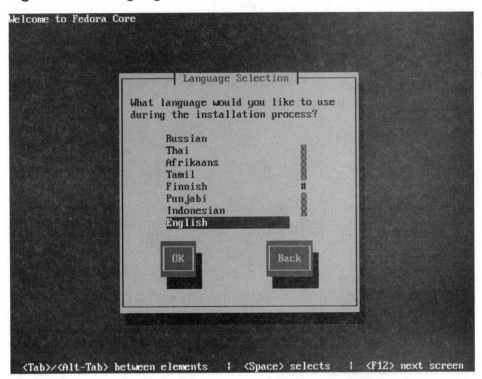

In the Language Selection screen, shown in Figure 1.23, use the up and down arrow keys to select a language. You can also use **Page Up** and **Page Down** to scroll through the options one page at a time, or type the first letter of the language you're looking for to be taken to the corresponding portion of the languages list. Use **Tab** to move to the OK button, and hit **Enter**.

Figure 1.24. Keyboard language selection in text mode.

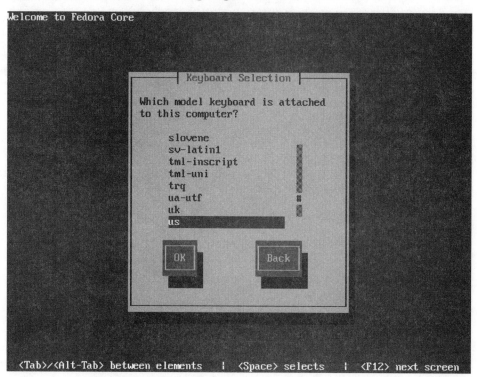

Like the graphical installation, Fedora's text installation offers dozens of languages both for the installation, and the keyboard, as shown in Figure 1.24.

Figure 1.25. Installation type selection in text mode.

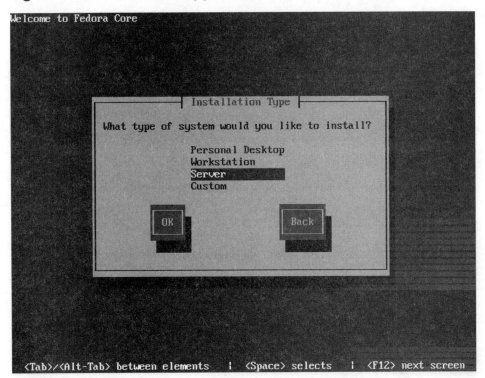

As with the graphical installation procedure, Fedora presents a number of "canned" options for installation types, as shown in Figure 1.25: Personal Desktop, Workstation, Server, or Custom. With typical granularity, each of these options is customizable: you can add or remove items from an installation type, exactly as we saw in the graphical installation process.

Figure 1.26. Setting up partitioning in text mode.

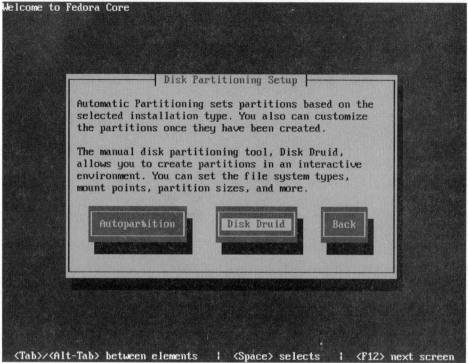

Like the graphical install, the text-based install offers options for auto-partitioning (/boot, / and swap), and Disk Druid-based manual partitioning, as shown in Figure 1.26. Should you choose Disk Druid, you'll need to navigate through the options using the keyboard. Obviously, the text-based Disk Druid doesn't provide a graphical representation of the current disk partition layout.

Figure 1.27. Manual partitioning in text mode.

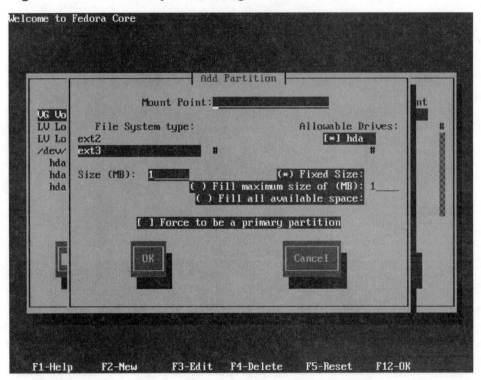

The text-based Disk Druid is not quite as helpful as its graphical counterpart, as Figure 1.27 illustrates. Whereas the graphical version provides drop-down lists pre-populated with the most common mount points, you'll need to manually enter each mount point into the Mount Point field for a successful text-based installation.

The Add Partition screen introduces a couple more text-based interface elements. The parentheses represent a set of radio buttons, or a set of options from which only one can be selected: (*) marks the selected option, while ( ) denotes an option that is not selected. The square brackets are similar, but behave more like checkboxes (i.e. more than one can be selected): [*] is a checked option, [ ] is an unchecked option.

Figure 1.28. The partition table in text mode.

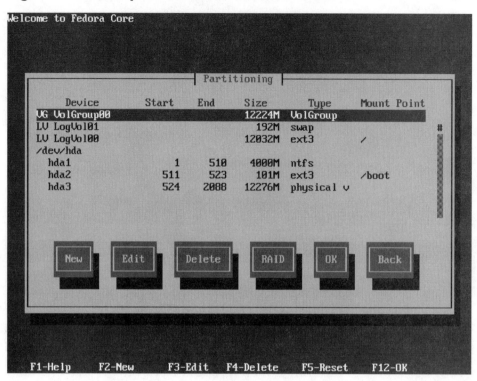

As noted in the graphical installation, everything on your Linux system resides within the top-level / directory. In this case, we've chosen a boot partition for the kernel and boot code, a swap partition, and the / partition. This is depicted in Figure 1.28.

Figure 1.29. The boot loader configuration in text mode.

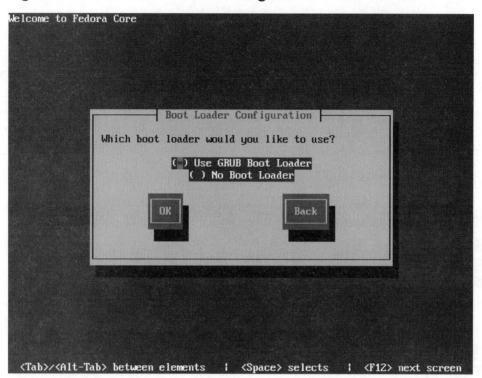

As Figure 1.29 shows, the boot loader options we saw in the graphical installation also apply to the text-based installation. If you've chosen to install a dual-boot system, the Windows operating system must be installed first—or already exist on the system—in order for your dual-boot system to work. For a dual-boot system, select the GRUB boot loader by tabbing to highlight the option, then pressing the space bar.

Figure 1.30. The boot loader configuration screen in text mode.

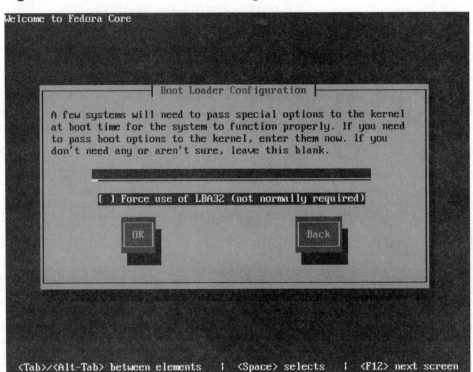

In a graphical installation, certain special options are presented in a single screen. For the sake of simplicity, the text-based installation breaks these options into separate screens, like the extra boot loader options screen shown in Figure 1.30. We'll discuss some of the options in Chapter 3, when we review instructions for adding them to a running system. For now, let's leave these options blank.

Figure 1.31. Boot loader password options in text mode.

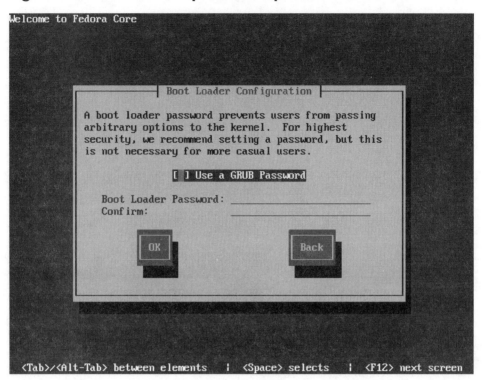

The screen shown in Figure 1.31 allows us to configure a boot loader password. This password will need to be entered if you want to change advanced boot features, such as the parameters passed to the kernel on boot. As in the graphical install, you should set a boot loader password to increase the security of your Web server.

Figure 1.32. Selecting an operating system in text mode.

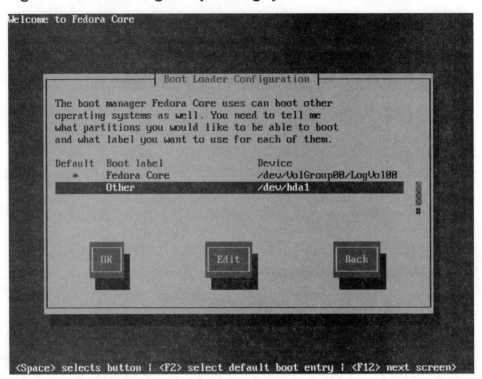

The text-based installer will show a list of all the operating systems on your machine, as Figure 1.32 shows, allowing you to select a default system. Again, this is useful only if you've chosen a dual-boot configuration. The selected system will boot automatically if the boot prompt times out while booting your Linux system.

Figure 1.33. Selecting a boot loader location in text mode.

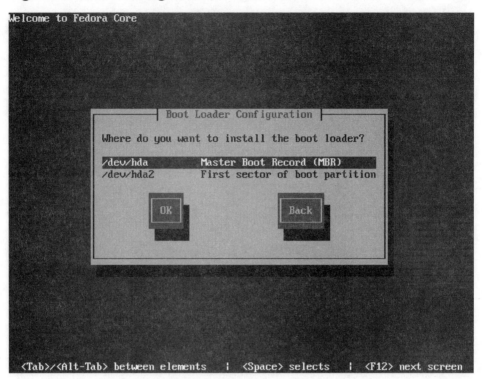

Linux offers flexibility even in the location of the boot loader code, as you can see in Figure 1.33. In most cases, you'll select the Master Boot Record (MBR) as the location of the boot loader. This is a requirement in the case of dual-boot systems.

Figure 1.34. The network configuration screen in text mode.

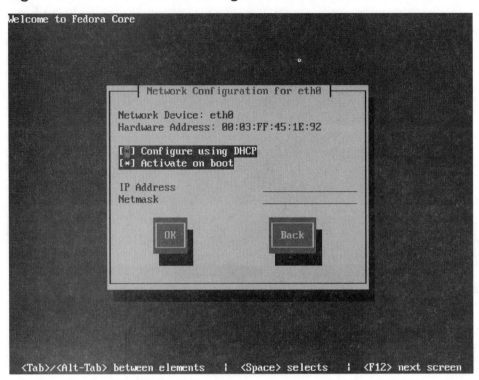

In the network configuration screen, shown in Figure 1.34, you can determine whether the system will gain an IP address via DHCP, or will use a static IP address. You'll also determine whether the Ethernet interface will start on system boot. Anaconda has done its work behind the scenes, providing a list of all the known Ethernet interfaces installed on the system.

The text-based installation again breaks single screens from the graphical installation into multiple text-based screens. Where the graphical installation allows the selection of DHCP and hostname configuration within the single screen shown in Figure 1.13, the text-based installation provides these options in consecutive menus.

Figure 1.35. Selecting firewall options in text mode.

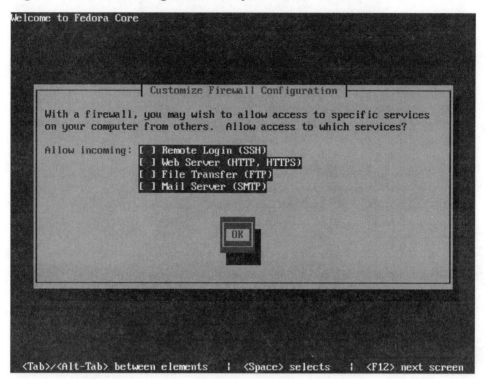

Like the graphical installation, the text-based installation gives you the opportunity to enable a firewall for your system, protecting it from outside intruders. If you choose to enable the firewall, you can specify what traffic is allowed by selecting the Customize button, which gives you the options shown in Figure 1.35. We'll cover the details of this firewall system (`iptables`) later in the book.

As discussed in the graphical installer section (the section called "Network Security"), you should allow only SSH and WWW traffic to enter the system from outside. This ensures that a minimal number of ports are open, while allowing the successful operation and remote administration of your Web server.

Figure 1.36. The Security Enhanced Linux options in text mode.

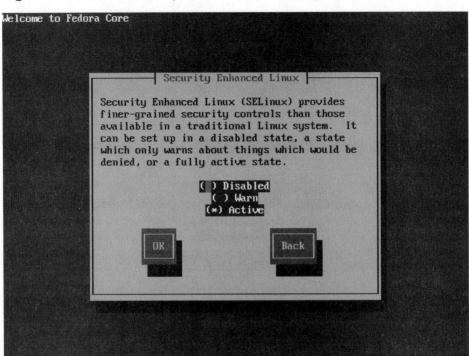

The next screen in the text-based installer sequence asks if you'd like to enable Security Enhanced Linux (SELinux). In the graphical installer, these options were part of the firewall options screen. This should be set to Active to enable the kernel's security-enhanced features.

Figure 1.37. The Time Zone Selection screen in text mode.

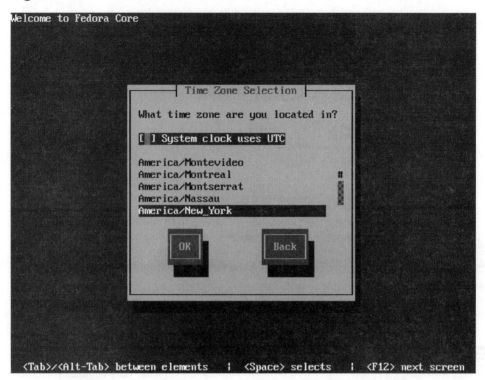

Unlike the graphical installation, which offers a map, the text-based installation provides time zone options in a list. If you'd prefer that your system use Coordinated Universal Time (UTC), highlight and select the System clock uses UTC option. To select a specific time zone in which the server is located, use the arrow keys to highlight a time zone, then **Tab** to the OK button, pressing **Enter** to finalize the selection.

Figure 1.38. Entering the root account password in text mode.

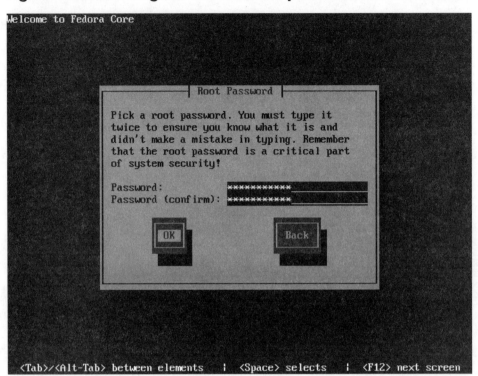

Enter your root account password in the screen shown in Figure 1.38, bearing in mind the warnings given in the graphical installation section: create a secure password to help ensure the integrity of your Web-connected system.

Figure 1.39. The Package Group Selection screen in text mode.

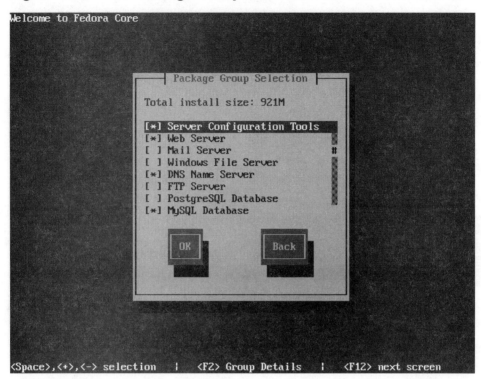

Following a brief scan of the installation medium, the text-based installer will provide you with all the existing package groups for the selection you've made. In Figure 1.39, we've selected all the essential tools for administering and maintaining a Web server, including Apache, DNS, and SQL database servers. You can select individual packages inside each package group, as in the graphical installer, by hitting **F2** while the package group is highlighted.

Figure 1.40. The Required Install Media screen in text mode.

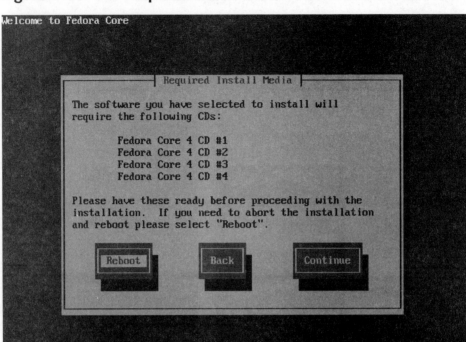

Next, you will be given one last chance to opt out of your Linux installation before Anaconda takes over and starts to install Linux. If you choose to continue, Anaconda will format your hard disk and/or set up the appropriate partitions, then install Linux as you have specified.

Figure 1.41. Linux installation progress bar.

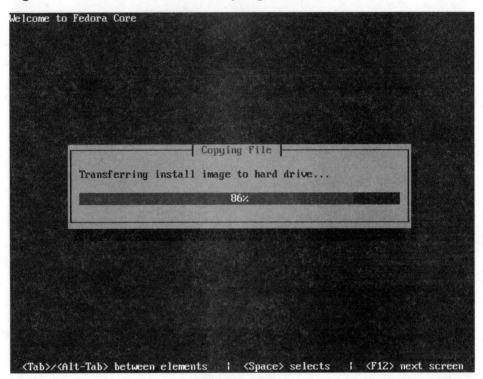

Your selection of specific installation options will create an install image for the installation process. This image contains a list of all the RPMs and dependencies necessary to install the Linux operating system on your machine in the configuration you've requested. In other words, all requested and required software is copied from the CD to the hard drive in preparation for installation, as illustrated in Figure 1.41.

Figure 1.42. The Package Installation progress display.

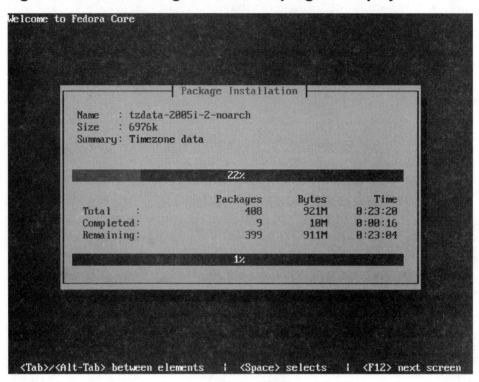

When the actual installation begins, the installer provides several pieces of potentially useful information, as shown in Figure 1.42. First, it presents a brief summary of the package being installed. Second is the progress of that package installation in a percentage-based progress bar. The high-level view of the overall installation is provided in a second progress bar. Installation progress, in terms of the number of packages, bytes, and approximate time remaining, is also presented as text between the progress bars.

If you've chosen to install your system without the X Windows system and a desktop manager—in other words, if you're installing a purely text-based system—the system will not provide the Setup Agent functionality. Instead, your first login will come in the form of a terminal screen. You'll log in using the "root" username and the password you created earlier in the installation.

Bear in mind that System Agent prompts you to create and configure a non-root user. Without System Agent, you'll need to perform this operation manually.

The creation of a non-root user is just as essential on a purely text-based system as it is on a graphical system. To create a new user from the command line, you first need to be logged in as root; then, run `useradd` *newusername*, replacing *newusername* with the username of the new user; you will be asked for a password and some details for that new user. Then, the user will be created.

Summary

The installation of a Linux system requires a little more up-front research than does a Windows installation. As many Linux device drivers are created through community-based reverse-engineering, rather than by those devices' manufacturers, it's important to check a number of hardware compatibility lists prior to commencing the installation. This will help you ensure that drivers exist for the devices on your server.

Linux support can take many forms, the most popular being Web-based lists and forums. This approach truly represents the spirit of community in the open source world, where user experience is relied upon to provide solutions to Linux issues. All commercial Linux distributors provide some level of paid support, though the support period may vary widely from one distributor to another.

Linux systems can be installed with a full complement of graphical tools, or as a minimal text-based system. The installers follow suit, providing options to complete an installation from a graphical environment, or from a purely text-based environment.

Unlike Windows systems, the desktop environment is not inextricably bound to the operating system kernel code. Instead, the X Windows and desktop management systems are distinct systems that run in their own space. This feature of Linux allows for the creation of a fully operational, text-based system, which boasts a very small installation code base. However, most users will opt for a graphical system based on X Windows and any of a number of desktop managers.

2

Day-to-day Usage

Unlike Windows, Linux doesn't offer a standard user interface, but provides a number of desktop environments that can be installed on top of the Linux kernel. Fedora Core comes with the KDE and GNOME desktop environments; in this book, we'll be looking primarily at GNOME.

The GNOME Desktop

Most graphical user interfaces are fairly similar; Microsoft Windows, Mac OS, and the GNOME desktop have a lot in common. You likely won't have much trouble finding your way around, but GNOME does do a few things differently. Here's a brief run-down of the GNOME basics to get you up and running.

A Tour of the Desktop

Figure 2.1. The GNOME desktop.

The GNOME desktop, shown in Figure 2.1, displays a bar at the top and a bar at the bottom; in GNOME, these bars are called **panels**.

The Bottom Panel

The bottom panel offers a clickable button for each window that's open, similar to the Windows Taskbar, as shown in Figure 2.2.

Figure 2.2. The bottom panel of the GNOME desktop.

On the right-hand side of the bottom panel is the **workspace switcher**, illustrated in Figure 2.3. A workspace (also known as a virtual desktop) is a way to organize your open windows.

As you open windows and move them around, you'll see a little illustration of the window layout appears in the first square. If you then click on the second square, all of the windows will disappear from the screen—the windows are still open, but you can't see them because you've switched to a different workspace. Click on the first square in the workspace switcher, and you'll see that your original windows return.

You can move windows between workspaces by right-clicking on a window's title bar and selecting a workspace from the Move to Another Workspace menu.

Figure 2.3. The workspace switcher displaying in the bottom panel.

By default, you have four workspaces, but you can change this default in the Workspace Switcher Preferences window (right-click on the workspace switcher and select Preferences... to access this).

The Top Panel

The top panel is divided into three sections: the menus and "shortcut" icons are shown on the left, while the notification area appears on the right, as depicted in Figure 2.4.

Figure 2.4. The top panel of the GNOME desktop.

Top Panel Menus

Figure 2.5. Locating Firefox through the Applications menu.

The top panel menus give us access to everything on the computer. The Applications menu shown in Figure 2.5 categorizes all installed applications as Games, Graphics, Internet, Office, and so on. If you installed Firefox, for example, you could find it in the Internet menu.

Figure 2.6. The Places menu.

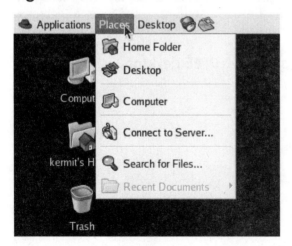

The Places menu depicted in Figure 2.6 lists file locations that may be useful: your home folder, your desktop, drives on the computer, and network locations.

The Desktop menu provides access to configuration—user preferences and system settings—as well as online help, screen locking, log out, and shut down options. These are shown in Figure 2.7.

Figure 2.7. The Desktop menu.

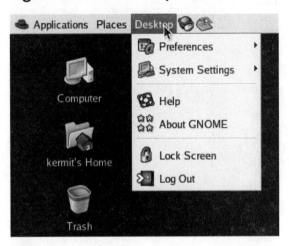

Top Panel Shortcut Icons

The shortcut icons, located in the Launcher Panel next to the menus, provide quick access to common applications.

Figure 2.8. Displaying shortcut icons in the Launcher Panel.

By default, the icons provide shortcuts to the Web browser (Firefox) and the email client (Evolution), as well as the three main OpenOffice.org applications (word processing, spreadsheet, and presentation tool packages) if you have these installed.

Using Windows

The display of windows that comprise the GNOME GUI is similar to the user interface on the Windows platform. Figure 2.9 shows the display of a GNOME window.

Figure 2.9. A GNOME window.

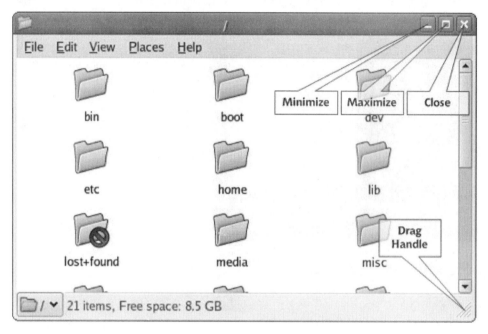

If you've used other operating systems, you're not going to have any trouble with GNOME's windows.

Starting Up and Shutting Down

Because Linux is a true multi-user system, you'll need to log into your system account before you use the system. In GNOME, the default application for handling this task is the GNOME Display Manager (GDM). The GDM login screen will open after all your system's devices and drives have been properly mounted. You'll log in to the system using the account name and password you created after installation.

Keep Out Of root!

It's never advisable to log in to your system as root. Remember that root is the omnipotent account in Linux, and is capable of performing any action on the system. Those actions include deleting system-critical files, which completely disables the system, making it very difficult to recover. root access should always be used sparingly. When logging in to your system, first log in to the user account; then, if necessary, you can perform administrative tasks by switching over to root temporarily.

Remember that it's important to shut down your Linux box gracefully, just as you would a Windows machine. This allows any buffered data to be written to the disk before the system shuts down. You can shut down either by selecting Desktop > Log Out, or through the command line. Let's look first at the graphical tool for shutting down your machine.

Selecting Log Out from the Desktop menu, as shown in Figure 2.10, will give you the options to log out of your system account (returning you to the login screen), to reboot the machine, or to shut down the machine completely.

Figure 2.10. Linux's logout options.

The Linux Filesystem

Drives and Partitions

If you're used to the drive-oriented layout of Windows, the Linux filesystem structure might be a bit confusing. There is no `C:` drive; in fact, there are no drives as such, only partitions. To muddy the waters a little more, the partitions' actual locations on the hard drive aren't identified clearly. The Linux filesystem is much more abstract than that.

Let me give you an example. My workhorse machine at home, `cortex`, contains two physical hard drives. One is an old 40GB drive that contains the operating system and all the programs I use. The other is a new, 160GB behemoth I added later, which is partitioned into two sections. The first section contains my personal files: the photos I've taken with my digital camera, my MP3 collection, and few odds and ends. I leave the second section free for temporary files created by my programs.

On a Windows system, these drives would most likely be seen by both the system and the user as `C:`, `D:` and `E:`. Windows would be installed at `C:\WINDOWS\`, Firefox would live in `C:\Program Files\Mozilla Firefox\`, my digital photos would reside in a directory called `D:\Photos\`, and so on. With Windows, the directory name is directly related to the partition, and therefore the hard disk, on which it's stored. This concept is illustrated in Figure 2.11.

Figure 2.11. How `C:`, `D:` and `E:` relate to my physical hard disks.

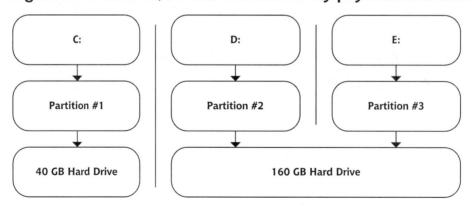

The Linux filesystem hides this unnecessary detail from you (until, of course, you want to see it). The operating system kernel is stored in a directory called `/boot/`, Firefox is in `/usr/lib/firefox-1.0.4/`, my photos and MP3s go into directories called `/home/`*username*`/photos/` and `/home/`*username*`/music/`, and temporary files go into a directory called `/tmp/`. There are no obvious signs that these directories reside in different partitions or on different hard disks.

The Linux filesystem assigns each partition a different **mount point**: a directory through which we access the partition. In our example, the `D:` in Windows is analogous to `/home/tony/` on our Linux system, `E:` is similar to `/tmp/`, and `C:` would be `/`, the top of the filesystem hierarchy. This structure is depicted in Figure 2.12.

Figure 2.12. The same partitions viewed in Linux.

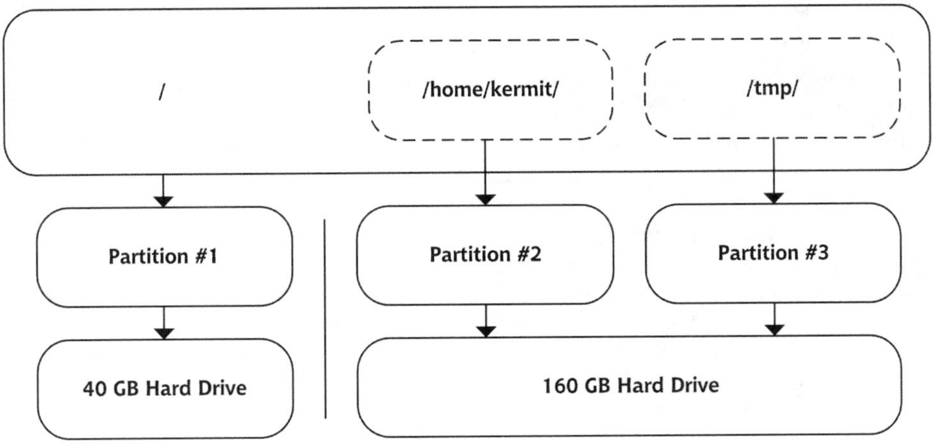

There's no doubt that it's confusing when you first make the transition from the physical disk-oriented view of Windows to the hierarchical filesystem of Linux. In time, however, you get over the shock and start to see the sense in viewing the system holistically, rather than as separate compartments.

The ext3 Filesystem

Linux is deservedly renowned for its ability to work with many different filesystems. A modern Linux distribution will read, write, and keep track of files in nearly all the Microsoft filesystems—from the original FAT through to NTFS—as well as filesystems used by Mac OS X, OS/2, and all sorts of esoteric operating systems. For Linux, it's a simple matter of loading the appropriate kernel module and mounting a partition. This makes it easy to handle files written on other systems on your Linux machine. In this section, we'll look at the filesystem that's native to your Fedora Core server: ext3.

The ext3 filesystem is an extension of the native Linux filesystem, ext2, and is now the default filesystem for Fedora Core. ext3 extends ext2 with a journaling layer that facilitates quick system recovery, and ensures a high level of data integrity. The journal is constantly updated with notes of file actions that are pending, and those that have been completed.

Journaling protects against data corruption with speed and ease. All pending and completed operations are logged to the journal. The system checks the journal when rebooting, and completes those operations that were pending at the time of a system failure or "dirty shutdown." This protects the consistency of the data that was buffered at the time the system went down.

Recovery time is also decreased by the use of a journaling layer. Rather than checking each file, bit by bit, for consistency, the system merely completes any pending writes noted in the journal. This reduces what was once a 20- to 30-minute reboot operation to mere seconds—an improvement that's especially critical in an enterprise environment.

Filesystems Galore

Other Linux distributions utilize different filesystems. SuSE Linux, for example, uses the ReiserFS filesystem by default. Extensive benchmarking has shown that ReiserFS can more efficiently handle large numbers of small files than can ext3. However, we won't have time to look at these other filesystems. If you'd like more information on the other filesystem options available for your Linux system, you can find a detailed list, descriptions and installation instructions online at Linux Gazette.[1]

A Quick Tour of the Filesystem

The Linux filesystem depicted in Figure 2.13 has a different structure than you're probably used to. Let's look at an outline of the filesystem structure, and explore its various functions and elements.

/ (The Root Directory)
This is the top level of any Linux system, known as the root directory. Unfortunately, there's also a directory named root. Don't worry: we'll explain the

---

[1] http://www.linuxgazette.com/issue68/dellomodarme.html

difference between these directories—and how to avoid confusion—in a minute.

/boot

This directory contains all the files necessary to boot the operating system, including the Linux kernel.

/bin and /sbin

These folders are similar in their contents—they both contain executable binary files—but differ in purpose. /bin contains executables that you're likely to use from the command line: commands such as **ls**, **mv**, and **cp**, which we'll be looking at in Chapter 3, live in this folder. /sbin contains commands and processes that are used by the operating system itself, so it might be best to stay away from this folder if you're just starting out.

/dev

These are the **device files**—abstractions of all the devices that are actually in the system, as well as all devices that could be added to the system. These files provide the operating system with a description of, and instructions for handling, each device.

/etc

This directory contains system-specific configuration files.

As an administrator, you're likely to spend quite a bit of time in the /etc directory, because it contains configuration instructions for most of the applications on the system. For example, the configuration file for Apache is located at /etc/httpd/conf/httpd.conf.

/home

This directory contains the home directories for each user of the system. For instance, our example user has the home directory /home/kermit, and other users on the same system have home directories /home/gonzo and /home/fozzie. By default, Gonzo or Fozzie can't read from or write to Kermit's files, and Kermit can't read from or write to theirs (only the root user has this ability).

/root (The root Directory)

This is the home directory of the root user, and is not to be confused with the other "root directory", /.

/lib

The /lib directory contains all the shared libraries that will be accessed by various applications in the system. It also contains libraries that will be used by the kernel in various system operations.

/media
/mnt

These directories serve as mount points for temporarily mounted filesystems. For example, the CD-ROM drive will be accessible from /media/cdrom.

/opt

This directory offers storage for packages that have been added to the system.

/tmp

This directory provides system-wide storage for temporary files.

/usr

Contains user commands and binaries, graphical interface files, include files for use in system applications, and optional source code files.

/var

The /var directory contains variable data files: files that may change during the operation of an application with which they're associated, including log files and mailbox files.

Tip

Mount Points

The concept of mount points may be a bit confusing, despite their existence in every operating system, including Windows. To avoid confusion, think of mount points as containers into which the contents of a device or filesystem will be emptied. For example, /media/cdrom is a mount point for the contents of the CD-ROM device. Emptying the contents of the device into the mount point makes the files accessible to the system and its users. In general, devices and filesystems must be mounted—attached to a mount point—before they can be used. In a later chapter, we'll discuss a way by which we can mount these devices and filesystems automatically in Linux.

Figure 2.13. The Linux filesystem displaying in the File Browser application.

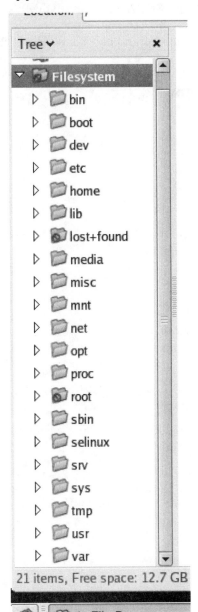

Navigating the Filesystem

Navigating the filesystem begins on the desktop with **Nautilus**, GNOME's graphical representation of the filesystem. There are two icons sitting on the desktop that act as starting points to Nautilus: Computer and *username*'s Home, as shown in Figure 2.14.

Figure 2.14. The desktop filesystem icons.

The Computer icon begins at the top level of the system, similar to My Computer in Windows; while the *username*'s Home icon begins within the current user's home directory.

Double-clicking the Computer icon presents us with a view similar to that shown in Figure 2.15. We see the removable media attached to the computer, as well as icons representing the root of the local filesystem and any other filesystems to which we have access over the network.

Double-clicking on the Filesystem icon opens a new window displaying the root directory of the filesystem, as shown in Figure 2.16. Double-clicking any of these icons will open another window, providing a view of the contents of the chosen directory, just like Windows Explorer or Finder on a Mac.

Figure 2.15. The Computer icon's top-level view.

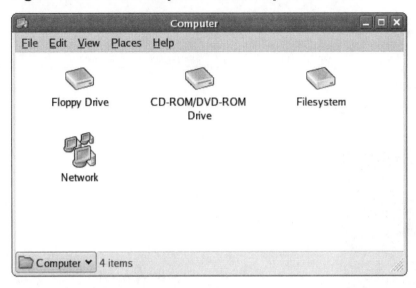

Figure 2.16. Viewing the Computer icon filesystem.

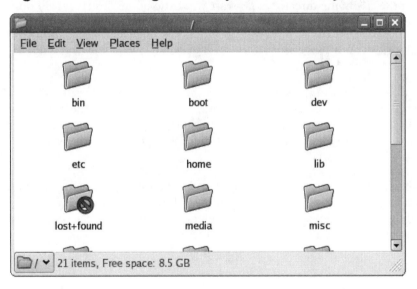

Figure 2.17. The Home icon view.

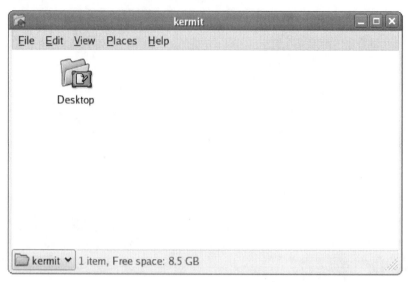

Double-clicking on the *username*'s Home icon on the desktop will jump straight to the current user's home directory. To start with, the home directory will only contain one visible folder icon, Desktop, as depicted in Figure 2.17.

Handling Linux Files

Literally everything in a Linux system is a file, including directories, links, and so on. Even the commands are files, ranging from the simple to the extremely complex. Because of the nature of the Linux system and its files, it's important to understand the processes of file handling and editing on your new system.

In this section, we'll take a quick spin through the file permissions structure, get a grip on the system's ability to link from one file to another, and explore some of the more common text editing applications for Linux. Because everything in Linux is a file, it's very important that you understand how files are accessed and edited. These are skills you'll find yourself using nearly every day.

File Permissions

Linux utilizes one of the most granular file permissions systems of any computer operating system. As we've already seen, that granularity is due, in part, to the fact that everything in Linux is a file. Commands, configurations, device files: all are editable, depending upon who the editing user is, and how the permissions on the file have been set. Accordingly, it's important to understand the permissions structure and how it will affect both your and your users' interaction with system files.

At their most basic, Linux permissions are broken into three sets of permissions. These are:

Owner (or user)   The permissions granted to the user who owns the file (usually the user who created the file).

Group   The permissions granted to a specified group of users. Users can be added to any number of available groups, each of which can have permissions on files.

Other   The permissions granted to anyone who isn't the owner, or a member of a group that has permissions to access the file.

Each of these sets can grant any combination of the following, self-explanatory permissions:

❏ read

❏ write

❏ execute

What's especially interesting in the Linux permissions structure is how these three sets of three permissions interact. A particular user may belong to a group that can only read a particular file, but if that user also happens to be the file's owner, the owner permissions of the file might also grant the user access to write to the file's contents.

Figure 2.18. Default permissions for a text file.

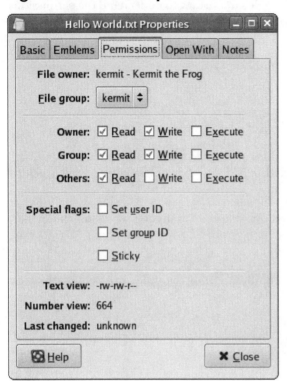

As an example, let's look at the default permissions structure of a simple text file. Open the gedit application by choosing Applications > Accessories > Text Editor from the menu. Enter some text into gedit, then save the file in your home directory. Locate the file in Nautilus, right-click on the file, and select Properties. Click the Permissions tab to see the permissions that have been given to the file as shown in Figure 2.18.

Let's take an in-depth look at this dialog.

File owner
This identifies the user who owns the file. By default, the owner is the user who created the file; however, a user that has sufficient privileges—root, for example—can change the file ownership details.

File group

The group of users that has access to this file: in this case, a group named `kermit`. When you create a user, Linux will automatically create a group with the same name as that user. This allows us to give a user access to another user's files. For example, if we added the user `gonzo` to the group `kermit`, Gonzo would have access to Kermit's files.

Owner, Group and Others

These checkboxes allow the actual setting of permissions. You can grant the owner, the group you've selected, or everyone else any combination of read, write, and/or execute permissions. That combination of three sections of three permission types results in 512 possible combinations for the permissions on this file. That's a pretty flexible structure! We'll look more closely at file permissions in a moment.

Special flags

Special extensions to the permissions system allow us to flag a file for special treatment by the filesystem. We won't need to use these flags within this book.

Text view and Number view

These alternative ways of viewing file permissions will be familiar to anyone who's dealt with file permissions via the command line.

The text view is made up of ten characters. The first indicates the file type: if the file is a directory, this character will be `d`; if the file is a regular file, it'll be `-`. The remaining nine characters indicate the read, write, and execute permissions for the owner, the group, and everyone else. For example, `-rw-rw-r--` represents a regular file with read and write permissions for the owner, read and write permissions for the group, and read-only permission for everyone else. You can see this view change as you change the checkboxes above.

The number view is a more compact view of the text view. The numbers represent, from left to right, the permissions given to the owner, the group, and to everyone else. This view, too, changes as you change your selections in the checkboxes.

Last changed

This field identifies the date and time at which the file was last changed. As this file hasn't been reopened and modified, Linux doesn't consider it to be changed yet. Open the file and modify it to see this date change.

Symlinks, or Linking Files: More Abstraction

Most people who have ever worked with Windows understand the concept of shortcuts. A shortcut is really a pointer from one location to a file in another area of the system. In fact, some users understand and become so obsessed with shortcuts in Windows that their desktops are eventually covered with them! The ability to launch a file from somewhere other than its real location clearly has value for computer users. And Linux offers such capabilities, too. As an administrator, you'll find Linux's shortcuts nearly as exciting as those in Windows.

A shortcut in Windows and a symbolic link in Linux really amount to the same thing: they're abstractions—mere representations—of the original file. Creating a shortcut in Windows doesn't actually move the executable file to the desktop. Similarly, in Linux, we can write for a file an abstraction that appears to be the file itself. The file doesn't really exist in the new location, it just operates as if it does.

One important difference between the way Windows and Linux create shortcuts is that a Linux **symbolic link** (normally called a **symlink**) can be treated exactly as if it were the file for most purposes. For example, if you open a symlink in your editor, and make changes to the file, the editor will edit the actual file to which the symlink points. If you try that under Windows, you're likely to get a surprise when the editor opens up the shortcut file for editing, rather than the file that to which the shortcut links! Symlinks are used frequently under Linux because they're a powerful abstraction that can make it seem as if a file is in multiple places at once.

You can create a symbolic link in Nautilus by right-clicking on a file or folder, and selecting Make Link, as shown in Figure 2.19. This will create a symlink with "link to" at the start of the filename, as depicted in Figure 2.20. You can drag and drop this file anywhere, and rename it as you choose.

Figure 2.19. Creating a symlink in Nautilus.

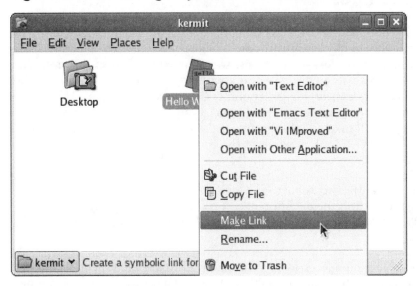

Figure 2.20. A newly created symlink.

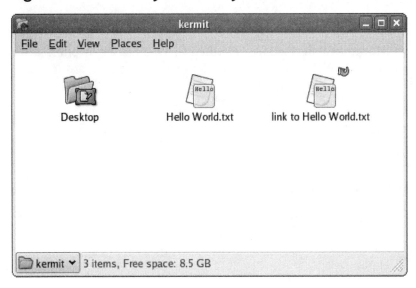

Editing Text Files

A reasonable command of a Linux-compatible text editor will be crucial to the success of your day-to-day administration. As most of the configuration in a Linux system is done via text files, you'd be wise to find one that works for you. In fact, Linux is replete with text editors: editors without a GUI, editors with a GUI, editors intended primarily for programmers, editors targeted at HTML developers—there's no shortage of tools to make your administrative tasks easier. In this section, we'll take a look at some of the GUI-based text editors that are available to you. We'll look at some of the command line-based editors a little later.

Fedora Core provides two robust GUI text editors in the default installation: **gedit** and **Kate**. gedit is the default text editor for the GNOME desktop environment, and Kate is the default for KDE, but both will work in either desktop environment.

If you were a longtime Notepad or Wordpad user in Windows, you'll find that many of the same features are available in Linux's GUI text editors, plus much, much more.

gedit

gedit is GNOME's default text editor. Pictured in Figure 2.21, it offers a full range of features, including:

❑ Full support for internationalized text, including UTF-8

❑ Tabbed multi-document interface

❑ Syntax highlighting

❑ Plugins and a plugin manager

❑ A complete preferences interface

In addition to these standard features, the following plugins can be added to extend the gedit application:

❑ Spell checker

❑ Insert date and time

❏ Word count

❏ Change case of selected text

❏ Indent or unindent blocks of text

❏ Ascertain the differences between two documents or files

❏ Insert output from the command line

❏ Markup language tag lists for common markup languages such as HTML, LaTeX, etc.

Figure 2.21. The main gedit screen, ready to edit the Apache configuration file.

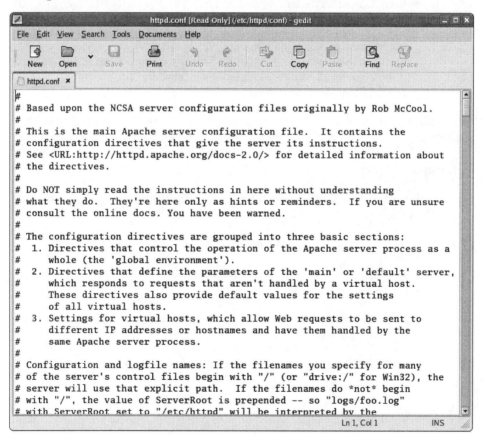

Mind your Gs and Ks

You'll quickly realize that most GUI applications for Linux are written specifically for one desktop environment or another. The naming conventions for these applications remain fairly consistent, and reasonably obvious. Most applications written for the GNOME desktop environment will begin with the letter "G," while applications written specifically for the KDE desktop environment will begin with the letter "K."

Kate

The KDE counterpart to gedit is Kate, the "KDE Advanced Text Editor," pictured in Figure 2.22. If it's not available in the Applications menu, you can start it by selecting Applications > Run Application... and entering **kate**.

Can't Start Kate?

The Kate text editor, originally a standalone application, is now included in the kdebase package. It's not available as a separate download. In order to use Kate, you'll need to have all the KDE libraries and base applications installed. To install additional applications, select Desktop > System Settings > Add/Remove Applications.

Like gedit, Kate is a multi-view editor: it will allow you to open and edit multiple documents in the same window. As well as that single, very useful feature, Kate offers a full range of other capabilities that make it a very powerful text editor. Its features include:

☐ Kate allows you to edit all kinds of text files, even if they're *big*. Kate can open a 50MB file in a few seconds.

☐ Kate's powerful syntax highlighting engine is extensible via XML files.

☐ The editor offers code folding capabilities for many programming languages, including: C++, C, PHP, etc.

☐ Kate offers split window views, allowing you to view different parts of the document simultaneously.

☐ Kate allows users to choose the encoding we want to use for each file via the save/open dialog.

☐ Kate boasts built-in terminal emulation.

❏ Kate's sidebar displays a list of open documents, a filesystem browser, and more.

❏ Kate provides a handy plugin interface that allows third party plugins.

❏ The editor provides project handling capabilities (which can be overridden by project handling plugins).

Figure 2.22. The main Kate screen, in which the Apache configuration file is being edited.

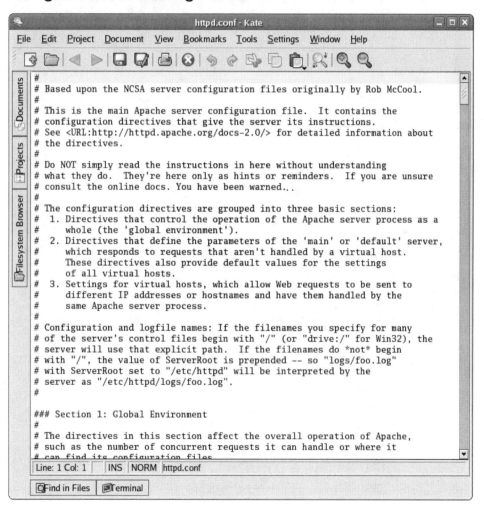

Ultimately, Kate is a bit more friendly, and offers greater flexibility for editing configuration files and writing shell scripts, than do some other editors. The syntax highlighting capabilities are unsurpassed, as Kate makes available a full range of programming languages and styles. Additionally, Kate provides such features as an open document listing (shown in Figure 2.23) and an integrated filesystem browser (Figure 2.24).

Figure 2.23. Kate's Documents tab.

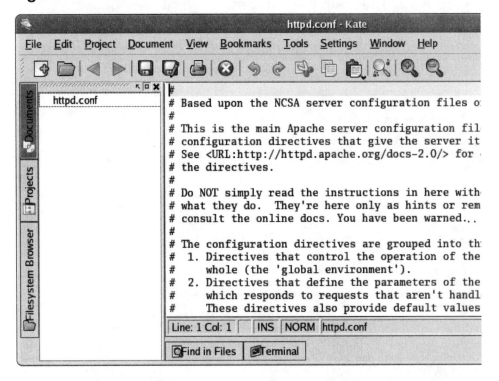

While Linux does provide other GUI text editing options, gedit and Kate are two of the most powerful and user-friendly on offer. Either will suit your Linux text-editing purposes well.

Figure 2.24. Kate's Filesystem Browser tab.

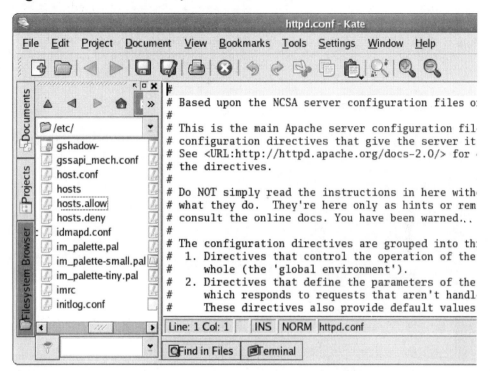

Summary

It takes time to understand Linux, and the first stage in the process is to find your way around what may, at first, be a slightly unfamiliar desktop. In this chapter, we've discussed some of the basics of Linux, Fedora, and the GNOME desktop from a user's point of view. Next it's time to look at what you need to know in your role as the administrator of a Linux server.

3

The Command Line

So far, our interactions with Linux have been through a pretty desktop environment, and it's been reasonably easy for experienced Windows users to get their heads around the system. Things haven't always been this way, though: the roots of the Linux user interface are firmly stuck in its command line.

What is the Command Line?

Unlike Windows, the GUI is completely optional in Linux. If you're feeling particularly competent, or you have certain requirements (or very old hardware), you can run your Linux machine with no graphics at all. As Linux has evolved, a variety of GUIs have been built on top of it, but the command line remains the administrator's best friend: a quick, easy, powerful way to perform actions that aren't always easily available from the desktop.

Figure 3.1. Accessing the GNOME Terminal.

Throughout this book, we'll use the GNOME Terminal application to gain access to the command line. You can access this application from Applications > System Tools > Terminal, as shown in Figure 3.1. The terminal itself is depicted in Figure 3.2.

 Tip

Tweaking the Terminal

The GNOME desktop environment is fully customizable—and that includes the appearance of the terminal. You can determine the font that's used, change the foreground and background colors of the window—you can even set the level of transparency of the window itself, so that it's possible to see the desktop image behind the window! Within the terminal, you can find these settings in Edit > Current Profile....

Figure 3.2. The GNOME Terminal application.

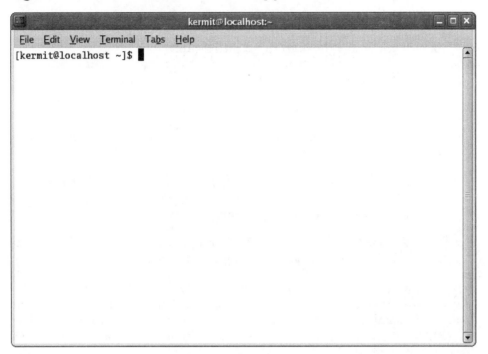

Let's look at a real-life example that uses the command line to meet a specific need. Once you understand the components of the command (and the complexity of the graphical alternative), you'll begin to understand the practical utility of the terminal and the command line.

```
[kermit@swinetrek ~]$ find /var/backups/* -ctime +5 -exec rm {} \;
```

I use this command regularly to remove from my system backups that are more than five days old. The command uses the find tool to search for files in the /var/backups directory that are more than five days old. For each file that the find tool locates, it runs the rm command: rm is the standard "remove file" command. Running this command regularly helps to save system storage space by deleting backups that, after five days, have become unnecessary. Of course, this command should be run in conjunction with an automated process that creates these backups every day or so.

Let's compare the use of this command to the process of utilizing a graphical tool to accomplish the same task.

1. Reach from the keyboard for the mouse.

2. Double-click on the Computer icon on the desktop.

3. Double-click on Filesystem to get to the root directory.

4. Double-click the var folder to open it.

5. Double-click the backups folder.

6. Ensure that the resulting window displays the creation time of the files by selecting View > View as List.

7. Holding down **Ctrl**, select the files with a creation date older than five days.

8. Right-click and select Move to Trash from the context menu.

9. To *really* delete the file, return to the desktop and empty the trash by right-clicking on the Trash icon and selecting Empty Trash.

You don't need to understand the intricacies of the Linux filesystem to see the advantage of the command line. The graphical approach involves at least nine—likely many more—mouse clicks. Rather than viewing the process of finding and deleting these files as single operation, you're forced to break the process down into its individual components. Add to that the inefficiency of using the mouse to locate, point at, and click targets on the screen, as compared to the swift simplicity of entering commands via the keyboard, and you start to understand how the command line can be a valuable and efficient tool for system administration.

This, however, doesn't even address the real beauty and power of the command line. You don't believe that I actually run the rm command three times a week, do you? That would also be terribly inefficient: I'd be relying on my own porous memory to make sure that the backups were removed! In fact, most of the commands you'll use in Linux are fully scriptable, with minimal modification. In reality, I've asked my system, via the cron utility (which we'll cover in depth in Chapter 4) to execute the command three times each week. This is much like the Scheduled Tasks feature in Windows, but it's more powerful: it can do just about anything. As you can see, an understanding of Linux commands and command line concepts is essential, even if you only open a terminal window occasionally.

Using the Command Line

When you use the Linux command line, you're opening what can be thought of as an alternative window to the operating system—an alternative window through which you have access to much more powerful, lower level operating system functions. Graphical tools don't provide that power. A graphical environment is merely a high-level abstraction of an operating system environment, and the icons and menus to which we're all so accustomed provide only limited access into that environment. Those icons and menus represent operating system functions, but they're not the actual functions. In other words, graphical interfaces provide a limited, additional layer between operator and operating system, in which a restricted range of functions are represented by pretty pictures. To administer your Web server with maximum efficiency, it's useful to be able to work at the same level as your system.

High and Mighty, or Down and Dirty

When we talk about "high level" and "low level" functions, we imply a hierarchy of functionality. Functions of the lowest level communicate with the kernel directly, and therefore have great power and flexibility; higher level tools do more work themselves, offering more functionality and increased safety. Compare, for example, the low level rm command with the higher level Trash functionality in Nautilus. rm simply deletes a file: it's quick and easy, but there's no easy or guaranteed way to recover that file. Nautilus doesn't provide you with such functionality. It insists that you move files to the Trash, effectively marking the file for potential deletion. The deletion itself doesn't occur until you go to the desktop and empty the trash.

Logging in as root

We've already talked about logging into Linux as root. To do so from the GNOME terminal, you'll enter the su (switch user) command.

```
[kermit@swinetrek ~]$ su
Password:
```

You'll be prompted for the root password. Once you've entered it, you'll gain full access to the system: computing omnipotence! Use it wisely. Although there are certain things that can only be done as root, including many of your system administration tasks, it's important to observe good Linux hygiene: don't remain logged in as root any longer than you need to. Every Linux administrator has a horror story of a time when, logged in as root, he or she mistyped a command

and deleted everything on the machine (or some similar calamity). You want to avoid such disasters. Be careful, and don't stay logged in as root if you don't need to be. To switch back to your standard user account, use the `exit` command.

Some Practical Examples

Let's look at a few examples of the command line in action.

Orienting yourself with the `pwd` Command

In Nautilus, we can have multiple folder windows open at once. However, when using the command line, we can only work within one directory at a time. That active directory is called the **working directory**. To find out which directory you're currently in, use the `pwd` (print working directory) command.

```
[kermit@swinetrek ~]$ pwd
/home/kermit
```

Tip

Home, Sweet Home

Your home directory, `/home/`*`username`*, is often referred to as ~. Did you notice the ~ in the command prompt? It indicates that you're currently in your home directory. As we begin to navigate the filesystem, we'll see this command prompt change to reflect the name of the directory in which we're working. Thus, we won't have to constantly enter `pwd` to find out where we are.

Listing Files with the `ls` Command

The `ls` (which stands for list) command, used by itself, lists the contents of the working directory.

```
[kermit@swinetrek ~]$ ls
Desktop  Hello World.txt
```

You can retrieve a list of the files in another directory by adding the directory name to the command line. For example, `ls /` will return a listing of everything in the root directory.

```
[kermit@swinetrek ~]$ ls /
bin    dev  home  lost+found  misc  net  proc  sbin     srv    tmp  var
boot   etc  lib   media       mnt   opt  root  selinux  sys    usr
```

Using `ls` by itself will show you the names of the files contained in a folder, but little more. To view all of the files' details, we can add the `-l` option to the command, which returns a longer listing.

```
[kermit@swinetrek ~]$ ls -l
total 16
drwxr-xr-x  2 kermit kermit 4096 Sep  5 14:21 Desktop
-rw-rw-r--  1 kermit kermit   13 Sep  8 07:30 Hello World.txt
```

There's plenty of information here.

❏ The first column presents the permissions for each file in the format we discussed in Chapter 2. In summary, the first character tells us whether the file is a directory; the next nine characters show whether or not read, write, and execute permissions have been granted to the owner, group, and others.

❏ The next column is really only useful for directories; it reflects the number of files inside a directory. For files, this number will be 1.

❏ The next two columns identify the owner and the group assigned to the file. In this case, they're both `kermit`.

❏ The size of the file in bytes is displayed next. Here, we see that the file `Hello World.txt` is 13 bytes.

❏ Next, we see the date and time at which the file was last modified. In the example above, the `Desktop` directory was last modified on the September 5 at 2:21 p.m.

❏ Finally, we're given the name of the file.

`ls -l` is so useful that Fedora Core includes a built-in shortcut to it: `ll`.

Your home directory will contain a number of hidden files. In Linux, we can hide a file by starting its filename with a period: if we changed the name of `Hello World.txt` to `.Hello World.txt`, it would become hidden. It's in these hidden files that programs store user-specific configuration information. To see hidden files, use the all option (`-a`), which can be use in conjunction with the `-l` option, or as an option to `ll`.

```
[kermit@swinetrek ~]$ ll -a
total 212
drwx------ 13 kermit kermit 4096 Sep  8 09:16 .
drwxr-xr-x  5 root   root   4096 Sep  6 13:48 ..
```

```
-rw-------   1 kermit kermit      5 Sep  8 06:21 .bash_history
-rw-r--r--   1 kermit kermit     24 May 10 10:15 .bash_logout
-rw-r--r--   1 kermit kermit    191 May 10 10:15 .bash_profile
-rw-r--r--   1 kermit kermit    124 May 10 10:15 .bashrc
drwxr-xr-x   2 kermit kermit   4096 Sep  5 14:21 Desktop
-rw-------   1 kermit kermit     26 Sep  6 14:20 .dmrc
drwx-x---   2 kermit kermit   4096 Sep  6 14:21 .eggcups
-rw-r--r--   1 kermit kermit    438 May 18 01:23 .emacs
-rw-------   1 kermit kermit     16 Sep  6 14:28 .esd_auth
drwx------   4 kermit kermit   4096 Sep  6 14:31 .gconf
drwx------   2 kermit kermit   4096 Sep  6 14:31 .gconfd
drwxrwxr-x   3 kermit kermit   4096 Sep  6 14:21 .gnome
drwx------   7 kermit kermit   4096 Sep  6 14:31 .gnome2
drwx------   2 kermit kermit   4096 Sep  6 14:20 .gnome2_private
drwxr-xr-x   2 kermit kermit   4096 Sep  6 14:21 .gstreamer-0.8
-rw-r--r--   1 kermit kermit    120 May 22 15:18 .gtkrc
-rw-rw-r--   1 kermit kermit    134 Sep  6 14:20 .gtkrc-1.2-gnome2
-rw-rw-r--   1 kermit kermit     13 Sep  8 07:30 Hello World.txt
-rw-------   1 kermit kermit      0 Sep  6 14:31 .ICEauthority
drwx------   3 kermit kermit   4096 Sep  6 14:21 .metacity
drwx------   2 kermit kermit   4096 Sep  6 14:22 .mozilla
drwxr-xr-x   3 kermit kermit   4096 Sep  6 14:21 .nautilus
-rw-------   1 kermit kermit     50 Sep  6 14:26 .recently-used
-rw-------   1 kermit kermit    497 Sep  6 14:21 .rhn-applet.conf
-rw-------   1 kermit kermit     66 Sep  8 09:16 .xauth3R8EvP
-rw-r--r--   1 kermit kermit    658 Jan 16  2005 .zshrc
```

At the top of this file listing appear two directories, named . and ... These are shortcuts to the current directory and the parent directory, respectively. We'll look at these in the next section.

Moving around the Filesystem with the cd Command

The cd command stands for change directory. It changes the current working directory to the one specified immediately after the command.

```
[kermit@swinetrek ~]$ cd /etc/httpd/
[kermit@swinetrek httpd]$
```

Used by itself, the cd command returns you to your home directory.

```
[kermit@swinetrek httpd]$ cd
[kermit@swinetrek ~]$
```

The commands **cd /home/kermit** and **cd ~** do the same thing. You can move to the working directory's parent directory using the **cd ..** command.

```
[kermit@swinetrek ~]$ cd ..
[kermit@swinetrek home]$
```

Printing with the echo and cat Commands

The echo command simply sends output to the screen.

```
[kermit@swinetrek ~]$ echo "Hello, World\!"
Hello, World!
```

Escaping Special Characters

Certain characters are reserved for special use on the command line, such as !. However, you'll often want to use these characters in command options or in filenames. To use these characters, you must **escape** them, that is, prefix them with a backslash (\) character. If you use spaces in filenames, you'll need to escape the spaces when dealing with those filenames on the command line: our file Hello World.txt needs to be accessed as Hello\ World.txt.

The cat command opens a file and writes its contents to the screen.

```
[kermit@swinetrek ~]$ cat Hello\ World.txt
Hello, World!
```

Copying and Moving Files with the cp and mv Commands

The copy command—cp—creates a copy of a file.

```
[kermit@swinetrek ~]$ cp Hello\ World.txt Copy.txt
[kermit@swinetrek ~]$ ls
Desktop  Hello World.txt  Copy.txt
```

Here, we've created an exact copy of Hello World.txt called Copy.txt. We can create a copy of a file in a different directory like so:

```
[kermit@swinetrek ~]$ cp Hello\ World.txt \
> /var/backup/Hello\ World.txt
[kermit@swinetrek ~]$
```

Splitting Long Commands

Because some commands are too long for the page width of this book, I have split them into multiple lines. If you ever want to do this on the command line, you need to end each line with a space followed by a backslash (\). When you press **Enter** when a line that ends this way, you'll get a > prompt to enter the rest of the command. Since you're not writing a book, you can just type these long commands as one long line (the terminal will wrap the command to the next line automatically as you type it).

You can use cp to copy an entire directory hierarchy. The following command will create a /var/backup/kermit directory, which will contain a copy of all of kermit's files.

```
[kermit@swinetrek ~]$ cp -r /home/kermit/ /var/backup/
[kermit@swinetrek ~]$
```

mv (which stands for move) moves a file from one location in the filesystem to another.

```
[kermit@swinetrek ~]$ mv Hello\ World.txt Moved.txt
[kermit@swinetrek ~]$
```

In the above example, the file Hello World.txt is being moved to a new file named Moved.txt in the same directory; effectively, we're just renaming the file. Unlike the cp command, when the mv command is used, the original file is not retained in its original location. To move the file to another directory, the command could be executed like so:

```
[kermit@swinetrek ~]$ mv Hello\ World.txt /var/backup/
[kermit@swinetrek ~]$
```

Switching Users with the su and exit Commands

We've already seen that su, used by itself, logs into the root account, and prompts you for the root user password:

```
[kermit@swinetrek ~]$ su
Password:
[root@swinetrek kermit]#
```

What the $#?

Note the changes to the prompt when you switch over to root: the character at the end of the prompt changes from a $ to a # to indicate that you're logged in as root. If you were in your home directory, the current directory in the prompt would change from ~ to your old username. This indicates that you're no longer your normal user in your home directory: you're root in another user's home directory. root's home directory is /root.

To switch back to your original user, use the exit command:

```
[root@swinetrek kermit]# exit
exit
[kermit@swinetrek ~]$
```

You can use su to switch to any other user, as long as you know that user's password.

```
[kermit@swinetrek ~]$ su gonzo
Password:
[gonzo@swinetrek kermit]$
```

Changing File Permissions with the chmod Command

We looked at permissions, and saw how to change them through the GUI, in Chapter 2. You can also change these permissions from the command line using the chmod (change mode) tool.

```
[kermit@swinetrek ~]$ chmod o+w Hello\ World.txt
[kermit@swinetrek ~]$ ll
total 16
drwxr-xr-x  2 kermit kermit 4096 Sep  5 14:21 Desktop
-rw-rw-rw-  1 kermit kermit   13 Sep  8 07:30 Hello World.txt
```

Here, we've granted all other users write access to Hello World.txt. We told chmod to do this by passing o+w to it. Let's take a look at what that means:

☐ The o character tells chmod to deal with the set of permissions for other users. This could be replaced with u for the user set, g for the group set, or a for all three sets.

☐ The + character tells chmod to grant permission. It can be changed to -, which will tell chmod to revoke permission.

☐ The w character tells chmod to deal with write permission. This can be changed to r for read permission, or x for execute permissions.

You can also combine these letters. For example, you can use ug-w to revoke write permissions for the user and group.

```
[kermit@swinetrek ~]$ chmod ug-w Hello\ World.txt
[kermit@swinetrek ~]$
```

Deleting Files with the rm Command

As we've already seen, the rm command removes a file. In the example below, rm would remove the file MyCopy.txt.

```
[kermit@swinetrek ~]$ rm MyCopy.txt
[kermit@swinetrek ~]$
```

In order to remove a directory and everything inside it, we must add the "recursive" (-r) option to the command, like so:

```
[kermit@swinetrek ~]$ rm -r untitled\ folder
[kermit@swinetrek ~]$
```

Ordinarily, you must have write permissions to a file in order to delete it; however, if you have write permissions on the directory containing the file, you can delete files if you confirm the action. If you attempt to delete a file to which you only have read permissions, you'll be asked if you really want to delete that file:

```
[kermit@swinetrek ~]$ rm Read\ Only.txt
rm: Remove write-protected regular file 'Read Only.txt'? y
[kermit@swinetrek ~]$
```

To force a deletion without further confirmation, add the -f option to the command. This can be combined with the -r option to delete a write-protected directory, too.

```
[kermit@swinetrek ~]$ rm -rf Read\ Only\ Folder
[kermit@swinetrek ~]$
```

Don't Force It!

Use the -f option with the rm command very carefully. When logged in as root, deleting directories or files without confirmation can result in serious damage to your installation. Confirming the deletion provides a safeguard against these accidental deletions.

Getting Help

Possibly the most useful of all command line tools is man, the online manual. If you ever need to find out what a command does or what options are available, just enter man *commandname* at the command prompt.

When reading the manual, the up and down arrow keys scroll through the text, the space bar scrolls through a page at a time, and **Q** quits the manual and returns you to the command prompt.

Introducing the Shell

In the same way that we can interact with Linux graphically through a desktop environment such as GNOME or KDE, we interact with the Linux command line through a **shell**. We've been using the shell throughout this chapter; let's now take a look at some of its more advanced features.

The default shell in Fedora Core (and, in fact, in most modern Linux systems) is **bash**, or the Bourne Again Shell. bash is a modern rewrite of the original Bourne shell, **sh**, which was written in 1977. While other shell environments exist, such as tcsh, csh and ksh, bash has become increasingly popular due to its useful featureset. We'll look in detail at some of those features here.

Tab Completion

One of the most useful features of many modern shells is tab completion. When a partial command or filename is entered on the command line, and the user presses the **Tab** key, the command or filename will be completed for you. For example, typing **cat Hello**, followed by **Tab**, will result in `cat Hello\ World.txt` being completed at the command line for you.

However, typing **cd /etc/ht**, followed by **Tab**, doesn't immediately return anything. That's because two directories begin with /etc/ht: /etc/httpd and /etc/htdig. Pressing the **Tab** key a second time will list the possible options:

```
[kermit@swinetrek ~]$ cd /etc/ht
httpd/  htdig/
[kermit@swinetrek ~]$ cd /etc/ht
```

We can use this list to continue typing until we've typed enough characters to identify a single directory; we can then press **Tab** again to have the filename completed.

Command History

The bash shell records a limited history of recently issued commands—up to 1000 by default. You can use the up arrow key to scroll back through the command history, and the down arrow key to scroll forward. When the desired command is found, you can execute it by pressing **Enter**.

To see the full history, simply enter the `history` command. All your recent commands will be displayed in chronological order, with the oldest at the top.

```
[kermit@swinetrek ~]$ history
    1   pwd
    2   ls
    3   ls /
    4   ls -l
    5   ll -a
    6   cd /etc/httpd/
    7   cd
    8   cd ..
    9   echo "Hello, World\!"
   10   cat Hello\ World.txt
   11   cp Hello\ World.txt Copy.txt
   12   cp Hello\ World.txt /var/backup/Hello\ World.txt
   13   cp -r /home/kermit/ /var/backup/
   14   mv Hello\ World.txt Moved.txt
   15   mv Moved.txt /var/backup/
   16   su
   17   su gonzo
   18   chmod o+w Hello\ World.txt
   19   ll
   20   chmod ug-w Hello\ World.txt
   21   rm Copy.txt
   22   rm -r untitled\ folder
   23   rm Read\ Only.txt
   24   rm -rf Read\ Only\ Folder
```

This history is also searchable. Hitting **Ctrl-R** will change the prompt to `(reverse-i-search)`'':`; now, try typing part of one of the commands in your history. The shell will find within the history the most recent command that contains the entered string, and display it. Just hit **Enter** to execute it, or **Esc** to return to the normal prompt. In the example below, I've entered **Hello** and found the last command that involved the file `Hello World.txt`.

```
(reverse-i-search)`Hello': chmod ug-w Hello\ World.txt
```

Some built-in history shortcuts can further maximize the efficiency with which you utilize the shell history. The `!!` command will execute the last command in the history file. For example, if the last command entered was `ll`, `!!` would re-run that command.

```
[kermit@swinetrek ~]$ !!
ll
total 16
drwxr-xr-x  2 kermit kermit 4096 Sep  5 14:21 Desktop
-rw-rw-r--  1 kermit kermit   13 Sep  8 07:30 Hello World.txt
```

!*partial-command* will execute the last command beginning with *partial-command*. For example, !ech would re-run the last echo command.

```
[kermit@swinetrek ~]$ !ech
echo "Hello, World\!"
Hello, World!
```

Programming the Shell

The shell itself can be quite a powerful little programming language. It supports looping, branching, variables—everything that constitutes a worthwhile programming environment. These shell programs, called **shell scripts**, are just text files on which execute permissions are set. The text files contain commands just like those you'd type on the command line:

File: **hello_world.sh**

```
#!/bin/sh
echo "Hello, World!"
```

The output of this script is exactly as you'd expect:

```
Hello, World!
```

Let's take a look at some of the shell's more programming language-like features. First, we'll create a new variable in the shell and print its value.

```
[kermit@swinetrek ~]$ COUNTER=0
[kermit@swinetrek ~]$ echo $COUNTER
0
```

Once the variable COUNTER is created, it's there until you close the terminal window. The value of the variable may change, as you'll see, but the variable itself remains until the terminal session is ended. This is true of any declared shell variable.

If we use the increment operator (++) to increment the value of COUNTER, then echo it again, you'll see that the shell does, in fact, track the values of these variables:

```
[kermit@swinetrek ~]$ let COUNTER++
[kermit@swinetrek ~]$ echo $COUNTER
1
```

Let's build a simple script, called counter_test.sh, that will keep on counting until we tell it to stop by pressing **Ctrl-C**.

Sorry to Interrupt...

You can abort any process on the command line by pressing **Ctrl-C**. This is referred to as sending the program an interrupt signal.

This same keyboard shortcut will throw away a command and start you on a new, blank prompt if you're not happy with what you've typed.

The first line of any shell script is what's commonly referred to as the **shebang**: a pound sign, followed by an exclamation point, followed by the path to the shell.[1]

```
#!/bin/sh
```

Every shell script must begin with this line. The next line of our script will set a value for the COUNTER variable:

```
COUNTER=0
```

In other words, we're starting the counter at zero. Next, we'll add a loop to the program. We'll make it an infinite loop, so the user will have to send an interrupt signal to quit the program.

```
while true;
do
   # contents of loop go here
done
```

Now all we need to do is define just what it is that the shell is going to do as long as the condition is true: print the value of COUNTER, increment COUNTER, and wait for one second:

```
while true;
do
   echo $COUNTER
```

---

[1] /bin/sh is a standard shortcut to the shell program on Linux systems. Usually, this file is just a link to the *actual* shell program (e.g. /bin/bash), but using the standard name ensures that you script will still work on a system that uses a different shell.

```
  let COUNTER++
  sleep 1;
done
```

If you're following along closely, you'll already know what we'll see on the screen: a count up from 0. Here's the script in its entirety:

File: **counter_test.sh**

```
#!/bin/sh

COUNTER=0
while true;
do
  echo $COUNTER
  let COUNTER++
  sleep 1;
done
```

We've created a good shell script, but we still have one loose end to tie up before we can run it. For our script to execute, we need to set the appropriate permissions.

```
[kermit@swinetrek ~]$ chmod u+x counter_test.sh
[kermit@swinetrek ~]$
```

Now we can run the script:

```
[kermit@swinetrek ~]$ ./counter_test.sh
0
1
2
3
4
```

This tells the shell to execute a file named counter_test.sh within the current working directory. You should see the screen start to count from zero, pausing for a second between increments. **Ctrl-C** will stop the counting.

That's but a small taste of the process of writing a shell script. Remember, as well, that shell scripts can access most of the single commands you'll utilize in your day-to-day Linux use. A script that elegantly combines these tasks into a single executable file can be a thing of beauty and a real time-saver.

If you've had previous programming experience, you're likely to find the shell a bit lightweight for programming purposes. Clearly, the shell isn't a powerful development environment. If it doesn't meet your needs, you should probably begin to dig more deeply into powerful scripting languages like Perl. Shell scripts, however, have the advantage of being a good hacker's tool. They're quick, they can accomplish many of the daily administrative tasks you'll face in Linux, and many pieces of each script can be tested directly in the shell prior to being rolled into a script.

Further exploration of the possibilities of shell scripting can be found in the detailed online tutorial *A Quick Guide to Writing Scripts Using the Bash Shell*.[2]

The PATH Environment Variable

Now, remember that all of the command line tools are binary files located somewhere in the filesystem: the ls command, for example, actually lives in the directory /bin. But how does the shell know to find /bin/ls when you type ls at the command prompt?

The shell looks through all the directories listed in its built-in PATH variable, in search of a file that has the same name as the command you're after. The PATH environment variable for a default Fedora Core installation will look something like this:

```
[kermit@swinetrek ~]$ echo $PATH
/usr/kerberos/bin:/usr/local/bin:/usr/bin:/bin:/usr/X11R6/bin
```

So when you type the ls command, the shell would first look for an executable file /usr/kerberos/bin/ls, without success. Is there a /usr/local/bin/ls? No. What about a /usr/bin/ls? Sorry. How about a /bin/ls? Bingo!

Remember that, when we ran our counter_test.sh script, we needed to prefix the script filename with ./ to tell the shell that the executable file was in the working directory. If we were to add this directory to the PATH variable, we could simply enter counter_test.sh to run this script regardless of the working directory.

Built-in variables such as PATH are known as **environment variables**. These are the variables that describe the environment in which a process is running. Examples of other environment variables are HOME, which contains the path of the user's home directory, and MAIL, which is the name of the file that stores the user's email. Environment variables work just like normal shell variables, except they can be accessed by programs that are launched from the shell too.

---

[2] http://pegasus.rutgers.edu/~elflord/unix/bash-tute.html

To set or modify an environment variable, you must use the `export` command:

```
[kermit@swinetrek ~]$ export PATH=$PATH:/home/kermit
[kermit@swinetrek ~]$ echo $PATH
/usr/kerberos/bin:/usr/local/bin:/usr/bin:/bin:/usr/X11R6/bin
:/home/kermit/bin:/home/kermit
```

Note how we've used the PATH environment variable's existing value ($PATH) in specifying its new value. This technique allows us to tack an additional directory onto the end of the existing PATH. You can see that the /home/kermit directory has been added to the PATH variable. You should now be able to run counter_test.sh as easily as you'd run ls.

```
[kermit@swinetrek ~]$ counter_test.sh
0
1
2
3
4
```

Setting the PATH environment variable in this way will allow you to run a shell script from any directory for the remainder of this terminal session, but the modified PATH will be lost as soon as you exit the terminal. In Chapter 4, we'll see how to modify the default PATH used whenever a new shell is launched.

Summary

As useful as it is, the Linux command line can seem pretty cryptic when you first open a terminal. There is logic to the commands, but it will likely take a bit of experimentation before you feel comfortable with them. In order to set you on the right path, we've laid out some of the most common terminal commands, and explained their use in your Linux system, in Appendix A.

It's possible to use a Linux system without going anywhere near the command line. If you do so, however, you'll forego accessing the true power of the operating system. Linux's roots lie in the command line interface. Certainly, you can use the terminal to achieve tasks more efficiently than would be possible using the graphical interface, but, even more importantly, the command line allows you to execute tasks that would be impossible to complete via the gui.

In a discussion on the intuitiveness of interfaces in the comp.os.linux.misc newsgroup, Mark van Hoeij wrote "How do I type '**for i in *.dvi do xdvi i done**' in a GUI?", and his point is a valid one; the command line lets you do things easily that the GUI does not. Mastery of the command line is a big step on the ladder to achieving status as a Linux guru.

4

System Administration

So far, we've looked at installing Linux, and we've become reasonably comfortable with both the graphical and the command line interfaces. Now, it's time to delve a little deeper into administrating our Linux Web server.

Creating New Users and Groups

The concepts of users and groups are important in Linux and, as an administrator, you'll surely find the need to add new users as you become more comfortable with the system, or begin to share some of your server's administrative duties. As with other tasks, you can add new users with either a graphical or text-based interface.

The User Manager Tool

Figure 4.1. Opening the User Manager.

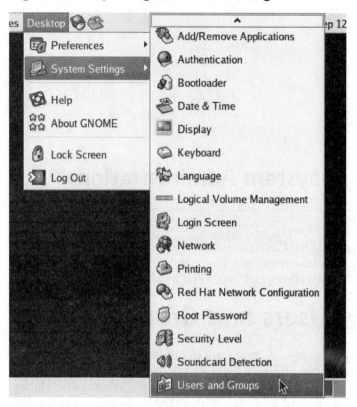

In Fedora Core, user and group management tasks are handled by the User Manager tool, which you can start by selecting Desktop > System Settings > Users and Groups, as depicted in Figure 4.1.

Getting Authorized

System Administration tools will often require root access. When they do, GNOME will prompt you for the root password via the dialog shown in Figure 4.2.

Figure 4.2. GNOME displaying a prompt for the root password.

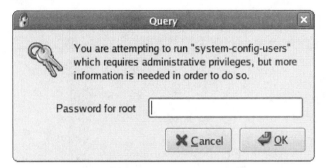

Provided you enter the password correctly, you'll become authorized to perform system configuration actions as root without having to re-enter the root password. That authorization is signified by the badge icon in the top right panel, like that shown in Figure 4.3. Once you're done making configuration changes, you can end this authorization by clicking on the badge icon, then clicking the Forget Authorization button on the dialog that appears. The badge icon should then disappear.

Figure 4.3. Displaying the authorization badge.

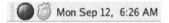

Managing Users

Figure 4.4. The user listing.

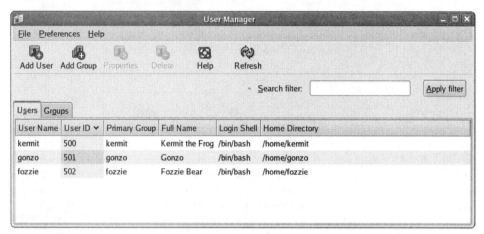

The User Manager, shown in Figure 4.4, displays all the user accounts that currently exist on your system. It also displays for each user the User ID number, the group to which that user belongs, the user's full name (optional), the user's default shell, and the home directory. To add a user, click Add User. The dialog shown in Figure 4.5 will appear.

As you can see in Figure 4.5, a Fedora administrator has plenty of options to consider when adding a new user. These include defining the home directory, creating a private group for the user, manually assigning a user ID, and selecting the user's shell. While the defaults are perfectly acceptable in most cases, the process is very flexible and caters well for unusual cases.

Managing Groups

Users within a Linux system may be consolidated into groups, which can ease the management of file permissions for groups of users. You might, for example, create a "developers" group, into which you'll add all the Web developers who create code for your server. You'd give that group appropriate permissions to the files of your Web application, providing each developer the ability to edit those files without allowing ordinary users access to them.

Figure 4.5. The Create New User dialog.

Figure 4.6. The Create New Group dialog.

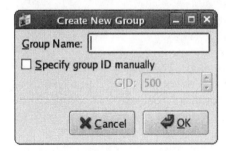

To add a new group, select Add Group from the User Manager window. The dialog shown in Figure 4.6 will appear.

First, you'll need to name the group. In our example, you might, for instance, name the group "Developers." You can also accept the pre-assigned group ID, or

GID (500, in this case), or check the Specify group ID manually checkbox to manually assign the group a group ID.[1]

To view the current groups, and add a user to an existing group, select the Groups tab in the User Manager window, as illustrated in Figure 4.7.

Figure 4.7. The User Manager's Groups tab.

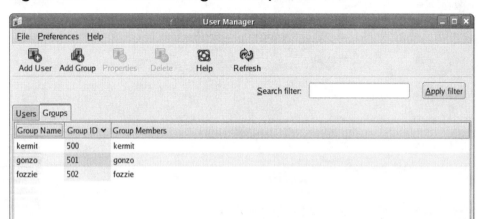

There are two methods by which we can add a user to a group. The first is to select a group in the User Manager and click the Properties button. In the dialog that appears, select the Group Users tab to see a list of users you can add to this group, as shown in Figure 4.8.

Ensure that you've checked all of the users you'd like to include as members of this group, and click OK.

The other way we can add a user to a group is via the User Manager's Users view. In the User Manager, click on the Users tab, select the user you'd like to add to a group, and click Properties. Clicking the Groups tab displays a list of all of the groups of which this user can become part, as shown in Figure 4.9.

Deleting a user or group within the User Manager window is as easy as creating one. Simply highlight the user or group, then click the Delete button in the User Manager window's toolbar.

---

[1] You'll almost always want to accept the pre-assigned ID, because it doesn't matter what a group's ID is, except in very rare cases. If you come across one of those rare cases, you'll know why you want a specific ID; otherwise, accept the suggestion.

Figure 4.8. Adding users to a group.

Figure 4.9. Adding a user to groups.

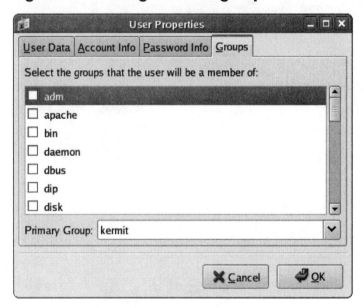

Managing Users from the Command Line

Creating Users and Groups with `useradd` and `groupadd`

To add users and groups from the command line, we use the `groupadd` and `useradd` commands.

Using `.bashrc`

Unfortunately, you can't use `groupadd` or `useradd` as easily as you might use `ls` in the default installation of Fedora Core. The `groupadd` and `useradd` tools are located in the directory `/usr/sbin`, which isn't part of the default PATH. To add this directory to the PATH variable, enter **export PATH=$PATH:/usr/sbin** at the command prompt, as we discussed in Chapter 3. This will only take effect for the current shell session; as soon as you close the terminal window, this value will disappear.

Figure 4.10. Opening `.bashrc` in gedit.

If you'd rather have this command run automatically every time you start the shell, you can add the command to .bashrc, a hidden file that's automatically executed every time you start up the bash shell. To open this file in gedit, select File > Open.... In the Open File... dialog, right-click in the area in which the files are listed, and click Show Hidden Files, as depicted in Figure 4.10.

Locate .bashrc and open it. Add the export command to the end of the file, as shown below.

File: .bashrc

```
# .bashrc

# User specific aliases and functions

# Source global definitions
if [ -f /etc/bashrc ]; then
    . /etc/bashrc
fi

export PATH=$PATH:/usr/sbin
```

The next time you open a terminal window, this command will be executed automatically. Note that this won't affect any shells you have open at the moment—you'll need to close and reopen them in order for the command to execute.

Let's look at an example of these commands, which we'll run as root.

```
[kermit@swinetrek ~]$ su
Password:
[root@swinetrek kermit]# groupadd muppets
[root@swinetrek kermit]# useradd -G muppets -c "Miss Piggy" \
> misspiggy
[root@swinetrek kermit]# passwd misspiggy
Changing password for user misspiggy.
New UNIX password:
Retype new UNIX password:
passwd: all authentication tokens updated successfully.
[root@swinetrek kermit]# exit
exit
[kermit@swinetrek ~]$
```

In this example, we can see that the groupadd command has been used to create a group called "muppets." Remember that groupadd is located in /usr/sbin, so you might need to enter /usr/sbin/groupadd instead.

Next, we use the `useradd` command to create a user called "misspiggy," and add her to the "muppets" group (as specified by the `-G` option) with the full name "Miss Piggy" (as specified by the `-c` option). When a user is created using `useradd`, that user's password is locked; we need to change it in order to unlock it. To do so, we use the `passwd` tool.

Deleting Users and Groups with `userdel` and `groupdel`

You can delete users and groups using the `userdel` and `groupdel` commands. Note that `userdel` will leave the users' home directory intact; you might want to delete this directory while you're logged in as root:

```
[kermit@swinetrek ~]$ su
Password:
[root@swinetrek kermit]# groupdel muppets
[root@swinetrek kermit]# userdel misspiggy
[root@swinetrek kermit]# rm -rf /home/misspiggy/
[root@swinetrek kermit]# exit
exit
[kermit@swinetrek ~]$
```

Mounting and Filesystems

We briefly touched on the concepts of devices, mount points and filesystems in Chapter 2. In Linux, when we insert removable media of any kind, we need to mount the filesystem stored on that media device. This concept is fairly unfamiliar to Windows users, but once you get the hang of it, it becomes second nature. In fact, Windows does the same thing; the difference is simply that the Windows operating system automates the mounting process, so users are usually unaware that it takes place. Nautilus largely automates this process, too, but it's still important for system administrators to know how devices are mounted, and how mounting is accomplished from the command line.

Mounting a Filesystem with the mount Command

Let's look at the process of mounting a floppy disk from the command line:

```
[kermit@swinetrek ~]$ su
Password:
[root@swinetrek kermit]# mount -t vfat /dev/fd0 /media/floppy
[root@swinetrek kermit]# exit
```

```
exit
[kermit@swinetrek ~]$
```

The mount command loads a device's filesystem into our server's filesystem. In this case, the device is the floppy disk drive (/dev/fd0), and that device's filesystem is loaded into /media/floppy—the mount point. We also need to tell Linux what kind of filesystem is can expect to find on the device. In this case, we're using a disk formatted as FAT32, and we've specified this with -t vfat.

Let's take a closer look at what's going on here. We're using a floppy disk from an old Windows machine; a couple of directories are stored on the disk, as shown in Figure 4.11.

Figure 4.11. Viewing the floppy disk's filesystem in Windows.

As we saw in Chapter 2, there is no A: drive in Linux; removable media devices appear as part of the filesystem within the /media directory. So, when we mount the floppy disk, it appears inside the /media/floppy directory, as depicted in Figure 4.12.

Figure 4.12. The floppy disk's filesystem displaying as part of the Linux filesystem.

Unmounting a Filesystem with the `umount` Command

Before removing the floppy disk, we should unmount it, thereby removing it from the filesystem. We can do so using the `umount` command—note the missing "n"—as shown below.

```
[kermit@swinetrek ~]$ umount /media/floppy
[kermit@swinetrek ~]$
```

For some devices, the unmounting process is very important. A floppy disk is a good example of this. It can take a long time to save a file to a floppy disk; the unmounting process ensures that any programs that are writing to the disk complete their writes before the device is removed.

The Filesystem Table (`fstab`) File

Many of the configuration options for your server's filesystem are contained in a single text file, `/etc/fstab`. As this file is critical to the operation of your system, the file is owned by root and only root can write to the file. That ownership and permissions structure prevents any potentially catastrophic alteration to, or deletion of the file by non-root users. It's strongly advised that you refrain from adjusting these permissions, and treat the file with the respect it deserves when logged in as root.

Tip

Editing Read-only Files

There are numerous ways to edit a text file as root. Perhaps the easiest is to launch your preferred text editor from the command line after switching to the root user. The text editor will run as if you were logged in as root, but GNOME will insist on returning to the terminal an ugly looking warning message:

```
[kermit@swinetrek ~]$ su
Password:
[root@swinetrek kermit]# gedit /etc/fstab

(gedit:2066): GnomeUI-WARNING **: While connecting to
session manager:
Authentication Rejected, reason : None of the
authentication protocols specified are supported and
host-based authentication failed.
```

There's absolutely no problem with using this approach to edit files. Kate, gedit, or the text editor of your choice will run without a problem. However, if you'd prefer to get rid of this warning, Bruce Wolk suggested the following script as a solution in the newsgroup linux.redhat.

File: ~/bin/xroot.sh

```sh
#!/bin/sh

if [ $# -lt 1 ]
then echo "usage: `basename $0` command" >&2
     exit 2
fi
su - -c "exec env DISPLAY='$DISPLAY' \
    XAUTHORITY='${XAUTHORITY-$HOME/.Xauthority}' \
    "'"$SHELL"'" -c '$*'"
```

Save this file as xroot.sh in a directory named bin inside your home directory. You'll probably need to create this directory yourself, and you'll also need to give yourself execute permissions on this file. You can do so by running **chmod u+x ~/bin/xroot.sh**, or by changing the file's permissions in Nautilus.

Because /home/*username*/bin is automatically included in the PATH environment variable, you should be able to run this from the command line simply by typing **xroot.sh**.

```
[kermit@swinetrek ~]$ xroot.sh gedit
Password:
```

fstab, which is an abbreviation of "filesystem table," provides instructions to the operating system as to where devices should be mounted.

The /etc/fstab file will appear similar to the following:

File: /etc/fstab

```
# This file is edited by fstab-sync - see 'man fstab-sync' for
# details
/dev/VolGroup00/LogVol00  /              ext3    defaults          1 1
LABEL=/boot               /boot          ext3    defaults          1 2
/dev/devpts               /dev/pts       devpts  gid=5,mode=620    0 0
/dev/shm                  /dev/shm       tmpfs   defaults          0 0
/dev/proc                 /proc          proc    defaults          0 0
/dev/sys                  /sys           sysfs   defaults          0 0
/dev/VolGroup00/LogVol01  swap           swap    defaults          0 0
/dev/fd0                  /media/floppy  auto    pamconsole,exec,
```

			noauto,managed 0 0
/dev/hdc	/media/cdrom	auto	pamconsole,exec,
			noauto,managed 0 0

Comments

In most Linux configuration files, lines that start with # are comment lines, and are ignored by the operating system.

Each line of /etc/fstab contains five fields which, together, specify the configuration of a single device. Let's look at what each field means.

1. The first element specifies the device.

    The second line, which starts with LABEL=/boot, is a special case—the label /boot is defined elsewhere in the system. You can treat this as a synonym for /dev/hda1.

2. The second item identifies the mount point for the device. The last two lines—/media/floppy and /media/cdrom—define the mount points for /dev/fd0 (the floppy disk drive) and /dev/hdc (the CD-ROM drive).

    The first line, which deals with the device /dev/VolGroup00/LogVol00 (this is the first partition on the first hard disk), tells the system to mount this disk as the root of the filesystem.

3. The third element defines the type of filesystem Linux should expect. Here we can see that /dev/VolGroup00/LogVol00 has an ext3 filesystem.

4. The fourth element lists mounting options for the device and the filesystem. Available options include:

    auto   This device should be mounted automatically when the system is started.

    noauto This device should not be mounted automatically when the system is started.

    owner   The device and filesystem may only be mounted by the owner of the device file.

    kudzu   The device will be checked for changes by the Red Hat kudzu system.

rw   The filesystem will provide read and write access.

ro   The filesystem will provide read only access.

There are several other options for mounting devices and filesystems, as you can see in the default `fstab` file, but these are the ones in which we're interested. In our example, many of the options are set to `defaults`. In a Fedora Core system, this is equivalent to `auto,owner,kudzu,rw`.

5.   The fifth column is used by the `dump` backup utility to determine if this filesystem should be included in its backups—the `0` value tells `dump` to ignore this filesystem for backup purposes.

6.   The final column indicates whether the filesystem should be checked with the `fsck` (filesystem check) utility. ext3 filesystems very rarely benefit from such a check. If you do want to perform such checks, you should number the filesystems in the order in which you'd like them checked—`1` for the first, `2` for the second, and so on.

With a correctly formatted `fstab` file, using the `mount` command becomes much easier:

```
[kermit@swinetrek ~]$ su
Password:
[root@swinetrek kermit]# mount /media/floppy
[root@swinetrek kermit]# exit
exit
[kermit@swinetrek ~]$
```

Here, we've specified only the mount point. `mount` is able to look in `fstab` to identify the device to which this mount point relates.

Whether or not you will be able to mount the device as a normal user depends upon the options noted in `fstab`, and the permissions on the device file. If the mount point is owned by root, and you attempt to mount a device on it as a normal user, you'll be presented with a `Permission denied` error.

Making a Mount Point

Until now, we've only talked about Fedora Core's conventions for mount points. Other Linux systems use different conventions, in order to make the mount point name slightly more recognizable. SuSE, for example, creates a `/floppy` mount point when the system is installed, as opposed to Fedora's `/media/floppy`. The fact that other distributions can use different conventions should tell you that the naming of mount points is not standard, nor should it be. Remember that a mount point is merely another directory on the system. If you're confused by the convention employed by the distribution you're using, use the convention you prefer.

For example, you can use the SuSE convention mentioned above on your Fedora system:

```
[kermit@swinetrek ~]$ su
Password:
[root@swinetrek kermit]# mkdir /floppy
[root@swinetrek kermit]# exit
exit
[kermit@swinetrek ~]$ mount -t vfat /dev/fd0 /floppy
[kermit@swinetrek ~]$
```

Here, we've mounted the floppy disk's filesystem at a new mount point: /floppy. We can edit fstab to make this change more permanent.

File: /etc/fstab

```
# This file is edited by fstab-sync - see 'man fstab-sync' for
# details
/dev/VolGroup00/LogVol00 /              ext3   defaults            1 1
LABEL=/boot              /boot          ext3   defaults            1 2
/dev/devpts              /dev/pts       devpts gid=5,mode=620      0 0
/dev/shm                 /dev/shm       tmpfs  defaults            0 0
/dev/proc                /proc          proc   defaults            0 0
/dev/sys                 /sys           sysfs  defaults            0 0
/dev/VolGroup00/LogVol01 swap           swap   defaults            0 0
/dev/fd0                 /floppy        auto   pamconsole,exec,
                                               noauto,managed      0 0
/dev/hdc                 /media/cdrom   auto   pamconsole,exec,
                                               noauto,managed      0 0
```

We can now mount a floppy disk by just entering mount /floppy.

Automatically Mounting Filesystems

We can use the auto option in fstab to make the mounting process automatic for some devices. To mount a CD-ROM automatically once it's inserted, change the options listed for /dev/hdc from noauto to auto.

```
                                                    File: /etc/fstab
# This file is edited by fstab-sync - see 'man fstab-sync' for
# details
/dev/VolGroup00/LogVol00 /              ext3    defaults         1 1
LABEL=/boot              /boot          ext3    defaults         1 2
/dev/devpts              /dev/pts       devpts  gid=5,mode=620   0 0
/dev/shm                 /dev/shm       tmpfs   defaults         0 0
/dev/proc                /proc          proc    defaults         0 0
/dev/sys                 /sys           sysfs   defaults         0 0
/dev/VolGroup00/LogVol01 swap           swap    defaults         0 0
/dev/fd0                 /media/floppy  auto    pamconsole,exec,
                                                noauto,managed   0 0
/dev/hdc                 /media/cdrom   auto    pamconsole,exec,
                                                auto,managed     0 0
```

Now, whenever you insert a CD-ROM, it will be mounted automatically.

Services

Like every modern operating system, Linux has quite a bit going on in the background. If you're an average computer user—on a Linux, Mac, or Windows system—you'll rarely have a compelling reason to interact with these background tasks. Most of the time, you won't even realize they're there. The tasks execute on their own and, provided you stay out of their way, they'll stay out of yours. Even as an administrator, you're not likely to need to do much more than start, stop, or restart these services. But don't let the lack of direct contact fool you: these services are critical to the operation of your system.

Linux's system services are generally referred to as **daemons**. They're applications that run in the background, providing such critical functionality as file and printer sharing, power management, automatic task scheduling, and system logging. For example, your Web server will be running httpd, the HTTP daemon that lies at the heart of Apache. If you make use of MySQL, you'll also need to run the MySQL daemon, mysqld.

The Service Configuration Tool

Figure 4.13. The Service Configuration tool.

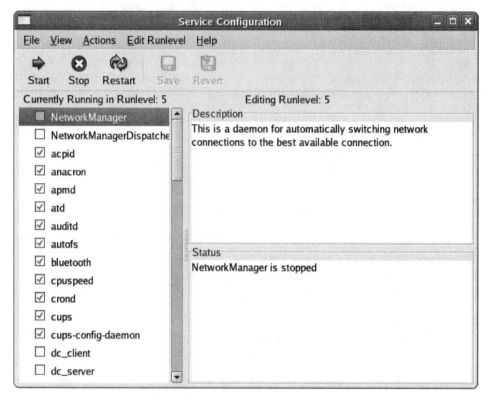

The Service Configuration tool, which you can start by selecting Desktop > System Settings > Server Settings > Services, can be used to stop and start services. The tool is shown in Figure 4.13.

To stop or start a service, select it from the list in the left-hand panel. A brief description, along with that service's current status, will be presented on the right. To start a stopped service, click the Start button at the top of the window; to stop a running service, click the Stop button. There is also a Restart button, which can be used to restart a service—an action that can be necessary for certain configuration changes to take effect.

You can also use this tool to configure services to start automatically when the machine is switched on. To do this, check the checkbox next to the service name, and click Save.

Services and Runlevels

Runlevels are basically a convenient way of describing the facilities that are currently available to the system. In runlevel 5, all system functions are available: multiple users can log in, networking features are available, and the GUI is up and running. As the system starts, and system functions become available, other runlevels are triggered:

Runlevel 1

This is known as **single user mode**. Only one user can be logged in at a time. No network resources are available.

Runlevel 2

Multiple users may be logged in simultaneously, but no network support is available. This is known as **multi-user mode**.

Runlevel 3

This is the same as runlevel 2, except that network resources have become available. This runlevel is sometimes referred to as **full multi-user mode**.

Runlevel 5

In addition to everything that's available in runlevel 3, the GUI server is also available at this runlevel.

What Happened to Runlevel 4?

There is no default runlevel 4—this is reserved for definition by system administration gurus.

Figure 4.14. Editing all runlevels.

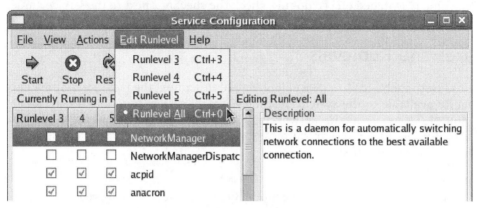

The Service Configuration tool allows us to set services to start at runlevels 3, 4, or 5. To alter the services that start at a given runlevel, select an option from the Edit Runlevel menu. You can choose to edit a single runlevel at a time, or edit all three at once by selecting Runlevel All, as shown in Figure 4.14.

Check the boxes to specify which daemons you'd like to have start automatically, and when you'd like them to start, then click Save at the top of the window. Note that if you want a daemon to run in runlevels 3, 4, and 5, you need to check all three boxes. If you only check the box for runlevel 3, the service will be stopped when the system reaches runlevel 5.

Using service to Start and Stop Services

To stop, start, or get the status of a service from the command line, you can use Fedora Core's service tool, which is located in the /sbin directory. Remember that, if you added /sbin to the PATH environment variable, you won't need to prefix the command name with /sbin/ to run it.

```
[kermit@swinetrek ~]$ su
Password:
[root@swinetrek kermit]# /sbin/service httpd status
httpd is stopped
[root@swinetrek kermit]# /sbin/service httpd start
Starting httpd:                                          [  OK  ]
[root@swinetrek kermit]# /sbin/service httpd status
httpd (pid 2928 2927 2926 2924 2923 2922 2921 2920 2917) is
running...
[root@swinetrek kermit]# /sbin/service httpd stop
```

```
Stopping httpd:                                          [  OK  ]
[root@swinetrek kermit]# exit
exit
[kermit@swinetrek ~]$
```

This tool takes two parameters: the name of the daemon (in this example, httpd) and the action to execute. All services will support the actions start, stop, re-start, and status.

Using ntsysv to Start Services Automatically

ntsysv is an unusual command line tool in that it offers an interface similar to the text-based install discussed in Chapter 1, as you can see in Figure 4.15.

Figure 4.15. ntsysv running in the terminal.

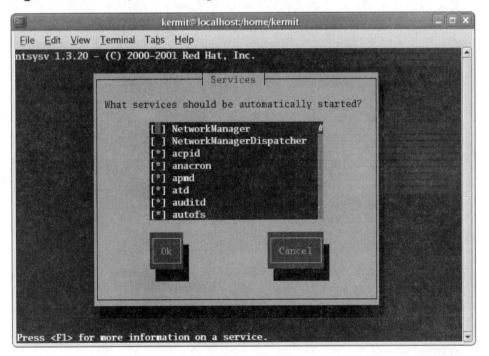

By default, ntsysv only edits runlevel 5. You can change this by starting ntsysv with the --level option. For example, ntsysv --level 3 will edit runlevel 3.

Automatically Starting Services with `chkconfig`

The more traditional command line equivalent of `ntsysv` is `chkconfig`.

```
[kermit@swinetrek ~]$ su
Password:
[root@swinetrek kermit]# /sbin/chkconfig --level 345 httpd on
[root@swinetrek kermit]# exit
exit
[kermit@swinetrek ~]$
```

This command sets `httpd` to start at runlevels 3, 4, and 5. You can get a list of the services that start at each level by running **`chkconfig --list`**.

Automating Routine Tasks

Computers are intended to do things for us. Yet, we spend much of our computing lifetimes repeatedly performing the same tasks, many of which are, in the end, rather mindless. System administration can sometimes become a chore chock-full of tedium and routine: the same keystrokes, the same checks, the same results. Wouldn't it be ideal if we were able to put the computer to its intended use, and have it do these things for us?

Linux provides an abundance of ways to automate tasks. Shell scripts can help, but the real power lies in two particular facilities: cron and, to a lesser extent, `at`. These are tools you'll rely upon to perform such routine tasks as archiving logs, updating the system database with newly installed applications, writing server statistics, and much, much more.

cron

cron is a Linux system daemon that executes scheduled scripts. The cron daemon, or `crond`, runs as a service that starts when your system starts. Every minute, it checks its own schedule database for tasks that need to be performed.

The heart of cron is the `/etc/crontab` file, which is shown below from the default, unaltered Fedora Core installation:

File: **`/etc/crontab`**

```
SHELL=/bin/bash
PATH=/sbin:/bin:/usr/sbin:/usr/bin
MAILTO=root
```

```
HOME=/

# run-parts
01 * * * * root run-parts /etc/cron.hourly
02 4 * * * root run-parts /etc/cron.daily
22 4 * * 0 root run-parts /etc/cron.weekly
42 4 1 * * root run-parts /etc/cron.monthly
```

The crontab file first defines some environment variables: the shell in which the tasks will run, the PATH environment variable, the system account to which mail notifications will be sent, and the home directory to use. After the run-parts comment, the command schedule is listed.

The crontab Command Schedule Syntax

Believe it or not, a single line in this file provides all the information required for the system to perform a full set of tasks. In order to understand it, we need to break this line out into fields.

24-Hour Time

cron always deals in 24-hour time: 7:24 means 7:24 a.m., and 19:24 means 7:24 p.m.

1. The first field defines how many minutes of each hour must pass before the task will be performed. In the above default crontab file, the first task is scheduled to start one minute past the hour; the last task is scheduled to commence at 42 minutes past the hour.

2. The second field defines the hour in which the task will be completed. From this, we can tell that the second task is scheduled to run at 4:02.

    An asterisk indicates that the task should be executed every hour. Therefore, we can tell that the first task is scheduled to be run at 0:01, 1:01, 2:01, and so on, all the way to 23:01, after which it starts all over again.

3. The third field defines the day of the month—numbered from 1 to 31—on which the task will run. The last command is scheduled to run at 4:42 on the first day of the month. Again, an asterisk indicates that the task should be run every day of the month.

4. The fourth field determines the month in which the task should run; as you'd expect, the months are numbered from 1 to 12. If you had a task to perform only once a year, say in July, this field would contain a 7. If you had a task

to perform every day in December, this field would contain twelve. Since, in our example, this field always contains an asterisk, we know that all of our tasks will be performed every month.

5. The fifth field defines the day of the week on which the task will run. 0 represents Sunday, 1 represents Monday, and 6 represents Saturday. Our third task has a 0 in this field: it will be executed at 4:22 on Sundays. Once more, an asterisk in this field indicates that the task will be performed on every day of the week.

6. The next field identifies the user who will complete the task. In all cases here, it's root.

7. The final field defines the actual task that is to be run. Here, we use `run-parts` to execute every script inside the /etc/cron.*schedule* directories. Scripts inside the /etc/cron.hourly directory are run every hour, scripts inside /etc/cron.daily are run daily, and so on.

Adding to `crontab`

Let's put this to more practical use with the scenario mentioned back in Chapter 3. You may remember that we introduced the power of the command line with the command `find /var/backups/* -ctime +5 -exec rm {} \;`, which I use to remove backups that are more than five days old three times a week. This automated process is powered by cron, so let's take a look at how this is configured on my system:

File: **/etc/crontab**

```
SHELL=/bin/bash
PATH=/sbin:/bin:/usr/sbin:/usr/bin
MAILTO=root
HOME=/

# run-parts
01 * * * * root run-parts /etc/cron.hourly
02 4 * * * root run-parts /etc/cron.daily
22 4 * * 0 root run-parts /etc/cron.weekly
42 4 1 * * root run-parts /etc/cron.monthly
12 5 * * 2,4,6 root find /var/backups/* -ctime +5 -exec rm {} \;
```

The first two fields tell us that this task will be run at 5:12—for purity's sake, I've scheduled the task to run at a time when I'm not using the system, though it probably won't make much of a difference in terms of performance. The next two fields are filled with asterisks, meaning they'll be run regardless of the date. The potentially interesting value here, though, is the fifth "day of week" field, which has the value 2,4,6—this means that the task is scheduled for Tuesday, Thursday, and Saturday. crontab also allows for ranges. 1-5 in the fifth would schedule a task to run Monday to Friday.

cron can just as easily execute shell scripts. Let's create a script named backup.sh to actually create these backups. Save this file in the /home/*username*/bin directory—you may need to create this directory if you haven't done so already.

File: ~/**bin**/**backup.sh**

```
#!/bin/sh

# Create a directory for this backup.
# Its name depends on the date and time so backups can't overwrite
# each other, unless they're executed in the same minute.
DATE=`/bin/date +%Y%m%d%H%M`
mkdir /var/backup/$DATE
# Backup the Apache logs.
mkdir /var/backup/$DATE/apache-logs
for f in /var/log/httpd/*;
do
   cp -fr "$f" --target-directory /var/backup/$DATE/apache-logs
done
# Backup kermit's home directory
mkdir /var/backup/$DATE/kermit-home
for f in /home/kermit/*;
do
   cp -fr "$f" --target-directory /var/backup/$DATE/kermit-home
done
```

This above script achieves several tasks:

❏ DATE=`/bin/date +%Y%m%d%H%M` declares a variable named DATE and fills it with the output of the date command. The +%Y%m%d%H%M option on the date command instructs it to format the date in YYYYmmddHHMM format. That is, the minute before midnight on December 31, 2006 becomes 200612312359. The backticks, or backward quotes around the date command, tell the system that this is a command embedded in your script that should be run to obtain the required text value.

❏ Next, mkdir /var/backup/$DATE creates a directory for our backups based on this date.

❏ `mkdir /var/backup/$DATE/apache-logs` creates a subdirectory for Apache logs.

❏ The `for f in /var/log/httpd/*;` line sets up a loop to go through each file in the `/var/log/httpd` directory. Inside this loop, the variable `f` will refer to the current file.

❏ `cp -fr "$f" --target-directory /var/backup/$DATE/apache-logs` copies the current file (`f`) to the target directory, `/var/backup/current-date/apache-logs`.

❏ The previous three steps are then repeated, copying everything in `/home/kermit` to `/var/backup/current-date/kermit-home`.

Before we go ahead and run this script, we need to create the `/var/backup` directory, grant everyone write access to this directory, and make the `backup.sh` script executable:

```
[kermit@swinetrek ~]$ su
Password:
[root@swinetrek kermit]# mkdir /var/backup
[root@swinetrek kermit]# chmod a+w /var/backup
[root@swinetrek kermit]# exit
exit
[kermit@swinetrek ~]$ chmod u+x ~/bin/backup.sh
[kermit@swinetrek ~]$
```

Let's test the script before we modify the `crontab` file to ensure that it works as we think it should:

```
[kermit@swinetrek ~]$ backup.sh
cp: cannot stat `/var/log/httpd/*': Permission denied
[kermit@swinetrek ~]$
```

We get this error message because we don't have access to the `/var/log/httpd` directory; we need to run this script as root:

```
[kermit@swinetrek ~]$ su
Password:
[root@swinetrek kermit]# backup.sh
[root@swinetrek kermit]# exit
exit
[kermit@swinetrek ~]$ ls /var/backup
200612312359
[kermit@swinetrek ~]$
```

In the file listing, we can see that a directory has been created with the current date and time. Delve deeper into this directory until you're satisfied that the script is working as expected.

The last step in the process is to add the execution of the script to the `crontab` file on the schedule we've already defined:

File: **/etc/crontab**

```
SHELL=/bin/bash
PATH=/sbin:/bin:/usr/sbin:/usr/bin
MAILTO=root
HOME=/

# run-parts
01 * * * * root run-parts /etc/cron.hourly
02 4 * * * root run-parts /etc/cron.daily
22 4 * * 0 root run-parts /etc/cron.weekly
42 4 1 * * root run-parts /etc/cron.monthly
12 5 * * 2,4,6  find /var/backups/* -ctime +5 -exec rm {} \;
32 5 * * * root /home/kermit/bin/backup.sh
```

This entry differs from the original only in that it executes a script rather than executing a lone command. Because the script can contain commands and logic, it's a sound approach to solving more complex routine operations.

Using the /etc/cron.*schedule* Directories

We've already discussed what the default `crontab` entries do. The first line runs the command `run-parts /etc/cron.hourly` every hour: `run-parts` will go into the `/etc/cron.hourly` directory and execute every executable file it finds there. Entries also exist for `cron.daily`, `cron.weekly`, and `cron.monthly` directories. If you prefer, you can simply store your `backup.sh` script in the `/etc/cron.daily` directory. It will run with the other daily scripts.

Anacron

Anacron is, to some extent, an extension of cron. Like cron, it's intended to execute commands on a schedule, taking care of routine tasks. However, unlike cron, Anacron makes no assumption that the machine is up and running 24/7. In that sense, Anacron provides some measure of redundancy to the functions of cron.

Like other Linux applications, Anacron gets its direction from a text configuration file. In Fedora, this file is /etc/anacrontab. At first glance, the anacrontab file looks less daunting than crontab, even though we know how simple the crontab file can actually be.

File: **/etc/anacrontab**

```
# /etc/anacrontab: configuration file for anacron

# See anacron(8) and anacrontab(5) for details.

SHELL=/bin/sh
PATH=/usr/local/sbin:/usr/local/bin:/sbin:/bin:/usr/sbin:/usr/bin

1       65      cron.daily      run-parts /etc/cron.daily
7       70      cron.weekly     run-parts /etc/cron.weekly
30      75      cron.monthly    run-parts /etc/cron.monthly
```

As in crontab, the first few lines of this file define some environment variables: in this case, SHELL and PATH. The remaining lines describe, over a number of fields, the jobs that Anacron must carry out. From left to right, these fields are as follows:

period

The period field identifies the number of days that constitute the "period" in which the job will run once. In this example, the first job will be run every day, the second job will run once every seven days, and the last job will run once every thirty days.

delay

When it's time for a task to be executed, Anacron will wait this many minutes before executing the task. This is potentially useful when a machine is turned on after a long period of being switched off. For example, imagine if our machine was turned off for more than thirty days. When we turn it back on, Anacron will realize that it's time to execute all of it's scheduled tasks. It will execute the daily tasks in 65 minutes time, the weekly tasks in 70 minutes time and the monthly tasks in 75 minutes time. This staggering stops the machine becoming bogged down by three competing jobs.

job identifier

The job identifier field is as it sounds: a means by which the system can identify each Anacron task. This field can contain any character, barring spaces, tabs and slashes.

command
>   Finally, similar to `crontab`, `anacrontab` specifies the command that will be executed. Again, Anacron will execute `run-parts` to work its way through the scripts in `/etc/cron.daily`.

The operation of Anacron is pretty straightforward. When run, it reads the list of jobs from `/etc/anacrontab` and checks whether or not each job has been run in the last specified number of days. If not, Anacron runs the job after waiting for the delay period. If the job has been run in the specified time period, it leaves it alone. It's pretty simple.

We can start the Anacron daemon using one of the service tools we looked at earlier in this chapter. By default, it should be set up to start with your machine, but you can change this setting if you like.

Running cron and Anacron Together

By default, both cron and Anacron are configured to run all of the scripts in the `/etc/cron.schedule` directories. However, only one of cron or Anacron will actually run the scripts.

Each of these directories contains a script to keep Anacron up to date. For example, whenever cron runs the scripts in `/etc/cron.daily`, one of those scripts updates the file that Anacron uses to record when the task was last run. Later, when Anacron goes to run these scripts, it will see that cron has already run them, so it won't run them again.

at

Now, we've got cron to perform regularly scheduled tasks on your system. We've got Anacron to pick up cron's slack if the machine isn't up and running 24/7. That seems like a pretty full complement of task scheduling methods, doesn't it? As true as that may be, we've still left one piece out of the automated task puzzle: `at`.

`at` is a classic Linux hack, intended to take up where other applications leave off. In the cases of both cron and anacron, it's not a trivial task to add a simple, one-off task to the schedule. Let's say, for example, that you need to download a very large file, and you want to do it at a time when there's no-one else on the network, so plenty of bandwidth is available. You could add an entry to `/etc/crontab`, but you'd have to remember to remove it in order to avoid downloading the same file again in the future. `at` serves this niche purpose perfectly. Better yet, the syntax for using `at` couldn't be simpler:

```
[kermit@swinetrek ~]$ at 3:00
at> wget http://sitepoint.com/verylargefile.zip
at> <EOT>
job 1 at 2005-12-31 03:00
[kermit@swinetrek ~]$
```

<EOT>

<EOT> stands for end of transmission, and is triggered by hitting **Ctrl-D**. Use this to indicate that you have finished entering commands to be executed at the given time.

at schedules the task for the next instance of the time you specify. In the above example, at would execute the given command at 3:00 a.m.

24-Hour Time

Remember that at, like cron and Anacron, uses 24-hour time.

In summary, if you're looking to schedule tasks, Linux has you well covered. You have cron and Anacron for repeating tasks, and at for those one-off, occasional jobs.

Sending Email

By default, mail on Fedora Core 4 is handled by the sendmail program. sendmail can be configured to perform very complicated tasks, like running all the email for a company or an ISP. Entire books can (and have) been written about it. However, you're unlikely to want to make your LAMP server double as your mail server, and you're already likely to have a mail server. Some services on your LAMP server will generate email; for example, if a cron job fails, it will often email a description of its error to root@localhost, the root user's account's mailbox. That mail needs to be read, sometimes urgently, and it would be a pain to have to log in to your server to do so. The best approach is to ensure that all mail that goes to your Web server is sent to an address at which the system administrator can read it. We'll set up the Web server so that all the mail it receives is forwarded automatically to another email address.

The aliases File

Mail direction is controlled by the file /etc/aliases, which is shown below.

File: **/etc/aliases**

```
#
#  Aliases in this file will NOT be expanded in the header from
#  Mail, but WILL be visible over networks or from /bin/mail.
#
#       >>>>>>>>>>      The program "newaliases" must be run after
#       >> NOTE >>      this file is updated for any changes to
#       >>>>>>>>>>      show through to sendmail.
#

# Basic system aliases -- these MUST be present.
mailer-daemon:  postmaster
postmaster:     root

# General redirections for pseudo accounts.
bin:            root
daemon:         root
adm:            root
...
marketing:      postmaster
sales:          postmaster
support:        postmaster


# trap decode to catch security attacks
decode:         root

# Person who should get root's mail
#root:          marc
```

Each line in this file is an email alias; the line `postmaster: root` means "if mail comes to the postmaster account, put it in root's mailbox." By default, Fedora's `aliases` file ensures that mail for all the "system" accounts on the machine (i.e., all the accounts that the computer creates, rather than the ones that you create) goes to root's mailbox. This is very useful, because then, all you have to do is ensure that the mail that's sent to root ends up in the administrator's mailbox. This is a two-step process. First, record in the aliases file that root's mail should go to the administrator's mailbox. To do so, uncomment the last line in `/etc/aliases`, and change `marc` to the administrator's email address.

File: **/etc/aliases** (excerpt)

```
# Person who should get root's mail
root:           kermit@myisp.net
```

Second, tell `sendmail` that the `aliases` file has changed by running the command `newaliases`:

```
[kermit@swinetrek ~]$ su
Password:
[root@swinetrek kermit]# newaliases
/etc/aliases: 77 aliases, longest 16 bytes, 785 bytes total
[root@swinetrek kermit]# exit
exit
[kermit@swinetrek ~]$
```

That's all that's required. From now on, any mail that's sent to root by any cron jobs (or similar) on your Web server will end up in your mailbox. If you've created additional accounts on your server (say, for individual system administrators), then you may wish also to add those accounts to `/etc/aliases`, making them forward their mail to root or other email addresses. Remember to run `newaliases` after you make the change.

File: **/etc/aliases** (excerpt)

```
# Person who should get root's mail
root:        kermit@myisp.net
kermit:      root
gonzo:       gonzo@myisp.net
fozzie:      fozzie@myisp.net
```

Other Services

As you might expect, your Fedora Core system installs with a full set of graphical tools to ease the administration of various services on the system. There are too many tools to cover in depth here; instead, we'll look at the tools you'll use most frequently to configure and maintain both your system and the services it provides.

Tip

Preferences vs Settings

In Linux, the general convention is to call user-specific options "preferences." Those that affect the whole system are called "settings."

Samba

Samba allows you to share directories and printers with other machines. Typically, these machines are Windows machines, though they don't have to be. To start up the Samba Server Configuration tool shown in Figure 4.16, select Desktop > System Settings > Server Settings > Samba.

Figure 4.16. The Samba Server Configuration tool.

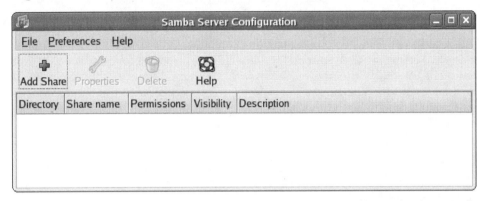

To share a directory on your Linux server with others, click the Add Share button. The dialog shown in Figure 4.17 will display.

Figure 4.17. The Create Samba Share dialog.

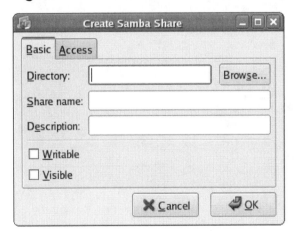

The main Samba Configuration window displays a list of all the shares you've defined. By highlighting a share, you can glean more information about it; you can adjust its settings by clicking on the Properties button.

NFS

NFS, or Network File System, is the Linux-native equivalent to Samba. It allows client machines to mount parts of your machine's filesystem as if they were other devices.

The interface for the NFS configuration (accessible via Desktop > System Settings > Server Settings > NFS) is much the same as that provided for Samba configuration. The directory, the allowed hosts, and the permissions are all displayed in the main window. You can add or delete a share and, as with the Samba configuration, check and alter the properties of existing shares.

Tip

Mounting NFS Shares

You can mount NFS shares quickly and easily using the `mount` command. Instead of specifying a device file, such as `/dev/fd0`, you simply specify a server name and the name of the shared directory, separated by a colon.

```
[root@swinetrek kermit]# mkdir /mnt/kermit-oldserver
[root@swinetrek kermit]# mount oldserver:/home/kermit \
> /mnt/kermit-oldserver
[root@swinetrek kermit]#
```

Apache Web Server

Figure 4.18. The graphical HTTP configuration tool.

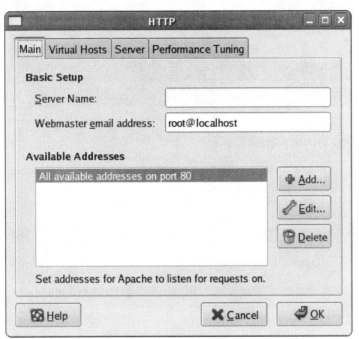

The Server Settings menu includes an HTTP option, which launches the graphical tool shown in Figure 4.18, allowing you to configure your Apache server.

We won't dig too deeply into the configuration tool here: we'll cover it in depth in Chapter 5. However, you can see that nearly every configuration option for your Apache server is available in this window.

Package Management

Figure 4.19. The Package Management tool.

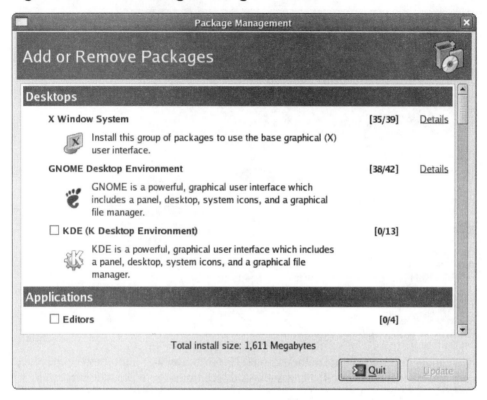

The Package Management tool shown in Figure 4.19 is available by selecting Desktop > System Settings > Add/Remove Applications.

This tool provides a means to add and remove applications from your system. You can adjust individual packages within groups, or remove an entire group.

Boot Configuration

Figure 4.20. The bootloader configuration tool.

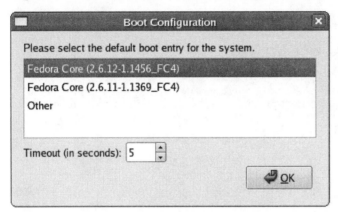

The Boot Configuration tool shown in Figure 4.20 is available from Desktop > System Settings > Bootloader. It's a very simple tool for configuring the GRUB bootloader we discussed in Chapter 1, allowing you to select the kernel your system will use at boot.

When automatic updates to the Linux kernel are allowed, it's likely you'll end up with multiple kernels on the system. By default, the system will choose the newest kernel version when booting, but this tool allows you to select from any of the kernels installed on the system. It also provides a tool to set the boot timeout: the period of time the system will wait for you to select a kernel during boot before automatically booting the default kernel version.

Date and Time

Figure 4.21. The Date/Time Properties window.

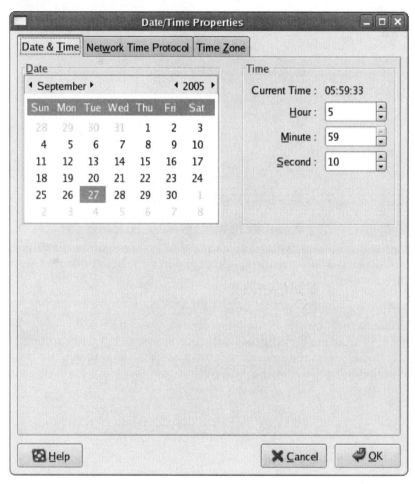

The Date/Time Properties tool (Desktop > System Settings > Date & Time), shown in Figure 4.21, serves several purposes. First, it provides a means to immediately adjust the system date and time. This is important for time-stamping and logging activity on the server.

In the Network Time Protocol tab, you can configure the server to make use of the Network Time Protocol (NTP) so that your system will connect with NTP servers around the world to automatically adjust its own internal clock. This will help ensure near-atomic-clock time accuracy on the server. To make use of NTP, check the Enable Network Time Protocol checkbox in the Network Time Protocol tab. Below this checkbox is a list of NTP servers to use; you can manage this list with the Add and Delete buttons.

Finally, in the Time Zone tab, the Date/Time Properties tool allows you to select the time zone in which the server is located. If you prefer that the server keep time based on the Coordinated Universal Time (UTC), check the System clock uses UTC checkbox.

Display Settings

Figure 4.22. The Display settings dialog.

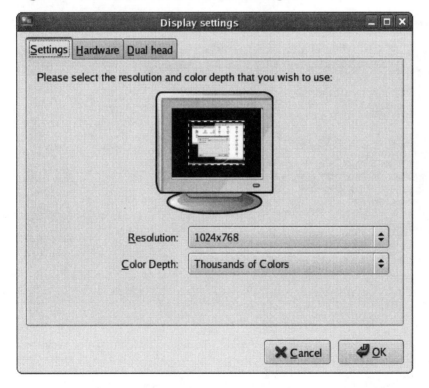

The Display settings tool in Fedora Core (Desktop > System Settings > Display), shown in Figure 4.22, allows you to set the resolution and color depth, identify the hardware you're using (which has probably been auto-detected by the system), and set up "dual head" (or dual monitor) systems.

Network Settings

The network settings on your machine can be configured via the graphical Network Configuration tool shown in Figure 4.23 (Desktop > System Settings > Network).

This tool allows you to configure all elements of your network devices, from the actual hardware, to IP addressing, to DNS and DHCP. Additionally, the devices can be activated or deactivated from within the graphical interface. Advanced operations, such as configuring individual interfaces to allow activation by normal users, or on system start, can also be performed.

Figure 4.23. The Network Configuration tool.

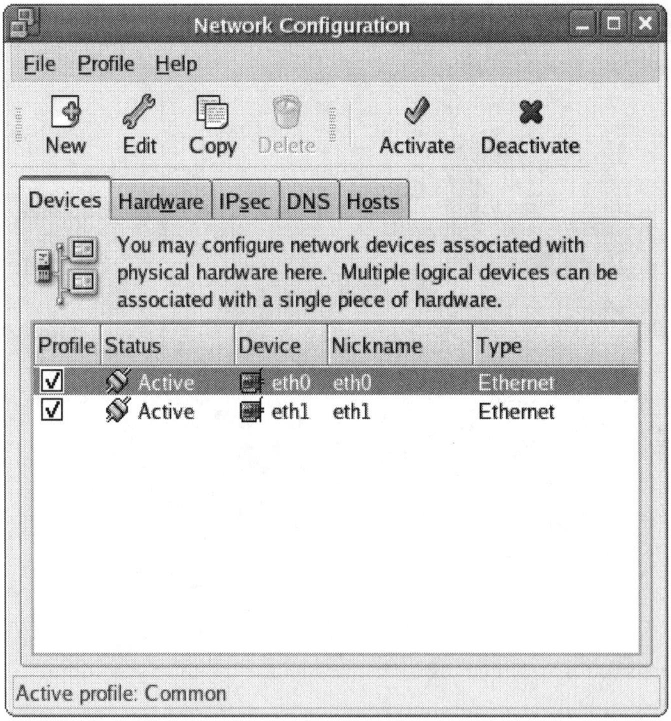

Printers

Fedora provides the tool depicted in Figure 4.24 to configure the printers on your system (Desktop > System Settings > Printing).

Figure 4.24. The Printer configuration tool.

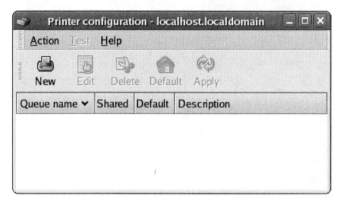

The New button will launch a wizard that allows you to use a printer that's connected directly to the server, or one that's on the network.

Security Level Configuration

Figure 4.25. The Security Level Configuration tool.

The firewall and Security Enhanced Linux (SELinux) are configured using the Security Level Configuration tool shown in Figure 4.25. To launch it, select Desktop > System Settings > Security Level.

This tool is a graphical front end for the `iptables` command-line tool and SELinux configuration.

`iptables` provides the capability to limit the network traffic coming in and out of your system to known traffic types, to specific ports, and/or to specific devices. This is all configured in the Firewall Options tab of the Security Level Configuration window. Clearly, if you're configuring and administering a Web server, it's important to allow WWW (HTTP) traffic on the machine. You can also optionally allow Secure WWW (HTTPS) traffic. For remote administration, it's useful to allow

SSH (Secure Shell) traffic: this will allow you to log into the machine from a remote location and perform administrative duties securely, as if you were sitting at the server. Telnet should seldom be allowed: this protocol has many, many known security issues.

If, instead of allowing traffic types, you'd prefer to allow all traffic across a specific interface (the first ethernet device, for example, or eth0), select that option from the Trusted devices list. Note that this is less secure than limiting traffic to specific protocols, as all traffic across the chosen interface will be allowed.

You may also want to allow traffic through specific ports. You can define these ports in the Other ports text field of the Security Level Configuration window, separated by commas. Of all the options in the Firewall Options tab, this is the most secure, as it limits traffic to very specific entry points. We'll look at this in more detail in Chapter 9.

SELinux is a new addition to Fedora Core, available as a standard option only since Fedora Core 3. It's a series of security related enhancements to the Linux kernel, largely written by the US National Security Administration (NSA). SELinux is such a rich tool that detailed configuration information is beyond the scope of this book. You can access more information about SELinux, including an extensive FAQ list, online at http://www.nsa.gov/selinux/.

Archive Manager

Figure 4.26. The Archive Manager application.

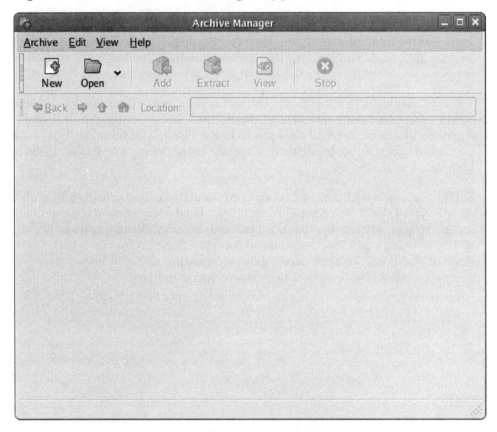

The Archive Manager depicted in Figure 4.26 is used to create archives of files on your system. It can handle a number of different archive formats, from the `.zip` format with which Windows users will be familiar, through to Java's `.jar` format, and Unix's `.tar`.

It's available from Applications > System Tools > Archive Manager.

The Archive Manager can be used to create a new archive or to add files to an existing archive. It's also used to view the contents of existing archives. To create a new archive, click on the New icon, then select the name and location of the new archive.

Next, you'll want to click the Add button in the main Archive Manager toolbar. In the resulting window, click to the location in which you'd like to store the new archive, and give it a name.

You can add files one at a time by clicking the Add button, or by dragging and dropping files or folders from Nautilus, as shown in Figure 4.27.

Figure 4.27. Adding a directory.

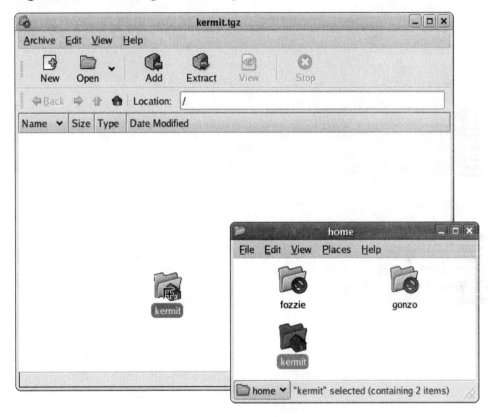

Figure 4.28. Archive Manager's Extract dialog.

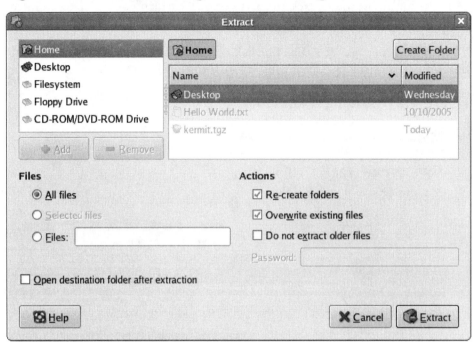

The Archive Manager can also be used to view or extract the contents of an archive. Click Open and select an archive, then click Extract on the toolbar. Archive Manager will display the Extract dialog which, as you can see in Figure 4.28, contains many options for extracting archived files.

Floppy Formatter

Figure 4.29. The Floppy Formatter.

To format a floppy disk, enter the path to the floppy device in the Floppy device text box; if the machine has only a single floppy, /dev/fd0 will be grayed in this text field. Select the density, the filesystem type and, if desired, add a volume name. You can also select the mode for formatting, including quick, standard, or thorough. When all the parameters are complete, click the Format button to complete the format. The Floppy Formatter, which is shown in Figure 4.29, is available from Applications > System Tools > Floppy Formatter.

Hardware Browser

Figure 4.30. The Hardware Browser.

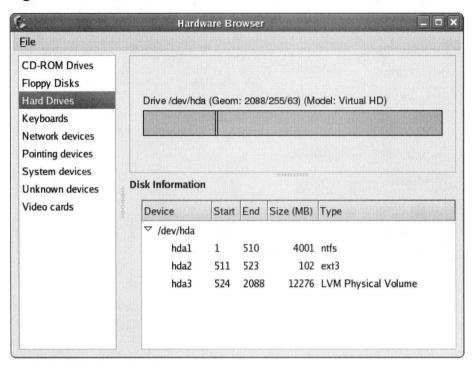

Fedora Core's Hardware Browser provides a view of all the hardware installed on your system. Detailed views can be gained by highlighting a device, as seen in the Hard Drive view in Figure 4.30.

Pointing devices, network devices, printers, and all other hardware devices are viewable from this window. You can launch the Hardware Browser by selecting Applications > System Tools > Hardware Browser.

Network Devices and Internet Connection

Fedora, of all the Linux distributions, is especially easy to configure for Internet access. The Internet Configuration Wizard shown in Figure 4.31 (Applications > System Tools > Internet Configuration Wizard) provides a complete, step-by-step walkthrough for configuring Ethernet cards, dialup and DSL modems, wireless cards, and other connection types.

Figure 4.31. The Internet Configuration Wizard.

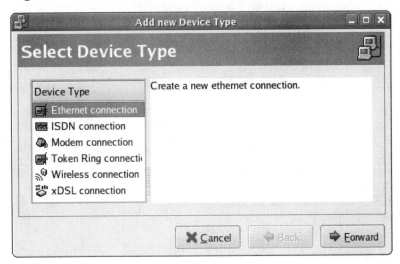

Fedora's parent distribution, Red Hat, pioneered the process of probing and detecting hardware devices. Network devices are no exception, as can be seen in Figure 4.32. The majority of commercially available network devices can be detected and displayed within this window.

Figure 4.32. Probing network devices.

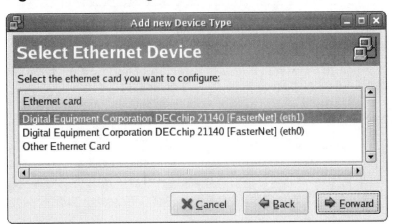

The Configure Network Settings dialog (shown in Figure 4.33), within the Internet Configuration Wizard, allows you to select your connection type—DHCP or static—and to provide a hostname for identification on the network.

Figure 4.33. The Configure Network Settings dialog.

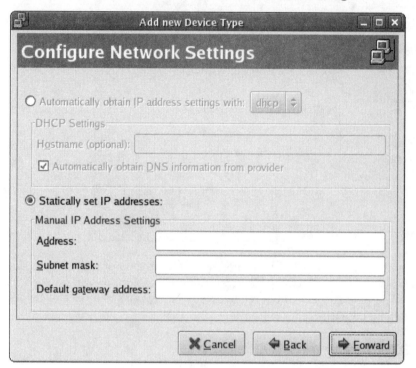

Kickstart

Fedora provides a tool that's intended primarily for administrators in a large environment: the Kickstart Configurator shown in Figure 4.34.

 Tip

Need a Kick?

Kickstart is not included in the standard server installation of Fedora Core 4. If you need to install it, run the Package Management application discussed previously, and select the system-config-kickstart package from the Administration Tools group.

Figure 4.34. The Kickstart Configurator.

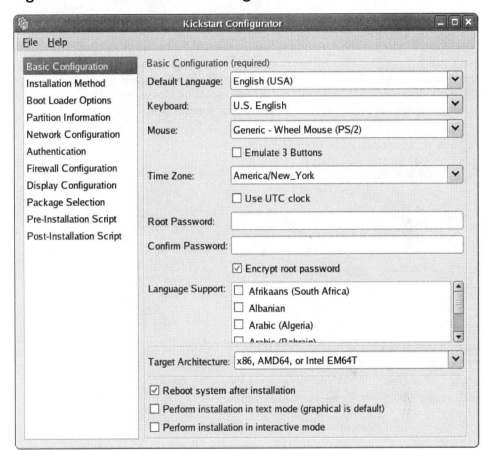

Kickstart provides a way to create a common system configuration that can later be leveraged in the installation of Fedora on multiple systems across a network. All the installation options are contained in a single text file that's written by the Kickstart Configurator tool. The parameters of the text file include boot loader options, partition information, network configuration, authentication, firewall configuration, display, RPM package selection, and other items. This is a favorite Fedora tool, as the Configurator makes it possible to install Fedora on all the machines in an entire office without ever leaving the server room.

System Monitor

The System Monitor shown in Figure 4.35 provides a constantly updated view of the processes running on your system. This can be useful when you sense, but can't quite quantify, a lag in your system. The listing displays the process name, the user under which the process is running, the memory used, and the process ID for each application currently in use. As an administrative user, you can view your processes, all processes, or only the active processes.

Figure 4.35. The System Monitor.

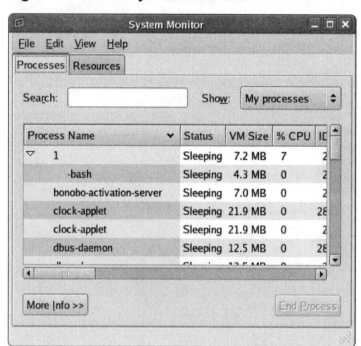

You can obtain detailed information on any process by highlighting the process and clicking the More Info button in the process listing window. If necessary, a running process can be stopped by highlighting the process and clicking the End Process button.

Figure 4.36. The Resources tab of the System Monitor.

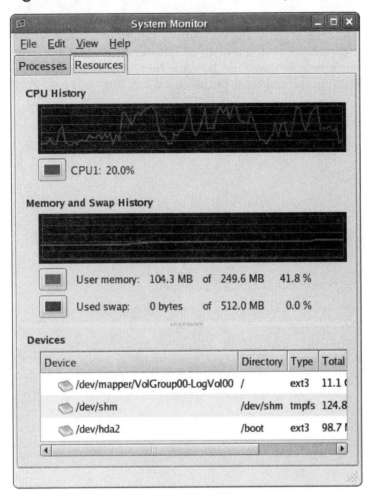

The Resources tab of the System Monitor provides high-level, real-time graphs of your system's resource usage, like those shown in Figure 4.36. CPU and memory usage are shown in graphs that are updated at regular intervals. The lower pane in the window contains a view of hard drive usage, including the percentage of space used on each device.

Summary

Linux is a powerful operating system, and can fulfil a variety of server roles. In this chapter, we've discussed the basics: how to administer a Linux system, how to configure it to provide new services, and how the filesystem is put together. Now it's time to move on to the real topic of this book: building your own Web server.

5

Building The Server

Now that we've constructed the Linux environment, it's time to build the Apache server. In this chapter, we'll cover all bases, from installation to configuration, from basic concepts to advanced server issues. The Linux element of the build is important, but it's probably not the aspect with which you'll work most often. If the Linux installation is stable, as it should be, the majority of the changes you'll make to your machine will be related to the server software. It's important to understand the basic concepts, and to establish a roadmap that will help you work through the issues that can—and will—arise.

As with the Linux chapter, we'll start with a bit of history about Apache, and the Apache project. This study will provide behind-the-scenes insight into the philosophy that underpins the most popular and reliable Web server on the Internet.

Apache: a Brief History

Apache, like Linux, has its roots in the open source philosophy. It exemplifies all the elements of the classic open source approach, including collaborative development and freely available source code. Apache is also developed by volunteers—primarily, interested users—and succeeds without a paid staff dedicated to product development or marketing. The Apache Group exists as an assembly of volunteer directors who communicate, plan, and coordinate the development of the server software from around the world.

As the World Wide Web's popularity flourished in the early 1990s, the most widely-used server software was the NCSA HTTP daemon (NCSA HTTPd) written by Rob McCool. McCool was yet another in the long line of students involved in open source application development. He created the HTTPd application while working for the National Center for Supercomputing Applications (NCSA). McCool was also intimately involved in a number of projects at Netscape, maker of the most popular browser of the day.

McCool left NCSA in mid-1994, and development on the project subsequently stalled. With the increasing need for a reliable Web server, Webmasters and administrators around the globe continued to develop patches and extensions for the server. These all occurred outside the official realm of the project, though the extensions and fixes found their way around the 'Net, and were implemented on servers throughout the world.

Recognizing the need to consolidate all the fixes, the Apache Group was formed over email in early 1995. The group used NCSA HTTPd version 1.3 as a base, rolling all the fixes and patches that were deemed practical into the new Apache server. In fact, the name Apache was chosen because the initial software was indeed "a patchy server." Development continued throughout 1995, culminating in the release of Apache 1.0 in December, 1995. Since then, Apache has been the top server software on the Internet.

For the purposes of this book, we'll be using the latest release of Apache version 2.

Installing Apache

Apache is available with nearly every Linux distribution. In the case of Fedora, you probably installed the RPM version of the software during the installation of your operating system.

Requirements

Apache requires the following of your Linux machine:

- [ ] 50MB free temporary disk space. This is necessary only for the installation of Apache. Once installed, Apache will only use about 10MB of disk space.

❑ An accurate clock on your server. Pieces of the HTTP protocol are expressed as time of day. In order to assure the proper operation and logging of your server, it's recommended that you utilize the Network Time Protocol (NTP) daemon to maintain system time. You can configure this using the Date/Time Properties tool, available from Desktop > System Settings > Date & Time.

All in all, the requirements for building the Apache server are minimal and can be met by most Linux systems.

When installing Apache on Fedora Core, you have several options: the installation can be accomplished via the RPM packages included with the Fedora Core distribution, or you can download the source code from the Apache site,[1] compiling and building the server to suit your specific needs. Compiling and installing the server yourself, though, is unlikely to constitute a good use of your time; the packaged version of Apache will probably meet all your needs, unless you're running a very high-volume or complex site. We won't discuss self-compilation of Apache in this book.

Installing Apache from RPM Packages

Apache 2 is included in the Fedora Core distribution, which makes for an easy installation. However, you're not bound to the version that's included on the installation CDs. Apache's open source nature allows for a constant stream of improvements and fixes, and the software is always moving forward through incremental releases. By the time you're ready to install the Fedora distribution, it's likely that the Apache server will have reached another incremental release. And, like the source distributions of the server, the incremental RPM releases are available for download.

One easy way to acquire and install the latest version of Apache is to use the updating tool, yum, which downloads updates directly from Red Hat. First, we'll check if any Apache updates are available.

```
[kermit@swinetrek ~]$ su
Password:
[root@swinetrek kermit]# yum check-update httpd
Setting up repositories
updates-released    100% |===========================| 951 B    00:00
extras              100% |===========================| 1.1 kB   00:00
base                100% |===========================| 1.1 kB   00:00
Reading repository metadata in from local files
```

---

[1] http://httpd.apache.org/

```
primary.xml.gz      100% |=========================| 307 kB   00:04
updates-re: ##################################### 949/949
Added 949 new packages, deleted 0 old in 18.67 seconds
primary.xml.gz      100% |=========================| 751 kB   00:10
extras    : ##################################### 2119/2119
Added 2119 new packages, deleted 0 old in 51.33 seconds
primary.xml.gz      100% |=========================| 824 kB   00:12
base      : ##################################### 2772/2772
Added 2772 new packages, deleted 0 old in 37.78 seconds

httpd.i386                  2.0.54-10.2         updates-released
[root@swinetrek kermit]#
```

The first time you run yum, it will need to download information about the available packages from Red Hat. Once it's analyzed the list of available packages, it will present a note of the packages for which updates are available. Above, we see that the httpd.i386 package has been updated to version 2.0.54-10.2. Getting and installing this latest Apache package is as simple as entering **yum update httpd** at the command prompt:

```
[root@swinetrek kermit]# yum update httpd
Setting up Update Process
Setting up repositories
updates-released   100% |=========================|  951 B   00:00
extras             100% |=========================|  1.1 kB  00:00
base               100% |=========================|  1.1 kB  00:00
Reading repository metadata in from local files
Resolving Dependencies
--> Populating transaction set with selected packages.
       Please wait.
---> Package httpd.i386 0:2.0.54-10.2 set to be updated
--> Running transaction check
--> Processing Dependency: httpd = 2.0.54-10 for package: mod_ssl
--> Processing Dependency: httpd = 2.0.54-10 for package:
       httpd-manual
--> Restarting Dependency Resolution with new changes.
--> Populating transaction set with selected packages.
       Please wait.
---> Downloading header for httpd-manual to pack into
       transaction set.
httpd-manual-2.0.54 100% |=========================|  91 kB   00:01
---> Package httpd-manual.i386 0:2.0.54-10.2 set to be updated
---> Downloading header for mod_ssl to pack into transaction set.
mod_ssl-2.0.54-10.2 100% |=========================|  23 kB   00:00
---> Package mod_ssl.i386 1:2.0.54-10.2 set to be updated
--> Running transaction check
```

```
Dependencies Resolved

===================================================================
 Package          Arch    Version         Repository       Size
===================================================================
Updating:
 httpd            i386    2.0.54-10.2     updates-released 935 k
Updating for dependencies:
 httpd-manual     i386    2.0.54-10.2     updates-released 1.7 M
 mod_ssl          i386    1:2.0.54-10.2   updates-released  92 k

Transaction Summary
===================================================================
Install     0 Package(s)
Update      3 Package(s)
Remove      0 Package(s)
Total download size: 2.7 M
Is this ok [y/N]:
```

yum will display a summary of the packages to be downloaded, and ask you to confirm that you would like to download them. If the download is very large, you may want to wait until a time at which plenty of bandwidth is available on your network, but since this download is only 2.7MB, we'll go ahead and download it now.

```
Is this ok [y/N]: y
Downloading Packages:
(1/3): httpd-2.0.5 100% |===========================| 935 kB  00:12
(2/3): httpd-manua 100% |===========================| 1.7 MB  00:22
(3/3): mod_ssl-2.0 100% |===========================|  92 kB  00:01
warning: rpmts_HdrFromFdno: Header V3 DSA signature: NOKEY, key ID
    4f2a6fd2
public key not available for httpd-2.0.54-10.2.i386.rpm
Retrieving GPG key from file:///etc/pki/rpm-gpg/RPM-GPG-KEY-fedora
Importing GPG key 0x4F2A6FD2 "Fedora Project <fedora@redhat.com>"
Is this ok [y/N]:
```

The RPM packages used to keep Fedora up-to-date are encrypted using GNU Privacy Guard (GPG), an open source implementation of the PGP (Pretty Good Privacy) cryptographic system. At this prompt, yum asks if it can download the Fedora Core public key that will allow it to decrypt the RPM. We'll be looking at cryptography again later in this chapter; for now, just answer **y**:

```
Is this ok [y/N]: y
Key imported successfully
```

```
Running Transaction Test
Finished Transaction Test
Transaction Test Succeeded
Running Transaction
  Updating  : httpd          ######################### [1/6]
  Updating  : httpd-manual   ######################### [2/6]
  Updating  : mod_ssl        ######################### [3/6]
  Cleanup   : httpd          ######################### [4/6]
  Cleanup   : httpd-manual   ######################### [5/6]
  Cleanup   : mod_ssl        ######################### [6/6]

Updated: httpd.i386 0:2.0.54-10.2
Dependency Updated: httpd-manual.i386 0:2.0.54-10.2
    mod_ssl.i386 1:2.0.54-10.2
Complete!
[root@swinetrek kermit]#
```

Once yum is finished, restart your new Apache server with the following command, again as root:

```
[root@swinetrek kermit]# /sbin/service httpd restart
Stopping httpd:                                          [  OK  ]
Starting httpd:                                          [  OK  ]
[root@swinetrek kermit]#
```

Starting and Stopping Apache

We've already looked at how services are stopped and started in Chapter 4, but there's another method that we can use to control apache: apachectl. Let's look at it now.

```
[kermit@swinetrek ~]$ su
Password:
[root@swinetrek kermit]# /usr/sbin/apachectl start
[root@swinetrek kermit]# /usr/sbin/apachectl restart
[root@swinetrek kermit]# /usr/sbin/apachectl stop
[root@swinetrek kermit]#
```

As you can see, it's pretty similar in syntax to the service tool, but apachectl stop will work across platforms. That is, it will work from the Windows command line just as it does in Linux; we can't say that about service httpd stop.

`apachectl` has other uses, as well. When you make changes to `httpd.conf`, the `apachectl` command can be used to check the syntax of your modified configuration.

```
[root@swinetrek kermit]# /usr/sbin/apachectl configtest
Syntax OK
[root@swinetrek kermit]#
```

Configuring the Server with MySQL and PHP

Today, dynamic Websites are more the rule than the exception. Most sites require some type of database back-end and use one scripting language or another. A bare-bones Apache configuration is perfectly suited to serving up static Web pages without any further configuration, but if you're looking to build a more dynamic site, a little more work is in order.

Installing MySQL and PHP

First, you'll need to make sure all of the appropriate packages for MySQL and PHP are installed. Here we're going for a pretty basic installation of MySQL and PHP; for a knock-'em-dead discussion of the finer details, see Kevin Yank's outstanding *Build Your Own Database Driven Website Using PHP & MySQL*[2] (SitePoint, ISBN 0–9579218–1–0).

---

[2] http://www.sitepoint.com/books/phpmysql1/

Figure 5.1. Displaying the packages in the Web Server group.

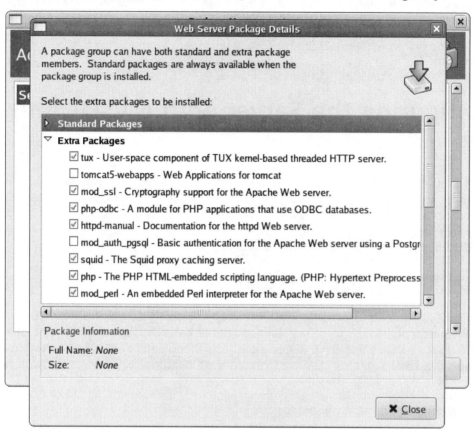

You can install the necessary PHP and MySQL packages using the Package Management tool we saw in Chapter 4 (Desktop > System Settings > Add/Remove Packages). Launch the tool, scroll down to Web Server, and click the Details button to display the packages in the Web Server group, as shown in Figure 5.1; most of these will probably already be installed.

Ensure that the php and php-mysql packages are ticked (tick them if they're not) and click the Close button.

Next, ensure that the MySQL Database package group is checked. As we're building a server to use MySQL exclusively, we can uncheck the PostgreSQL Database package group, too. Click the Details button for MySQL Database and make sure that php-mysql and mysql-server are checked.

Once you're done, click Update in the main window to install or remove any packages.

Tip PostgreSQL, Anyone?

If you'd rather make use of PostgreSQL than MySQL, there's no problem with that. In the Web Server package group, check php-pgsql to give PHP the ability to communicate with PostgreSQL databases. You can uncheck php-mysql to keep your server lean and mean, or leave it in, for added flexibility.

To complete your installation, restart the Apache service using your preferred method.

Testing your Installation of PHP

To test the installation of PHP, let's create a file named phpinfo.php in the /var/www/html directory; you'll need to switch to root to do this. The file should contain only the following three lines of code:

File: **phpinfo.php**

```
<?php
phpinfo();
?>
```

This page will call the built-in PHP function phpinfo() to display all the available information about your PHP installation. Run this page by opening **http://localhost/phpinfo.php** in your Web browser (Applications > Internet > Firefox Web Browser).

Figure 5.2. Displaying `phpinfo.php` in Firefox.

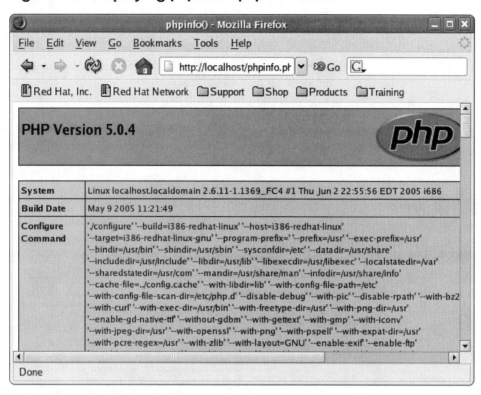

Firefox should display details about your server, as shown in Figure 5.2. If it does, congratulations: PHP is working! If not, check that the Apache service is up and running, then check Apache's error log (`/etc/httpd/logs/error_log`). Searching the Web for any error messages displayed in the error log will usually lead to a solution; alternatively, try your luck at SitePoint's friendly forums.[3]

Tip

Destroying the Evidence

Once you've checked the installation, it's a good idea to delete `phpinfo.php`, lest someone should stumble across the critical details of your PHP installation.

---

[3] http://www.sitepoint.com/forums/

Configuring Apache

At first glance, configuring Apache can appear to be an intimidating process. The configuration file (`httpd.conf`) contains almost 1000 lines. The directives that actually configure Apache are buried deep among lines of comments, and while those comments are useful—and deserve some serious and thoughtful consideration—they do help foster the myth that Apache configuration is a process best undertaken by administrative gurus. Fortunately, this simply isn't the case: Apache's configuration directives are actually quite easy to understand. The flexibility of the available directives assures that the end result of your configuration can be as complex or as simple as your needs dictate.

Configuring the Apache Server using the HTTP Configuration Tool

Whether you've installed the server via the RPM system, or have taken the plunge and decided to configure and build the server from source, Fedora Core offers a set of graphical tools that can lessen the intimidation factor faced by those configuring Apache servers. The other major distributions also offer graphical tools: SuSE rolls the Apache configuration into its YaST2 tool, and Mandriva offers a configuration tool in its Drak suite. As we've mentioned, Linux has matured to the point that most tasks can be achieved—at least in a fundamental way—with a strong set of graphical tools. In the case of Fedora, that tool is the HTTP configuration tool.

To launch the HTTP configuration tool, select Desktop > System Settings > Server Settings > HTTP.

Beware of inadvertently overwriting your edits!

The HTTP configuration tool makes direct edits to `httpd.conf`. Consequently, you should decide early on whether you'll use the tool, or edit the configuration file manually. If you choose to manually edit first, then tweak with the HTTP configuration tool later, your initial manual edits will be overwritten by the tool. In fact, manual edits to the file at any point in the process will be overwritten by subsequent use of the HTTP configuration tool.

Figure 5.3. The HTTP configuration tool.

The Main tab of the HTTP configuration tool, displayed in Figure 5.3, provides the means by which you'll set several critical parameters for your server.

The first field on this screen is Server Name. If your server will be live on the Internet, the Server Name text box should contain the fully qualified domain name of the server such as **www.mycompany.com**. If, on the other hand, the server will be used only internally for testing and development, you can assign any recognizable name you choose in this text field. You can also assign an email address for the server's Webmaster. You should enter a the address of a working email account.

Below these two fields is the Available Addresses section, where you can define the IP addresses and ports Apache listens on for incoming requests. Listening to all available addresses on port 80 is the default behavior for the Apache server. If you'd prefer to specify the specific addresses and/or ports for your server configuration, use the Add..., Edit... and Delete buttons to manage this list.

Default Ports

Port 80 is the default port for HTTP traffic; 443 is the default for HTTPS traffic. To send an HTTP request to another port, you must add *:port-number* to the server name in the URL. Entering **http://www.my-company.com:1024/** into your Web browser will send a request to my-company.com's server's port 1024.

Configuring Apache to listen only to certain IP address and port combinations is especially useful when running multiple Websites from the same server. You might enter one site's IP address and only allow traffic on port 80, but for another site, you may have two entries: one for port 80, and one for 443.

Figure 5.4. Defining a virtual host.

The Virtual Hosts tab of the HTTP configuration tool, shown in Figure 5.4, allows an administrator to create a **virtual host**, which is basically a Website that's hosted by your server. Virtual hosting makes it possible to serve requests for many Websites from the one server. To manage the list of virtual hosts, use the Add..., Edit..., and Delete buttons.

Figure 5.5. Setting virtual host options.

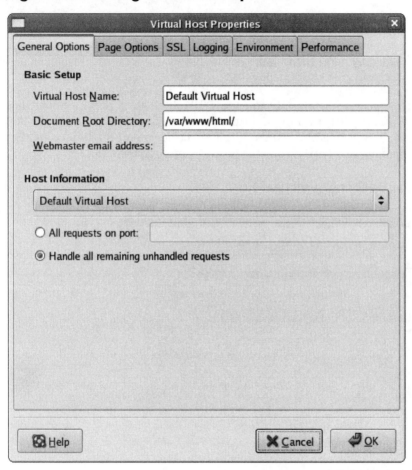

As you can see in Figure 5.5, several options are offered when adding or editing a virtual host. In the General Options tab, the administrator can specify whether this is an IP based Virtual Host, a Name based Virtual Host, or a Default Virtual Host via the Host Information drop-down list. Let's take a look at each of these options:

☐ An IP based virtual host is, perhaps not surprisingly, a virtual host with a unique IP address. If you select IP based Virtual Host from the drop-down, you'll be asked to enter the IP address of the virtual host, as well as its server name, which is the fully qualified domain we entered above.

❏ A name based virtual host does not have a unique IP address. Instead, Apache uses the server name to distinguish between the different virtual hosts that share any given IP address. Unfortunately, this means that such hosts can't use HTTPS, as the server name is part of the headers that are encrypted. When you select Name based Virtual Host, you'll be prompted for the host's name and IP address; you can also enter any number of aliases, or other names by which the host is known.

❏ A default virtual host will handle all the requests that remain unhandled by other hosts. You can optionally choose to limit a default virtual host to a particular port.

In the Basic Setup section, you can give your virtual host a name (this can be anything), and tell it where to find files. You can also enter the Webmaster's email address; again, this should be a working email address.

Figure 5.6. Virtual host site configuration options.

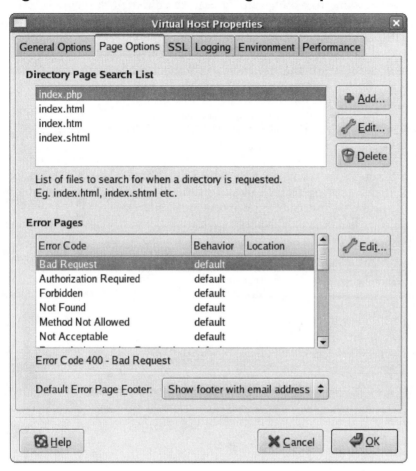

As shown in Figure 5.6, the Page Options tab provides the means to define both the default documents for a directory, and the error handling pages for a site.

In the Directory Page Search List, you can define the names and levels of precedence of the default pages for your directories. Normally, when you request a page from http://www.mycompany.com/example/, the server that runs www.mycompany.com will scan the directory example for the first file in this list. If the first file in the list isn't found, a search will be run for the second document in the list.

Error page handling for the virtual server is configured in the bottom half of the dialog. If you've taken the time to create custom error pages, you can direct the server to use these pages for specific error types: simply click the Edit... button in the right-hand pane. If you choose to use default error pages, you can specify how the footer on those pages appears: either with the Webmaster's email address, without the email address, or not at all.

Figure 5.7. Virtual host SSL options.

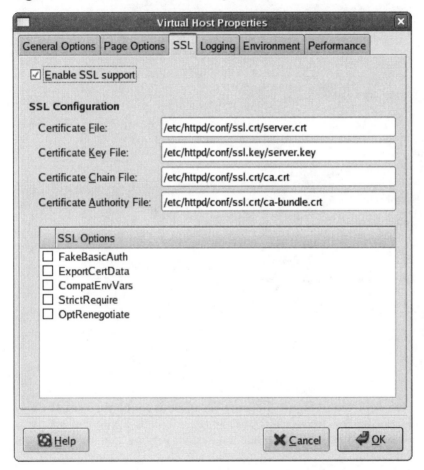

The HTTP configuration tool provides the means by which you can set up HTTPS communication with SSL, as shown in Figure 5.7. We'll be looking at SSL later in this chapter.

Figure 5.8. Virtual host Logging options.

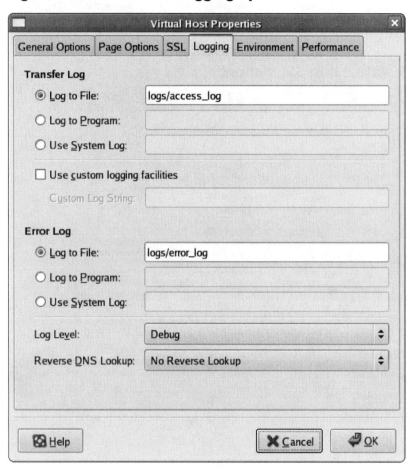

The Logging tab depicted in Figure 5.8 provides options for configuring the way in which the transfer (or access) and error logs are handled: you can specify a directory to which they'll be written, select a custom logging tool, or write them to a system log.

Importantly, the logging configuration also allows you to customize two other options. Log Level will determine which error messages are actually written to the logs. The log levels are listed in order of detail, from the very verbose Debug, through to Emergency, which will only log system failures. If you choose a more verbose logging level, you'll need to pay special attention to the size of the resulting logs, as disk space may become an issue. If, on the other hand, you choose a log level that's listed higher in the drop-down, the logging level will be much lighter, though you may not have all the details necessary to resolve a problem with the server. Choosing the correct log level is always a fine balance between having too much detail and not enough.

Finally, the logging options allow you to specify whether reverse or double-reverse DNS lookups should be performed. An example of a reverse lookup is a reverse dictionary lookup, in which a word would be found on the basis of its definition, rather than the other way around. Normally, DNS is used to translate domain names into IP addresses, so a reverse DNS lookup is used to lookup a domain name that corresponds with an IP address. A double-reverse DNS lookup not only looks up the domain name, but also performs a regular DNS lookup to ensure that the original IP address is returned.

If either reverse or double-reverse DNS lookups are enabled, domain names, instead of IP addresses, will appear in your sever logs. While this may be more user friendly, it also puts load on the server. It's recommended that you switch this functionality off if you anticipate your server experiencing heavy loads.

Figure 5.9. Virtual host environment variable options.

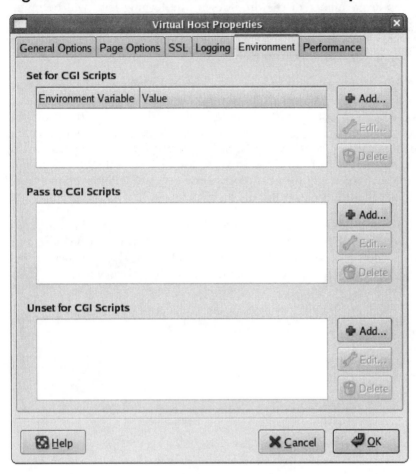

As shown in Figure 5.9, a full set of server environment variables can be defined for your virtual host. This may be necessary if you want to utilize CGI programs within your pages.

Figure 5.10. Virtual host directory options.

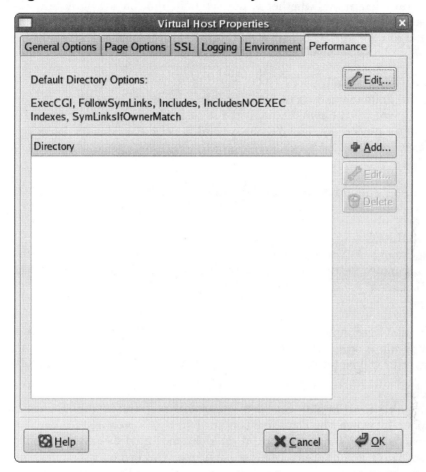

The last of the virtual host configuration tabs, Performance, is shown in Figure 5.10. It allows you to toggle Apache's directory options on and off for the entire site; simply click the Edit... button toward the top of the dialog to use this functionality. You can also set these options for specific directories. The options are:

ExecCGI

When turned on, this option allows the execution of CGI programs.

FollowSymLinks

This option determines whether or not symbolic links in the filesystem will be treated as part of the Website's filesystem. When this option is switched on, symlinks are treated as part of the filesystem; when it's off, symlinks are ignored.

SymLinksIfOwnerMatch

When the FollowSymLinks option is enabled, turning this option on ensures that the owner of the symlink file is the same as the owner of the symlink's target. If the owners don't match, the symlink is not included in the Website's filesystem.

Includes

This option should be turned on if you want to make use of server-side includes.

IncludesNOEXEC

The IncludesNOEXEC option is almost identical to the Includes option, the only difference being that use of the potentially dangerous `<!--#exec cmd="command"-->` directive is not allowed.

Indexes

This option determines what happens when no default document is found. If the option is on, a list of all files in the directory will be displayed. If it's off, an error will be returned. You'd most likely want this option turned off.

MultiViews

Turning this functionality on enables **content-negotiated multiviews**, a technique by which you can serve content in a user's preferred format. For example, say we have content in French and English saved as `content.html.fr` and `content.html.en`, and that MultiViews is switched on. Browsers requesting `content.html` that were set up for French would receive the French content, while browsers set up for English would receive the English content. Note that if we also had a file named `content.html`, this file would always be served, regardless of the browser's preferred language.

To change the options for a specific directory, click the Add... button to bring up the Directory Options screen shown in Figure 5.11.

Figure 5.11. Changing a directory's options.

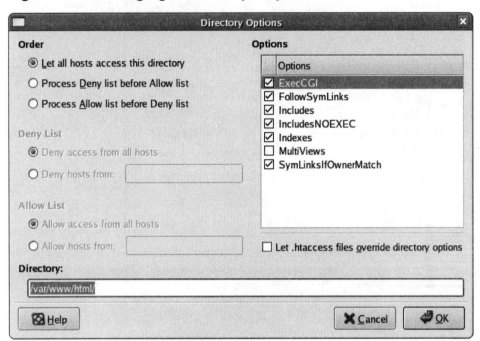

Enter the name of a directory in the text field toward the bottom of the dialog, then select the options you want from those listed in the right pane of the resulting window.

You can also restrict access to this directory via the Deny and Allow lists. Select the Process Deny list before Allow list option from the Order options at left; both the Deny List and Allow List fields will become enabled. Use the Deny hosts from and Allow hosts from fields to configure the IP addresses from which your virtual server will either accept or deny requests.

Finally, we can choose whether we want to allow these options to be overridden in .htaccess files, which we'll discuss in detail very soon.

Figure 5.12. Changing the server configuration options.

The Server tab of the HTTP configuration tool, shown in Figure 5.12, offers several lower-level configuration options for your server. The first is the Lock File, created when the service starts up. The presence of this file prevents other instances of the server from starting up. The PID File provides process ID information to the system. The Core Dump Directory is the location to which a core file will be written in the event of a server crash. The core file will then contain a wealth of debugging information that may point you to the cause of the crash.

The Server tab also provides the facility to define the server user and group. While these can be set to any existing user and group on the system, it's generally a good idea to leave them in the default configuration. The user and group defined in the Server tab were created at the time your server was installed, whether via the RPM packages or from source. If you choose a user other than the default, you'll need to make sure the user and group exist on the system, or create them prior to changing the defaults in the Server tab.

Figure 5.13. Changing the performance tuning options.

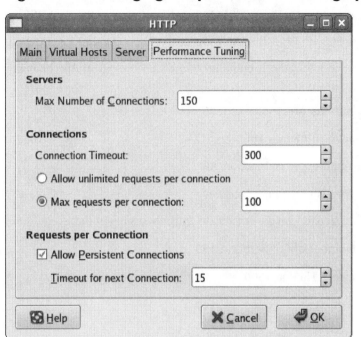

The final tab in the HTTP configuration tool, shown in Figure 5.13, provides several performance tuning options. These include the number of simultaneous server connections, the connection timeout in seconds, the maximum number of simultaneous requests per connection, and whether or not to allow persistent connections. By default, Apache will allow 150 connections simultaneously, each of which may make up to 100 requests, generating up to 15,000 requests at once. While this figure may seem large, the fact is that most servers—even those with three- or four-year-old processors and minimal RAM—can handle this default. You can increase or decrease this number for your system by changing either the maximum connection number, or the maximum requests per connection. In most cases, reducing or increasing the acceptable number of requests per connection is the preferred adjustment.

Tuning Up

Performance tuning in Apache can be an art unto itself. However, it's easy to provide some rough guidelines for your server, based on the age of the machine, the amount of RAM, and the speed of the connection to which the server is attached. Let's take three scenarios as examples:

1. An old PC with 128MB RAM, connected via a slow ADSL connection.

2. A reasonably new PC with 256MB RAM, also connected via ADSL.

3. A new PC with 512MB RAM, connected to the 'net via a T1 connection.

In the first scenario, the appropriate connection settings in Apache might be:

❑ Max Number of Connections: **50**

❑ Connection Timeout: **100**

❑ Max requests per connection: **50**

❑ Allow persistent connections: off

The second scenario, on the other hand, might best support these conditions:

❑ Max Number of Connections: **150**

❑ Connection Timeout: **300**

❑ Max requests per connection: **100**

❑ Allow persistent connections: on

The second machine has more RAM, so it's capable of handling more connections. As a result, the connection timeout can be slightly longer, too. However, because of the connection speed, it may not handle persistent connections, or high numbers of requests per connection, very well.

The third machine can easily handle the default settings:

❑ Max Number of Connections: **100**

❑ Connection Timeout: **200**

❑ Max requests per connection: **50**

❑ Allow persistent connections: off

Additionally, because of the higher connection speed, it may be acceptable to allow persistent connections on this machine. As you can see, there's a lot of trial and error involved in properly adjusting Apache's performance settings.

When the server is configured to your needs, click OK in the HTTP configuration tool, and restart the server using the method of your choice.

Further Configuration with `.htaccess` and `httpd.conf`

What happens if you have some special requirements for your server—configurations that should apply only to specific directories—or you need to quickly lock down directory access to all but a handful of users? In such cases, you can write directives into an .htaccess file, creating configurations on a directory-by-directory basis. The .htaccess file is often referred to as a distributed configuration file. In some cases, .htaccess files can make the maintenance and configuration of your server much easier.

An .htaccess file is a smaller and more targeted version of httpd.conf. It can contain any directive that's allowed in the global httpd.conf file. For example, the following are equivalent:

File: **httpd.conf (excerpt)**

```
<Directory /var/www/html>
  Options +ExecCGI
  AddHandler cgi-script .cgi
</Directory>
```

File: **/var/www/html/.htaccess (excerpt)**

```
Options +ExecCGI
AddHandler cgi-script .cgi
```

Directives in an .htaccess file apply to the directory in which the file is found and to all the subdirectories it contains. So, if this .htaccess file was located in /var/www/html, it would affect the configuration of /var/www/html, /var/www/html/navigation, /var/www/html/styles, and so on.

.htaccess files can also be used to restrict access to certain directories. For example, if we wanted to restrict access to /var/www/html/testing/admin, we could use the following .htaccess file like so:

File: **/var/www/html/testing/admin/.htaccess**

```
AuthType Basic
AuthName "Password Required"
AuthUserFile /etc/httpd/htpasswd
```

```
AuthGroupFile /etc/httpd/groups
Require Group admins
```

When used in this way, the .htaccess file will tell Apache that the user needs to enter a username and password for a member of the group admins. As specified in this example by the AuthUserFile and AuthGroupFile directives, username and password will be checked against the /etc/httpd/htpasswd file, then the user's membership will be checked in /etc/httpd/groups.

The /etc/httpd/htpasswd file is maintained using the htpasswd tool.

```
[root@swinetrek kermit]# htpasswd -c /etc/httpd/htpasswd kermit
New password:
Re-type new password:
Adding password for user kermit
[root@swinetrek kermit]# htpasswd /etc/httpd/htpasswd misspiggy
New password:
Re-type new password:
Adding password for user misspiggy
[root@swinetrek kermit]#
```

You must use the -c option when adding the first user. This tells htpasswd to create the password file. An example of the file produced by htpasswd is shown below.

File: **/etc/httpd/htpasswd**

```
kermit:phQeDvrsdvni6
misspiggy:Xzbbbk8ImxCcI
```

The /etc/httpd/groups file must be maintained manually, though a text editor. It's a pretty simple file: groups are listed at the beginning of each line, and the members of each group follow.

File: **/etc/httpd/groups**

```
muppets: kermit gonzo fozzie misspiggy
admins: kermit misspiggy
```

If you attempt to set this up in the default installation of Apache in Fedora Core, nothing will happen. By default, Apache is not configured to allow .htaccess files, but it's fairly simple to set this up in httpd.conf.

To allow .htaccess configuration in a directory, open the HTTP configuration tool and go to the Virtual Hosts tab. Select the virtual host you'd like to have make use of .htaccess files and click Edit... to bring up the Virtual Host Properties dialog. Switch to the Performance tab, click Add... and enter the directory you'd like to protect. You'll need to enter the name of the directory as it appears in your server's filesystem, which will most likely mean prefixing the name of the directory with `/var/www/html`. Check the Let .htaccess files override directory options checkbox, and click OK to save your changes.

Alternatively, you can make the changes to `http.conf` directly. Open `httpd.conf` and add the following directives to the end of the file.

File: **httpd.conf (excerpt)**

```
<Directory /var/www/html/testing/admin>
  AllowOverride AuthConfig
</Directory>
```

The `AllowOverride` directive instructs Apache to process .htaccess files within the specified directory, but the `AuthConfig` argument limits the directives that are allowed within the .htaccess file to those related to authorization. Other available arguments include:

FileInfo   Allows directives that relate to file type handling.

Indexes   Allows directives that control what happens if no default document is found in a directory.

Limit   Allows directives that control deny and allow lists.

Options   Allows directives that can control the options set in the Virtual Host Properties dialog's Performance tab.

All   Allows all directives.

None   Allows no directives; .htaccess files are ignored.

The .htaccess file isn't a panacea, though. There are some caveats to its use, including the performance hit created by the use of .htaccess files. When the `AllowOverride` directive allows the use of .htaccess files, the server will search every directory in the server filesystem for .htaccess files. While this may not create a real performance issue on servers handling a modest number of requests, it can cause serious performance slowdowns on high-traffic production servers.

Further, the server will be required to find all the .htaccess files in higher-level directories. This means that if you're using an .htaccess file in the `/var/www/html/testing/admin` server directory, Apache will look for

/var/www/html/.htaccess, /var/www/html/testing/.htaccess and /var/www/html/testing/admin/.htaccess. In effect, the use of .htaccess files creates three checks for a single page request. Again, the performance hit on high-traffic production servers can be significant.

Given that, why would you use distributed configuration files at all? Well, there are some legitimate uses. If, for example, you're providing hosting services for several users on a single machine via virtual hosts, .htaccess files can allow users to customize their individual server environments within the limitations you've created in the httpd.conf file.

With some careful planning, and an understanding of the httpd.conf directives, your Apache server will provide an environment that's secure, flexible, and easy to maintain. That planning will also minimize the work required of the server to meet your users' needs.

Configuring your Server for Secure Connections

With the advent of commerce over the Internet, it became necessary to create a protocol by which data could be sent securely between Web servers and browsers. This protocol is HTTPS, the secure version of HTTP. HTTPS encrypts the data to be sent using an agreed encryption protocol—most commonly Secure Sockets Layer (SSL)—then sends the encrypted data to its destination, where it's decrypted and processed.

Apache can provide secure Web services over HTTP using OpenSSL. Before we go and set this up, though, it's important that we understand the process involved in serving secure requests from our server.

A Brief Introduction to Public Key Cryptography

Two elements are required to encrypt the connection between server and browser: keys and certificates. These will allow the server to provide the browser with evidence of its identity, and establish a connection that utilizes public key cryptography.

The keys serve to encrypt the connection. There are two fundamental types of encryption: **public key encryption** and **symmetric key encryption**, also known as private key encryption. In the latter, both the server and the browser posses the encryption key, which is necessary to encrypt and decrypt data. While very secure, distributing the encryption key to all clients makes use of the symmetric key cryptography nearly impossible for public servers: how can you ensure that no one stole the encryption key while it was in transit? Symmetric key encryption is much more common in intranet environments or internal server usage.

With public key encryption, two keys exist: the public key and the private key. As their names imply, the private key is stored securely on the server, while the public key is made available for public access. Through a complex mathematical process, data that's encrypted with the public key can only be decrypted with the private key, and vice versa.

However, cryptography isn't the only element that's necessary to create a secure, trustworthy connection. A client needs assurance that the machine is really the one it claims to be. This can be accomplished by acquiring a public key certificate from a well-known and trusted certificate authority (CA). When requesting a certificate from a CA, you'll need to send proof of your or your company's identity, as well as payment for the service, in most cases. The CA will return a public key certificate for use on your secure server.

It's also possible to create your own public key certificates using OpenSSL, but such certificates are only appropriate for development and testing purposes: browsers will usually complain when confronted with a certificate issued by a CA that they don't consider "trusted," showing an error similar to that depicted in Figure 5.14. In this chapter, we'll be creating our own certificates using the genkey tool, which acts as a wrapper for OpenSSL.

Figure 5.14. The Website Certified by an Unknown Authority dialog.

Installing OpenSSL and genkey

In the Package Management tool, click on the Details button of the Web Server package group, and ensure that mod-ssl and crypto-utils are checked. Click the Close button, then click Update in the main window to install any packages you lack.

Creating your own Private and Public Key Pair

With everything installed, we're now ready to create our private and public keys. To run the genkey tool, open a terminal window and run genkey *servername* as root.

```
[kermit@swinetrek ~]$ su
Password:
[root@swinetrek kermit]# genkey www.mycompany.com
```

Figure 5.15. genkey's first screen.

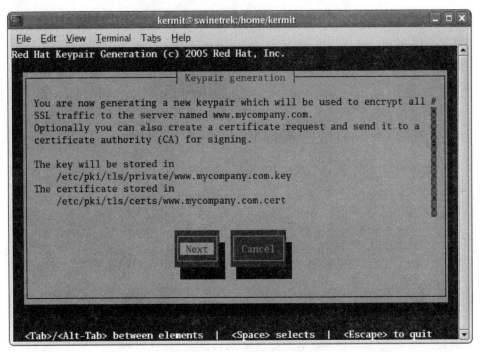

genkey's interface is similar to the text-mode installation we saw in Chapter 1. Move between options by pressing the **Tab** key, and select options by pressing **Space**.

genkey's first screen, shown in Figure 5.15, tells us that it will write the private key to /etc/pki/tls/private/*servername*.key and the public key certificate to /etc/pki/tls/certs/*servername*.cert. It's important to make a note of these filenames, as we'll need to know them when we configure Apache. When you're ready to proceed, select Next.

Figure 5.16. Selecting a key size in genkey.

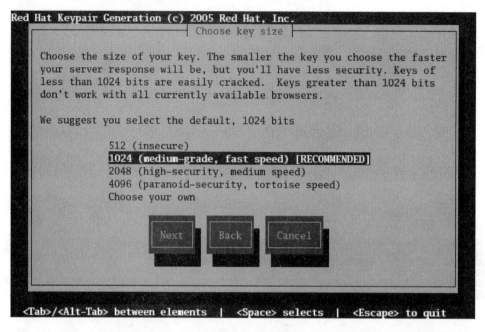

The next screen, shown in Figure 5.16, lets you select the size of your key. The larger they key, the more difficult your encryption is to crack, but few browsers support keys that are larger than 1024 bits. Select 1024 bits, and select Next.

Figure 5.17. genkey collecting random data.

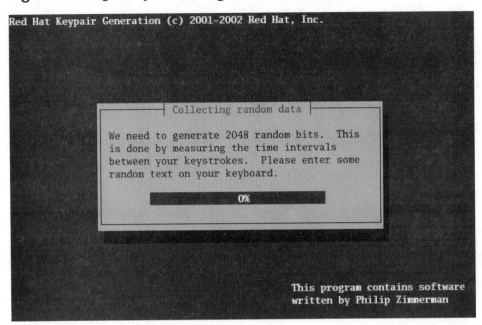

```
Red Hat Keypair Generation (c) 2001-2002 Red Hat, Inc.




              ┤ Collecting random data ├

         We need to generate 2048 random bits.  This
         is done by measuring the time intervals
         between your keystrokes.  Please enter some
         random text on your keyboard.

                   ┌─────────────────────┐
                   │         0%          │
                   └─────────────────────┘



                              This program contains software
                              written by Philip Zimmerman
```

genkey will now generate your keys. After spending some time generating random bits itself, genkey will ask you to type at your keyboard in order to collect some further random data, as shown in Figure 5.17. As you type, the progress meter will slowly tick over until it reaches 100%.

Next, you'll be asked if you want to send a certificate signing request (CSR) to a CA. We don't, so answer No to this question. If you did want to send a CSR, you'd answer Yes, then select the CA you'd be sending the request to (one of Equifax, Thawte, VeriSign, or Other).

Figure 5.18. Entering the details for your certificate.

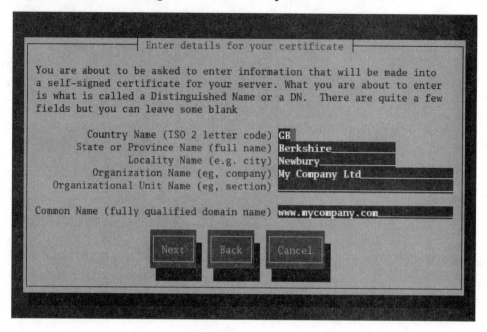

The next step is to enter the details of your certificate, as illustrated in Figure 5.18. The form is pre-populated with dummy details; overwrite them with information that's appropriate to your server.

Figure 5.19. Choosing whether or not to encrypt the private key.

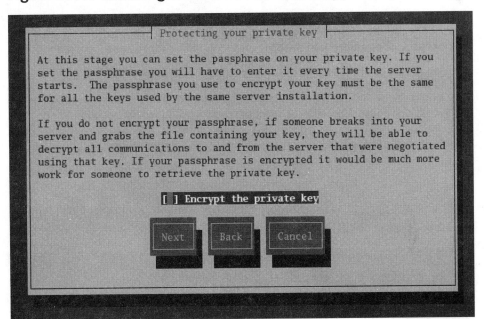

Next, you're asked if you want to encrypt the private key you've created. If a malicious party were to gain access to your private key and it was not encrypted, they would be able to decrypt the communication between the browser and the Web server. If you're running a secure site and trying to build a trustworthy reputation, this has obvious disastrous consequences. Encrypting the key ensures that, even if the malicious party compromises your system and gains access to the key, he or she cannot use it to decrypt communications without the key's passphrase. However, if you encrypt your private key, you'll need to enter the key's passphrase whenever Apache is restarted; therefore, Apache cannot start automatically after the server is rebooted. You need to decide which is more important for your server: security or ease of management.

In almost any case in which HTTPS is required, server security should be paramount, so we'll encrypt our private key. Hit **Space** so that an asterisk appears next to Encrypt the private key, then select Next.

Figure 5.20. Entering the private key's passphrase.

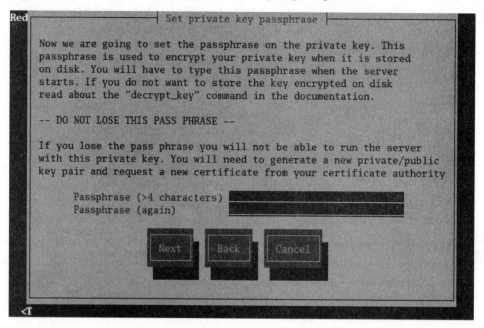

On the next screen, enter the private key's passphrase twice, then select Next to complete the key generation process.

Select Next and the process is complete! You're dumped rather unceremoniously at the command prompt. If you had generated a CSR, from this point you'd need to follow the CA's instructions as to how to obtain your certificate. If you've generated a self-signed certificate, as we have here, you're ready to configure Apache to use it.

IMPORTANT

Stopping Apache

If you've configured Apache to use an encrypted private key, you'll need to stop Apache's daemon from starting when the system is rebooted. If you don't stop it, you'll find that your system won't start properly at all!

Open the Service Configuration tool (Desktop > System Settings > Server Settings > Services), select Edit Runlevel > Runlevel All from the menu, locate httpd in the list and make sure that none of its checkboxes are checked. Be sure to click Save if you make any changes.

Configuring Apache

All we need to do now is to configure Apache to use these certificates instead of the dummy certificates that are included with Fedora Core. Make a backup of /etc/httpd/conf.d/ssl.conf, open the original file in a text editor, and locate the lines shown below.

File: **/etc/httpd/conf.d/ssl.conf** (excerpt)

```
#    Server Certificate:
#    Point SSLCertificateFile at a PEM encoded certificate.  If
#    the certificate is encrypted, then you will be prompted for a
#    passphrase.  Note that a kill -HUP will prompt again.  A new
#    certificate can be generated using the genkey(1) command.
SSLCertificateFile /etc/pki/tls/certs/localhost.crt

#    Server Private Key:
#    If the key is not combined with the certificate, use this
#    directive to point at the key file.  Keep in mind that if
#    you've both a RSA and a DSA private key you can configure
#    both in parallel (to also allow the use of DSA ciphers, etc.)
SSLCertificateKeyFile /etc/pki/tls/private/localhost.key
```

Here, SSLCertificateFile is the name of the public key certificate file, and SSLCertificateKeyFile is the name of the private key. Edit the file so that these lines refer to the files created by genkey.

File: **/etc/httpd/conf.d/ssl.conf** (excerpt)

```
#    Server Certificate:
#    Point SSLCertificateFile at a PEM encoded certificate.  If
#    the certificate is encrypted, then you will be prompted for a
#    passphrase.  Note that a kill -HUP will prompt again.  A new
#    certificate can be generated using the genkey(1) command.
SSLCertificateFile /etc/pki/tls/certs/www.mycompany.com.cert

#    Server Private Key:
#    If the key is not combined with the certificate, use this
#    directive to point at the key file.  Keep in mind that if
#    you've both a RSA and a DSA private key you can configure
#    both in parallel (to also allow the use of DSA ciphers, etc.)
SSLCertificateKeyFile /etc/pki/tls/private/www.mycompany.com.key
```

Save your changes and restart Apache using the apachectl command.

```
[root@swinetrek kermit]# /usr/sbin/apachectl restart
httpd not running, trying to start
Apache/2.0.54 mod_ssl/2.0.54 ( Dialog)
Some of your private key files are encrypted for security reasons.
In order to read them you have to provide the passphrases.

Server 127.0.0.1:443 (RSA)
Enter :

OK:  Dialog successful.
[root@swinetrek kermit]#
```

Controlling Apache

When you use an encrypted private key, you must start Apache with `apachectl` so that you can enter the private key's passphrase. You'll receive an error message if you try to start Apache with something other than `apachectl`.

Now, your Apache server is ready to serve documents over HTTPS. To test this, attempt to load your server's default page in Firefox with HTTPS by entering **https://localhost/** into the browser. If you've installed a self-signed certificate, you'll receive at least one warning that the certificate may be from an untrusted source. Click Examine Certificate... to see the details of the certificate; you should see many of the details you entered while generating the certificate.

Summary

Linux servers are a mainstay of the Internet. Since the creation of the robust open-source HTTPd package in the early 1990s, Apache servers have gained an increasing share of the server market with each passing year.

The Apache server is highly configurable: it can handle secure requests, encrypting all communications between the server and the client. This has made it a popular choice for ecommerce-related sites, which pass sensitive data across the Internet; it also plays well with other server-related components such as scripting languages and databases. A full complement of graphical tools for configuring the Apache server is supplied with Fedora Core.

In the next chapter, we'll look at the many tools available for administering and hardening your server. We'll also look at backups, logging, traffic reporting, and accessing your server remotely.

6

Server Administration

Meeting the needs of your users, ensuring that the system is at full operational capability, and keeping up to date with any new security and feature patches: these are the tasks of daily server administration. Fortunately, tools to help automate and simplify these processes exist in abundance. The Linux system itself is chock-full of useful tools to make the administration of your server a reasonably painless task.

In this chapter, we'll look at Webmin—a third-party tool designed to ease the burden of keeping your server in a fully operational state—and yum, a command line tool designed to help you keep your system up to date.

Webmin

Webmin is a browser-based system administration tool that offers a range of capabilities. The interface is easy to use, and, while it offers a variety of tools itself, Webmin also supports plugins that can be used to extend and customize the program's functionality. Webmin can help you perform the full range of administrative tasks, from user management to backups, and everything in between. Nearly every server I've built or administered over the past four years has contained a Webmin installation: it really is invaluable.

In this section, we'll touch on some of the functionality that Webmin offers. For a more in-depth look, I highly recommend the excellent title, *The Book of Webmin (Or: How I Learned to Stop Worrying and Love UNIX).*[1]

Installing Webmin

Webmin is available for download from http://www.webmin.com/ as an RPM package. You can choose to download the source code and compile Webmin for yourself, but with a Red Hat-based system like Fedora Core, the preferred method is to install the package using the RPM system. This will write an entry to the RPM database, allowing the easy upgrade and, if necessary, rollback or removal of the package later on. We'll discuss these tasks a little later.

Getting the Right File

Two RPM packages will be available at the Webmin site: `webmin-version.src.rpm` (the source code package) and `webmin-version.noarch.rpm`, which is the installable version. Be sure to grab the installable package.

To install the package, just double-click on the RPM file. You'll be guided through a series of simple dialogs, and Webmin will be installed.

Webmin Basics

Webmin installs a small, purpose-specific Web server on the machine on port 10000. You can access it via **http://*servername*:10000/**.

Can't Get Through?

In order to access this Website externally, you'll need to allow port 10000 access through the firewall. To do so, open the Security Level configuration tool from Desktop > System Settings > Security Level, and enter **10000:tcp** in the Other ports field.

From this page, shown in Figure 6.1, you can log in to Webmin by entering your root username and password. Once you do so, you'll see the Webmin screen pictured in Figure 6.2.

---

[1] http://www.swelltech.com/support/webminguide/

Figure 6.1. The Login to Webmin page.

Figure 6.2. The Webmin home screen.

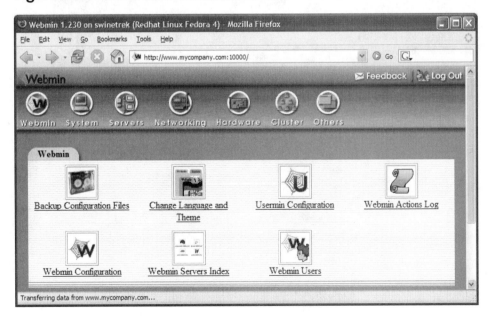

Webmin User Administration

If other users are going to administer the system, it's a good idea to create separate logins for each of those users. To add a new Webmin user, click the Webmin Users link on the main page, then click Create a New Webmin User from the resulting page. You'll see the screen shown in Figure 6.3.

Figure 6.3. Creating a new Webmin user.

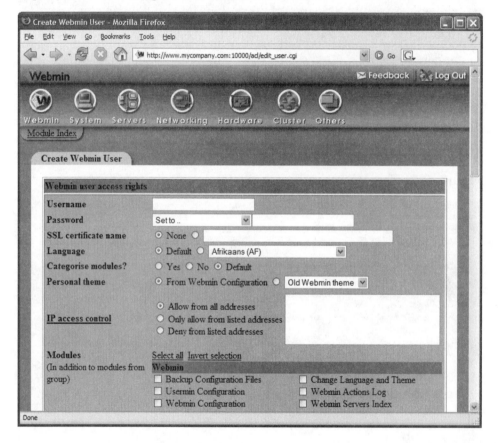

As you can see, many options are available in the creation of a new user. Here, we'll cover two basic options: creating a Webmin-only user, and creating a Webmin user who's synchronized with a Linux user.

Creating a Webmin-only user is pretty straightforward. Fill out the Username field, select Set to... from the Password drop-down, enter the user's password, and leave the default settings in the other fields. Further down the page, in the Modules section, you'll see a collection of checkboxes that allow you to specify the features to which this user will have access. Check the appropriate checkboxes (or click the Select all link to select all of the checkboxes), and click the Save button at the bottom of the page.

Creating a Webmin user profile that's synchronized with a Linux user profile is a similarly straightforward process. Enter the Linux user's username into the Username field, and select Unix authentication from the Password drop-down. Don't enter a password: this will be taken from the Linux user profile. Select the appropriate module checkboxes, and click Save to create the user.

In keeping with the Linux model, Webmin users can be grouped, and access can be assigned to these groups. To create a new Webmin group, click the Create a new Webmin group link on the Webmin Users page, enter the name of the group, and select the modules to which that group will have access. Existing users can be added to the new group from their user page—just click on the username and the Member of group drop-down will appear in the top-right corner.

Step up to Security

There are many other steps that you should take to effectively secure the installation of Webmin if you intend to use it on your server. Most of these steps are outlined in *The Book of Webmin (Or: How I Learned to Stop Worrying and Love UNIX)*.[2]

Webmin Features

The real beauty of any Web-based tool is usually its interface, and this is certainly the case with Webmin. As the browser is one of the most well-known interfaces in computing these days, the learning curve involved in moving around within the Webmin interface is minimal. The Web-based nature of Webmin also allows an administrator to perform necessary tasks from anywhere on the network, or—provided the package is properly installed and secured—from anywhere in the world.

---

[2] http://www.swelltech.com/support/webminguide/

Figure 6.4. The Webmin sections.

The Webmin modules are broken into several groups, which can be accessed via the icons at the top of the Webmin interface, shown in Figure 6.4. Let's take a look at the modules behind four of the most important groups for server administration: System, Servers, Networking, and Hardware. We'll use these modules in later sections of this chapter, so consider the next few pages an overview of the features offered by Webmin.

Figure 6.5. Webmin modules available in the System group.

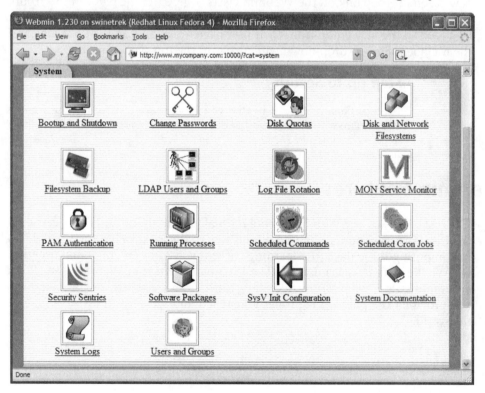

System Group Modules

The System Group provides access to important system-wide configuration tools, as shown in Figure 6.5.

Bootup and Shutdown

This tool displays a list of all services, describes each, and identifies whether or not that service is currently configured to start at boot. This page allows you to start and stop these services, and configure them to start (or not start) when the system starts. Toward the bottom of the page is a drop-down list of all the runlevels; you can use this to view and configure what happens at each runlevel. Finally, you can use this screen to shut down or reboot the system.

Change Passwords

This tool displays a list of all users, and allows an administrator to change the password for each.

Disk and Network Filesystems

This tool provides a description—and identifies the current status—of the various filesystems on the server. It also provides the ability to mount and unmount existing filesystems and mount new filesystems.

Filesystem Backup

This tool displays a list of all the currently configured filesystem backups, and provides the administrator with a means to create new backups. These backups are created either with the dump command, or as TAR archives.

Running Processes

This tool lists all the processes running on the system, along with each process's Process ID (PID), the process owner, and the command used to start the process. By default, the processes are displayed in a hierarchy, but the display can be sorted by user, memory use, and CPU time; it's also searchable. You can also use this module to execute a command as a specified user.

Scheduled Commands

This tool displays all the currently defined at jobs, and provides a page on which you can define more.

Scheduled Cron Jobs

All the cron jobs that are active on the server are displayed in this tool; it also allows you to create new jobs.

Software Packages

This tool provides an interface that allows you to search for RPM packages installed on the system. Also provided are tools to install new packages, upgrade existing packages, and to search for individual file elements of an installed package.

Users and Groups

This tool provides a full complement of tools to manage users and groups, including a tool to manage multiple users at once using batch files.

Servers Group Modules

Figure 6.6. Webmin modules available in the Servers group.

Webmin's Servers modules, pictured in Figure 6.6, allow you to configure and maintain several different software packages that act as servers for other client applications. We'll use Webmin to configure several of these packages later in this chapter, and to establish a strong level of system security later on. For now, let's walk through some of the features of the Servers section of Webmin.

Apache Web Server

The Apache module, like many of the modules in the Servers group, contains so many options that it's almost another module group in itself. It even offers the ability to edit the `httpd.conf` file via the Edit Config Files page. You can see some of the other options offered in the Apache module in Figure 6.7.

Figure 6.7. The Apache Webserver Webmin module.

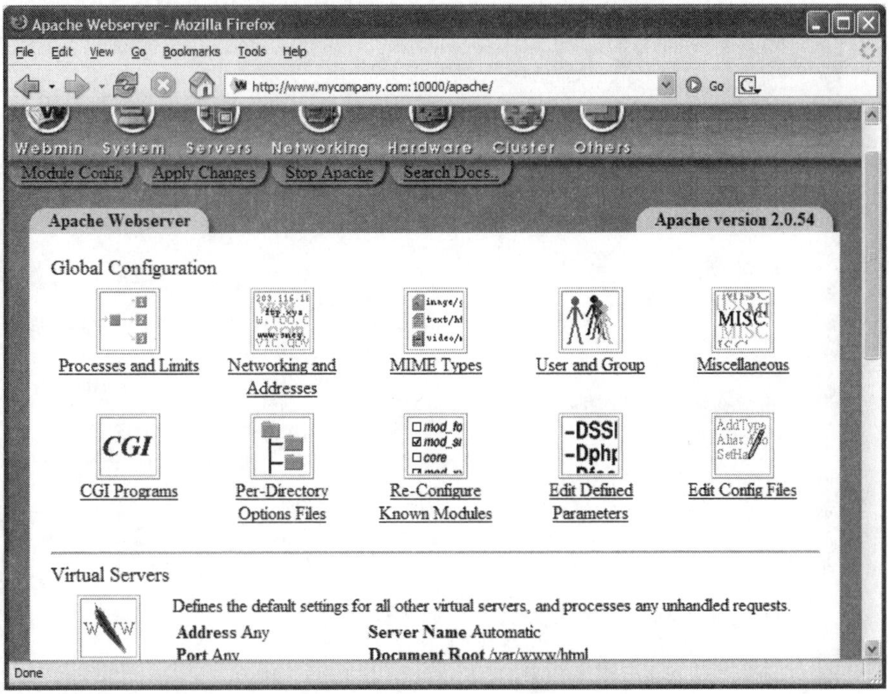

CVS Server

CVS (Concurrent Versioning System) is a tool that's used widely by developers to track changes in code. The CVS Server page provides options for creating CVS users, user access control, and server configuration. It also allows the logged-in user to browse the repository, or library of code currently in CVS.

Majordomo List Manager

Majordomo is an email list manager and has long been recognized as the standard in Linux. The Majordomo List Manager page in Webmin allows you to create new lists and to define the parameters of existing email lists.

MySQL Database Server

Figure 6.8. The Webmin MySQL module.

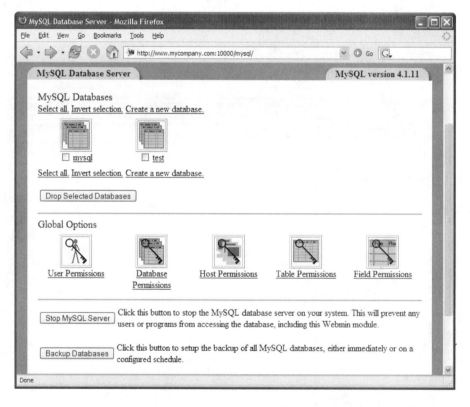

In the top part of the page shown in Figure 6.8, the MySQL module displays an icon for each database that's hosted on the server. Clicking on a database icon displays new icons that represent each of the tables in that database; these can be clicked on to display the structure of that table. From here, you can edit the structure of the table, or edit the data in that table. At each point along the way, an administrator has access to a full complement of tools with which to manipulate MySQL, its databases and tables; you can drop a database or table, create a database backup, create a new database or table, execute SQL statements, and more.

Postfix Configuration
QMail Configuration
Sendmail Configuration

Webmin provides the means to configure several mail servers. Sendmail is the longtime standard for Linux, while Postfix and Qmail are newer, more easily configured alternatives. The Webmin configuration interfaces for these servers provide all the tools necessary to configure and secure your mail server.

ProFTPD Server
WU-FTP Server

ProFTPD and WU-FTP are the two FTP services that can be configured via the default Webmin installation. Administrators can use these tools to add or remove FTP users and establish user home directories.

SSH Server

SSH is the secure shell. It allows remote users to work within the shell environment on the server over a secure connection. The SSH Server module of Webmin allows you to configure authentication, access control, and much more. We'll take a detailed look at SSH in Chapter 7.

Samba Windows File Sharing

We briefly discussed Samba back in Chapter 4. Samba is a utility for sharing files and printers with Windows machines on the network. The Samba Windows File Sharing page in Webmin displays current shares, and allows you to create new shares, and configure or reconfigure all the working parameters of new and existing shares.

SpamAssassin Mail Filter

SpamAssassin is a robust tool to fight spam email. The SpamAssassin Mail Filter module in Webmin allows you to configure many aspects of SpamAssassin, including what is done with messages identified as spam email.

Webalizer Logfile Analysis

Webalizer is a Web server access log analysis tool. It can provide you with interesting and valuable insight into the usage of your server, and it's included in the default installation of Fedora Core 4. The Webalizer Logfile Analysis page in Webmin allows you to determine which log files will be analyzed, add new files for analysis, schedule regular analysis, and to manually generate a new log analysis report.

Networking Group Modules

Given the fact that you've created a Web server, the networking features of your machine are especially important. Webmin's Networking module group, pictured in Figure 6.9, includes modules for administering firewalls and other security features, bandwidth monitoring modules, and several special protocols for allowing access to the server machine.

Figure 6.9. Webmin modules available in the Networking group.

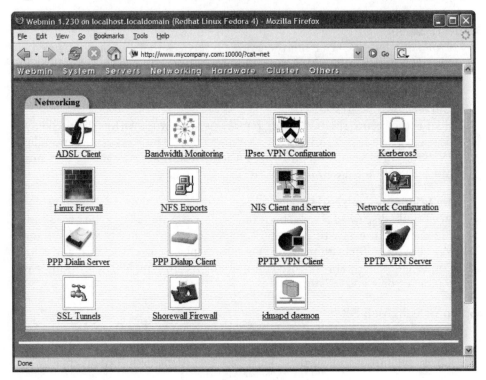

Bandwidth Monitoring

This page provides information about traffic received by the server, using `iptables` rules and a package called mrtg that's built in to the default installation of Fedora Core. mrtg provides a graphical representation of server traffic during administrator-selectable time periods, which is useful for analyzing the server's peak and low traffic periods. It also breaks that traffic into "downloaded" and "uploaded" segments.

Linux Firewall
Shorewall Firewall

The Linux Firewall module creates and administers `iptables` rules—the rules used by the Security Level Configuration tool. We'll be looking more closely at `iptables` a bit later on. Shorewall is a third-party package that provides services similar to `iptables`.

NFS Exports

NFS is the Network File System, a tool that allows your Linux server to share files with other servers on the network. We took a brief look at NFS in Chapter 4.

Network Configuration

The Network Configuration page in Webmin allows you to configure your network interfaces or devices, set up your server as a router or a gateway, configure how your server makes use of DNS, change your server's host name, and add host addresses.

Hardware Group Modules

Figure 6.10. Webmin modules available in the Hardware group.

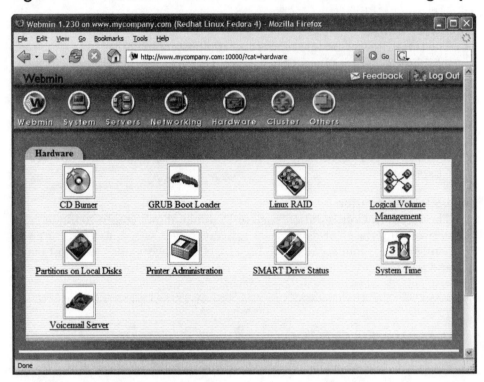

As critical as networking is to the operation of the server, it's all irrelevant if your hardware is misconfigured or somehow damaged. Webmin's hardware configuration and monitoring tools, shown in Figure 6.10, provide a good overview of the current operational state of the critical hardware devices on the server. Webmin also provides several great tools for configuring the hardware, including boot configuration, drive status, RAID, partition management, and logical volume management.

GRUB Boot Loader

The GRUB Configuration screen in Webmin displays the current kernel versions installed on the machine as icons. Select an icon to gain access to complete configuration options for all the GRUB parameters.

System Time

This comparatively simple module allows you to change the system time, set the system's time zone, and set up time synchronization with an NTP server.

Other Modules

Figure 6.11. Webmin modules available in the Others group.

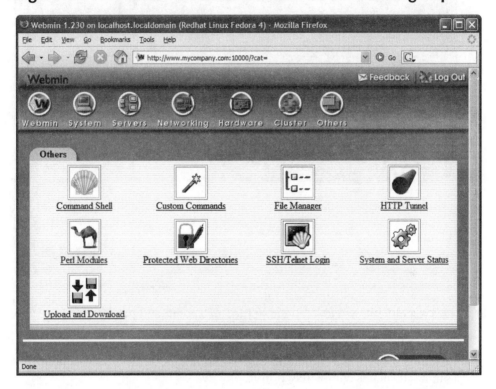

The Webmin application also provides tools that don't really fit into any of the other categories, so they're placed in the "Others" module group shown in Figure 6.11. They include:

Command Shell

Figure 6.12. Using Webmin's Command Shell tool.

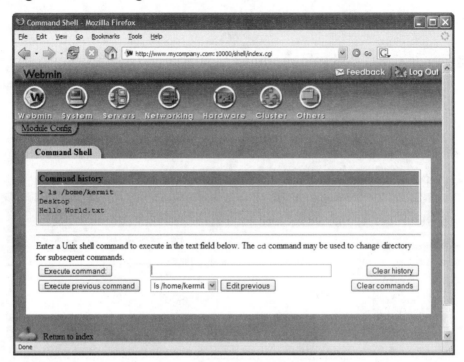

This is a rather low-tech implementation of a command prompt inside a Web browser. Enter a command into the text box at the bottom of the page, as depicted in Figure 6.12, and submit the form to see the command's output. Be sure not to enter a command that would require some interaction, as this command shell is completely non-interactive.

SSH/Telnet login

This tool comprises a Java applet that provides SSH or Telnet access to the server from the browser.

File Manager

This Java applet provides graphical access to the filesystem on the server in the style of the Windows Explorer or GNOME's File Browser.

System and Server Status

This module displays the status of the various services on the machine, allowing you to configure alerts and add monitors. For example, you could configure this module to send a message to a pager if Apache or the monitoring service itself goes down.

Perl Modules

This tool lists all of the Perl modules currently installed on the server, and provides a browser interface to CPAN, the Comprehensive Perl Archive Network. CPAN is an online collection of Perl modules used in all kinds of applications.

Webmin Configuration

Finally, you can completely customize the installation of Webmin to suit your tastes and needs from the Webmin section at the upper left of the main screen. As you can see in Figure 6.13, the customizable parameters include:

Change Language and Theme

Webmin is fully internationalized, with support for more than 30 languages. The look and feel of Webmin can also be customized, using one of three built-in themes, or one of any number of themes available online.

Webmin Configuration

The Webmin Configuration section is a rich interface for configuring nearly every element of the Webmin application, including network access, modules, authentication, certificates, and proxies.

Figure 6.13. Configuring Webmin.

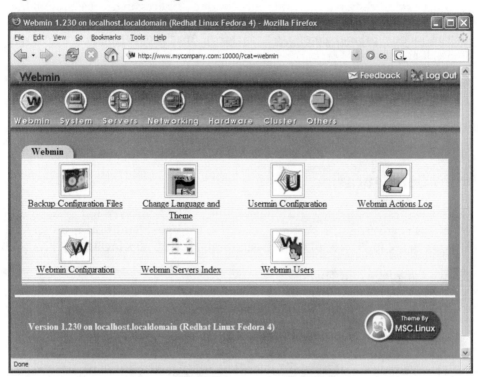

Keeping Software Up to Date

By now, you would almost certainly have noticed the small flashing exclamation mark icon in the top right corner of the Fedora desktop. Clicking this icon will launch the Red Hat Network Alert Notification Tool shown in Figure 6.14. This tool is designed to keep the RPM packages you've installed up to date.

Unfortunately, this applet, and its companion application up2date, contain a serious bug, so most of their functionality doesn't work. Hopefully, someone at Red Hat or a member of the Fedora community will fix it soon; you can check the status of this bug at Red Hat's Bugzilla bug-tracking system.[3]

If you proceed through the dialogs presented by accepting the Terms of Service and configuring any HTTP Proxies you may use, you'll see the Red Hat Alert

---

[3] https://bugzilla.redhat.com/bugzilla/show_bug.cgi?id=160873

Notification icon turn green, to indicate that it's checking for updates, and then turn blue, to indicate that there are no updates available, as shown in Figure 6.15. Unfortunately, this color change is likely to be a symptom of the bug mentioned previously. To make sure no updates are available, you can use Fedora's command-line updating tool, yum. Keep an eye out for this bug to be fixed in a future release of Fedora Core.

Figure 6.14. Red Hat Network Alert Notification Tool displaying on first launch.

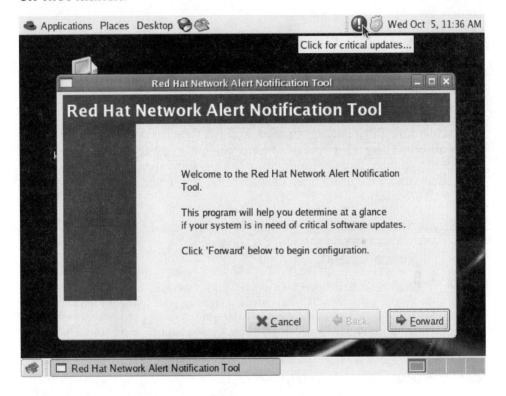

Figure 6.15. The Red Hat Network Alert notifier.

yum

yum (Yellow Dog Updater, Modified) is a relatively recent addition to the administration toolkit in many Linux distributions. Derived from a tool that was built for the PowerPC-based Yellow Dog Linux distribution, yum provides a way to keep your system packages up to date by utilizing a network of servers that host RPM packages. We used this tool in Chapter 5 to get the latest version of Apache. yum has some distinct advantages over other tools. These advantages make it a good choice for administrators—especially those who may not always be sitting at the server.

❑ The yum daemon (yumd) can be run in the background to check the repositories periodically for new software updates.

❑ yum can also run non-interactively: a simple command line switch will assume that your answer to each yum prompt is "yes."

❑ yum uses only RPM package headers to check the system software against the repository. This sets it apart from other updating systems, which create an index in addition to the headers stored in the RPM database. Using only the headers can save considerable disk space on the server, especially as the set of installed tools grows.

❑ The yum command set is very small, yet very powerful.

Tip

yum: a Caveat

While yum is a convenient tool, it can occasionally cause problems. For example, some MySQL updates may overwrite your configuration and, sometimes, even delete your data. If your installation depends on specific libraries in order to function, it's generally a good idea to check through the list manually before you install new packages.

Updating your Server with yum

To check the availability of updates to your server, enter **yum check-update** in a terminal window.

```
[kermit@swinetrek ~]$ su
Password:
[root@swinetrek kermit]# yum check-update
Setting up repositories
updates-released    100% |===========================|  951 B    00:00
```

```
extras              100% |=========================| 1.1 kB    00:00
base                100% |=========================| 1.1 kB    00:00
Reading repository metadata in from local files
primary.xml.gz      100% |=========================| 342 kB    00:09
updates-re: ######################################### 954/954
Added 954 new packages, deleted 0 old in 19.43 seconds
primary.xml.gz      100% |=========================| 829 kB    00:24
extras    : ######################################### 2324/2324
Added 2324 new packages, deleted 0 old in 41.74 seconds
primary.xml.gz      100% |=========================| 824 kB    00:16
base      : ######################################### 2772/2772
Added 2772 new packages, deleted 0 old in 37.56 seconds

MyODBC.i386                    2.50.39-25.FC4.1    updates-released
NetworkManager.i386            0.4-20.FC4.1        updates-released
NetworkManager-gnome.i386      0.4-20.FC4.1        updates-released
...
yum.noarch                     2.4.0-0.fc4         updates-released
zlib.i386                      1.2.2.2-5.fc4       updates-released
zlib-devel.i386                1.2.2.2-5.fc4       updates-released
[root@swinetrek kermit]#
```

All of this output is an indication that the system is working as it should. yum compares the versions of RPM software installed locally with those available for download, then lists all of the packages that have been updated. If the system is newly installed, you'll probably see quite a few packages for which updates are available. Updating the system with these new packages is just a matter of entering **yum update**, as root, at the command prompt:

```
[root@swinetrek kermit]# yum update
[root@swinetrek kermit]# yum update
Setting up Update Process
Setting up repositories
updates-released    100% |=========================|  951 B    00:00
extras              100% |=========================| 1.1 kB    00:00
base                100% |=========================| 1.1 kB    00:00
Reading repository metadata in from local files
primary.xml.gz      100% |=========================| 347 kB    00:04
updates-re: ######################################### 966/966
Added 966 new packages, deleted 0 old in 35.21 seconds
primary.xml.gz      100% |=========================| 855 kB    00:51
extras    : ######################################### 2361/2361
Added 2361 new packages, deleted 0 old in 52.41 seconds
primary.xml.gz      100% |=========================| 824 kB    00:11
base      : ######################################### 2772/2772
Added 2772 new packages, deleted 0 old in 47.62 seconds
```

```
Resolving Dependencies
--> Populating transaction set with selected packages.
       Please wait.
---> Downloading header for glib2 to pack into transaction set.
glib2-2.6.6-1.i386 100% |=========================| 21 kB   00:00
---> Package glib2.i386 0:2.6.6-1 set to be updated
---> Downloading header for spamassassin to pack into transaction
       set.
spamassassin-3.0.4 100% |=========================| 31 kB   00:00
---> Package spamassassin.i386 0:3.0.4-1.fc4 set to be updated
...
---> Downloading header for pam to pack into transaction set.
pam-0.79-9.5.i386. 100% |=========================| 62 kB   00:00
---> Package pam.i386 0:0.79-9.5 set to be updated
---> Downloading header for libraw1394 to pack into transaction
       set.
libraw1394-1.2.0-1 100% |=========================| 4.9 kB   00:00
---> Package libraw1394.i386 0:1.2.0-1.fc4 set to be updated
--> Running transaction check
--> Processing Dependency: python-numeric for package: pygtk2
--> Restarting Dependency Resolution with new changes.
--> Populating transaction set with selected packages.
       Please wait.
---> Downloading header for python-numeric to pack into
       transaction set.
python-numeric-23. 100% |=========================| 9.0 kB   00:00
---> Package python-numeric.i386 0:23.7-2 set to be updated
--> Running transaction check

Dependencies Resolved

================================================================
 Package          Arch    Version           Repository      Size
================================================================
Installing:
 kernel           i686    2.6.13-1.1526_FC4 updates-released 16 M
 kernel-devel     i686    2.6.13-1.1526_FC4 updates-released 4.2 M
Updating:
 MyODBC           i386    2.50.39-25.FC4.1  updates-released 59 k
 NetworkManager   i386    0.4-20.FC4.1      updates-released 181 k
...
 zlib             i386    1.2.2.2-5.fc4     updates-released 48 k
 zlib-devel       i386    1.2.2.2-5.fc4     updates-released 98 k
Installing for dependencies:
 python-numeric   i386    23.7-2            base             679 k
```

```
Transaction Summary
====================================================================
Install        3 Package(s)
Update       190 Package(s)
Remove         0 Package(s)
Total download size: 371 M
Is this ok [y/N]: y
Is this ok [y/N]:
```

At the end of this output, yum lists the packages that are available for download, including the version, repository, and size of each download. Here we can see that the total download size is 371MB, so we may not want to run this update until there's plenty of bandwidth available on the network. Answer **y** at this prompt if you wish to continue:

```
Is this ok [y/N]: y
Downloading Packages:
(1/193): glib2-2.6  100% |=======================| 568 kB 00:09
(2/193): spamassas  100% |=======================| 685 kB 00:09
(3/193): system-co    8% |==                     |  71 kB 00:02 ETA
```

yum will download all the listed packages.

```
(1/193): glib2-2.6  100% |=======================| 568 kB 00:09
(2/193): spamassas  100% |=======================| 685 kB 00:09
(3/193): system-co  100% |=======================| 307 kB 00:03
...
(192/193): pam-0.7  100% |=======================| 1.9 MB 00:27
(193/193): libraw1  100% |=======================|  37 kB 00:00
warning: rpmts_HdrFromFdno: Header V3 DSA signature: NOKEY, key ID
    4f2a6fd2
public key not available for glib2-2.6.6-1.i386.rpm
Retrieving GPG key from file:///etc/pki/rpm-gpg/RPM-GPG-KEY-fedora
Importing GPG key 0x4F2A6FD2 "Fedora Project <fedora@redhat.com>"
Is this ok [y/N]:
```

As we mentioned in Chapter 5, the RPM packages yum downloads are encrypted using a private key, so we need to import the public key to decrypt the package. Once yum has downloaded the public key, it can decrypt and install the packages.

```
Is this ok [y/N]: y
Key imported successfully
Running Transaction Test
Finished Transaction Test
Transaction Test Succeeded
Running Transaction
```

```
   Updating   : libgcc              #################### [  1/383]
   Updating   : tzdata              #################### [  2/383]
   Updating   : glibc-common        #################### [  3/383]
   Updating   : glibc               #################### [  4/383]
Stopping sshd: [  OK  ]
Starting sshd: [  OK  ]
   Updating   : zlib                #################### [  5/383]
   Updating   : glib2               #################### [  6/383]
...
   Updating   : mod_ssl             #################### [192/383]
   Updating   : dhcpv6_client       #################### [193/383]
   Cleanup    : glib2               #################### [194/383]
   Cleanup    : spamassassin        #################### [195/383]
...
   Cleanup    : pam                 #################### [382/383]
   Cleanup    : libraw1394          #################### [383/383]

Installed: kernel.i686 0:2.6.13-1.1526_FC4
     kernel-devel.i686 0:2.6.13-1.1526_FC4
Dependency Installed: python-numeric.i386 0:23.7-2
Updated: MyODBC.i386 0:2.50.39-25.FC4.1
     NetworkManager.i386 0:0.4-20.FC4.1 ...
     zlib.i386 0:1.2.2.2-5.fc4 zlib-devel.i386 0:1.2.2.2-5.fc4
Complete!
[root@swinetrek kermit]#
```

Your system is now up to date with all patches released by Red Hat.

Updating a Single Package

yum will also allow you to update individual packages. You can do this by including the package name in the command line, just as we did when we updated Apache in Chapter 5:

```
[root@swinetrek kermit]# yum update bind
Setting up Update Process
Setting up repositories
updates-released   100% |=========================| 951 B  00:00
extras             100% |=========================| 1.1 kB 00:00
base               100% |=========================| 1.1 kB 00:00
Reading repository metadata in from local files
Could not find update match for bind
No Packages marked for Update/Obsoletion
[root@swinetrek kermit]#
```

In this case, yum has found that the bind package on the system is up to date, but that's not always going to be the case. Here's what would happen if a new version of the bind package existed, and we decided to update the version we have on our server:

```
[root@swinetrek kermit]# yum update bind
Setting up Update Process
Setting up repositories
updates-released    100% |=========================| 951 B  00:00
extras              100% |=========================| 1.1 kB  00:00
base                100% |=========================| 1.1 kB  00:00
Reading repository metadata in from local files
primary.xml.gz      100% |=========================| 342 kB  00:04
updates-re: ######################################### 954/954
Added 1 new packages, deleted 12 old in 5.09 seconds
base      : ######################################### 2772/2772
Added 2772 new packages, deleted 0 old in 36.97 seconds
Resolving Dependencies
--> Populating transaction set with selected packages.
      Please wait.
---> Downloading header for bind to pack into transaction set.
bind-9.3.1-10_FC4. 100% |=========================| 38 kB  00:01
---> Package bind.i386 24:9.3.1-10_FC4 set to be updated
--> Running transaction check
--> Processing Dependency: bind-libs = 24:9.3.1-10_FC4 for
      package: bind
--> Processing Dependency: bind-utils = 24:9.3.1-10_FC4 for
      package: bind
--> Restarting Dependency Resolution with new changes.
--> Populating transaction set with selected packages.
      Please wait.
---> Downloading header for bind-utils to pack into
      transaction set.
bind-utils-9.3.1-1 100% |=========================| 28 kB  00:00
---> Package bind-utils.i386 24:9.3.1-10_FC4 set to be updated
---> Downloading header for bind-libs to pack into
      transaction set.
bind-libs-9.3.1-10 100% |=========================| 30 kB  00:00
---> Package bind-libs.i386 24:9.3.1-10_FC4 set to be updated
--> Running transaction check

Dependencies Resolved

=================================================================
 Package          Arch     Version          Repository     Size
=================================================================
```

```
Updating:
  bind              i386      24:9.3.1-10_FC4   updates-released   510 k
Updating for dependencies:
  bind-libs         i386      24:9.3.1-10_FC4   updates-released   779 k
  bind-utils        i386      24:9.3.1-10_FC4   updates-released   146 k

Transaction Summary
===============================================================
Install       0 Package(s)
Update        3 Package(s)
Remove        0 Package(s)
Total download size: 1.4 M
Is this ok [y/N]: y
Downloading Packages:
(1/3): bind-9.3.1- 100% |=========================| 510 kB  00:08
(2/3): bind-utils- 100% |=========================| 146 kB  00:02
(3/3): bind-libs-9 100% |=========================| 779 kB  00:09
warning: rpmts_HdrFromFdno: Header V3 DSA signature: NOKEY, key ID
    4f2a6fd2
public key not available for bind-9.3.1-10_FC4.i386.rpm
Retrieving GPG key from file:///etc/pki/rpm-gpg/RPM-GPG-KEY-fedora
Importing GPG key 0x4F2A6FD2 "Fedora Project <fedora@redhat.com>"
Is this ok [y/N]: y
Key imported successfully
Running Transaction Test
Finished Transaction Test
Transaction Test Succeeded
Running Transaction
  Updating  : bind-libs         ######################### [1/6]
  Updating  : bind-utils        ######################### [2/6]
  Updating  : bind              ######################### [3/6]
  Cleanup   : bind              ######################### [4/6]
  Cleanup   : bind-utils        ######################### [5/6]
  Cleanup   : bind-libs         ######################### [6/6]

Updated: bind.i386 24:9.3.1-10_FC4
Dependency Updated: bind-libs.i386 24:9.3.1-10_FC4
    bind-utils.i386 24:9.3.1-10_FC4
Complete!
[root@swinetrek kermit]#
```

Searching for and Installing Packages

So far, we've looked at updating currently installed software using yum, but we
can also use it to install software from its repositories. In order to locate such

software, we can use yum's search facility. Here, we're using **yum search mathml** to search for any packages that make mention of MathML in their metadata:

```
[root@swinetrek kermit]# yum search mathml
Searching Packages:
Setting up repositories
updates-released    100% |===========================|  951 B    00:00
extras              100% |===========================|  1.1 kB   00:00
base                100% |===========================|  1.1 kB   00:00
Reading repository metadata in from local files


mathml-fonts.noarch              1.0-18.fc4            extras
Matched from:
mathml-fonts
This package contains fonts required to display mathematical
symbols.  Applications supported include:

* mozilla (and netscape >= 7) to display MathML
* lyx
* kformula (koffice)
http://www.mozilla.org/projects/mathml/fonts/


mathml-fonts.noarch              1.0-15               extras
Matched from:
mathml-fonts
This package contains fonts required to display mathematical
symbols.  Applications supported include:
* mozilla (and netscape >= 7) to display MathML
* lyx
* kformula (koffice)
http://www.mozilla.org/projects/mathml/fonts/


gtkmathview.i386                 0.7.5-2.fc4          extras
Matched from:
A MathML rendering library
GtkMathView is a C++ rendering engine for MathML documents.
It provides an interactive view that can be used for browsing
and editing MathML markup.


mathml-fonts.noarch              1.0-17.fc4           extras
Matched from:
mathml-fonts
```

```
This package contains fonts required to display mathematical
symbols.  Applications supported include:
* mozilla (and netscape >= 7) to display MathML
* lyx
* kformula (koffice)
http://www.mozilla.org/projects/mathml/fonts/


gtkmathview.i386              0.7.5-3.fc4           extras
Matched from:
A MathML rendering library
GtkMathView is a C++ rendering engine for MathML documents.
It provides an interactive view that can be used for browsing
and editing MathML markup.
[root@swinetrek kermit]#
```

yum presents a list of all packages whose metadata contain the term "MathML."
Let's take a closer look at the last package that yum found. The first line of this
output provides the package name (gtkmathview.i386; the part after the dot
indicates the processor architecture for which this package is built), the version
of the package (0.7.5-3.fc4), and which repository the package was found in
(extras). If the package is installed, the repository will be displayed as installed.
Following this line, yum provides a description of the package.

To install this package, we use the yum install command. We can leave the
architecture out of the package name; yum is smart enough to figure out which
is the most appropriate package for this computer.

```
[root@swinetrek kermit]# yum install gtkmathview
Setting up Install Process
Setting up repositories
updates-released   100% |===========================|  951 B    00:00
extras             100% |===========================|  1.1 kB   00:00
base               100% |===========================|  1.1 kB   00:00
Reading repository metadata in from local files
primary.xml.gz     100% |===========================|  342 kB   00:07
updates-re: ######################################## 954/954
Added 5 new packages, deleted 17 old in 5.74 seconds
primary.xml.gz     100% |===========================|  855 kB   00:11
extras    : ######################################## 2361/2361
Added 37 new packages, deleted 0 old in 11.79 seconds
Parsing package install arguments
Resolving Dependencies
--> Populating transaction set with selected packages.
      Please wait.
```

```
---> Downloading header for gtkmathview to pack into
        transaction set.
gtkmathview-0.7.5- 100% |=========================| 8.4 kB    00:00
---> Package gtkmathview.i386 0:0.7.5-3.fc4 set to be updated
--> Running transaction check

Dependencies Resolved
=====================================================================
 Package          Arch     Version        Repository        Size
=====================================================================
Installing:
 gtkmathview       i386     0.7.5-3.fc4     extras            958 k

Transaction Summary
=====================================================================
Install      1 Package(s)
Update       0 Package(s)
Remove       0 Package(s)
Total download size: 958 k
Is this ok [y/N]: y
Downloading Packages:
(1/1): gtkmathview 100% |===========================| 958 kB    00:12
warning: rpmts_HdrFromFdno: Header V3 DSA signature: NOKEY, key ID
    1ac70ce6
public key not available for gtkmathview-0.7.5-3.fc4.i386.rpm
Retrieving GPG key from file:
    ///etc/pki/rpm-gpg/RPM-GPG-KEY-fedora-extras
Importing GPG key 0x1AC70CE6
    "Fedora Pre Extras Release <pre-extras@fedoraproject.org>"
Is this ok [y/N]: y
Key imported successfully
Running Transaction Test
Finished Transaction Test
Transaction Test Succeeded
Running Transaction
    Installing: gtkmathview                ######################### [1/1]

Installed: gtkmathview.i386 0:0.7.5-3.fc4
Complete!
[root@swinetrek kermit]#
```

Removing Packages

You can use yum to remove packages cleanly from your system.

```
[root@swinetrek kermit]# yum remove bind
Setting up Remove Process
Resolving Dependencies
--> Populating transaction set with selected packages. Please wait.
---> Package bind.i386 24:9.3.1-10_FC4 set to be erased
--> Running transaction check
Setting up repositories
updates-released   100% |===========================| 951 B    00:00
extras             100% |===========================| 1.1 kB   00:00
base               100% |===========================| 1.1 kB   00:00
Reading repository metadata in from local files
primary.xml.gz     100% |===========================| 800 kB   00:10
extras    : ########################################### 2247/2247
Added 2 new packages, deleted 79 old in 11.69 seconds
--> Processing Dependency: bind >= 9.1.3-0.rc2.3 for package:
        caching-nameserver
--> Processing Dependency: bind for package: caching-nameserver
--> Processing Dependency: bind for package: NetworkManager
--> Restarting Dependency Resolution with new changes.
--> Populating transaction set with selected packages.
        Please wait.
---> Package caching-nameserver.noarch 0:7.3-3 set to be erased
---> Package NetworkManager.i386 0:0.4-15.cvs20050404
        set to be erased
--> Running transaction check
--> Processing Dependency: NetworkManager = 0.4-15.cvs20050404
        for package: NetworkManager-gnome
--> Restarting Dependency Resolution with new changes.
--> Populating transaction set with selected packages.
        Please wait.
---> Package NetworkManager-gnome.i386 0:0.4-15.cvs20050404
        set to be erased
--> Running transaction check

Dependencies Resolved

=====================================================================
 Package          Arch    Version          Repository       Size
=====================================================================
Removing:
 bind             i386    24:9.3.1-10_FC4  installed        1.4 M
Removing for dependencies:
 NetworkManager   i386    0.4-15.cvs200504 installed        482 k
 NetworkManager-g i386    0.4-15.cvs200504 installed        180 k
 caching-nameserv noarch  7.3-3            installed         43 k
```

```
Transaction Summary
=====================================================================
Install      0 Package(s)
Update       0 Package(s)
Remove       4 Package(s)
Total download size: 0
Is this ok [y/N]: y
Downloading Packages:
Running Transaction Test
Finished Transaction Test
Transaction Test Succeeded
Running Transaction
  Removing   : caching-nameserver   ####################### [1/4]
warning: /etc/rndc.key saved as /etc/rndc.key.rpmsave
  Removing   : bind                 ####################### [2/4]
  Removing   : NetworkManager-gnome ####################### [3/4]
  Removing   : NetworkManager       ####################### [4/4]

Removed: bind.i386 24:9.3.1-10_FC4
Dependency Removed: NetworkManager.i386 0:0.4-15.cvs20050404
    NetworkManager-gnome.i386 0:0.4-15.cvs20050404
    caching-nameserver.noarch 0:7.3-3
Complete!
[root@swinetrek kermit]#
```

Other yum Functions

yum can clean up its cache of RPM package headers with the command yum clean all, like so:

```
[root@swinetrek kermit]# yum clean all
Cleaning up Everything
3 headers removed
3 packages removed
6 metadata files removed
0 cache files removed
3 cache files removed
[root@swinetrek kermit]#
```

Finally, yum also contains features that allow you to obtain information on specific packages:

```
[root@swinetrek kermit]# yum info gaim
Setting up repositories
updates-released   100% |=========================|  951 B    00:00
extras             100% |=========================|  1.1 kB   00:00
```

```
base                  100% |===========================| 1.1 kB    00:00
Reading repository metadata in from local files
primary.xml.gz        100% |===========================| 352 kB    00:19
updates-re: ######################################### 981/981
Added 27 new packages, deleted 12 old in 9.58 seconds
primary.xml.gz        100% |===========================| 876 kB    02:12
extras    : ######################################### 2436/2436
Added 92 new packages, deleted 17 old in 17.71 seconds
Installed Packages
Name    : gaim
Arch    : i386
Version: 1.5.0
Release: 1.fc4
Size    : 11 M
Repo    : installed
Summary: A GTK+ clone of the AOL Instant Messenger client.

Description:
 Gaim is a clone of America Online's Instant Messenger client.
It features nearly all of the functionality of the official AIM
client while also being smaller, faster, and commercial-free.


[root@swinetrek kermit]#
```

All in all, yum makes updating and maintaining the RPM packages on your system an easy process.

Summary

In an ideal world, servers wouldn't need administration. In this less-than-ideal world, they do; you'll want to install new software and tweak the services you already have running. In this chapter, you've seen some of the wealth of system administration tools available for Linux—tools that can help you keep your LAMP servers in tip-top shape.

7

Remote Administration

As we've seen, administering your servers is a vital part of their daily health. However, it's a lot more convenient to administer a server when you don't have to walk all the way to the server room to do so. While you can quite happily work with your Linux server when you're sitting in front of it, it's just as easy to administer a server at the other end of the corridor, or indeed, the continent. SSH and VNC make it possible to run your Linux server from across the network with hardly any need to visit it at all.

SSH

SSH, the Secure Shell, is a way of running commands on a remote computer. Using SSH in its most basic mode to connect to a remote machine across a network is essentially the same as being seated at that machine and opening a GNOME Terminal window. SSH is deliberately engineered to stop malicious parties intercepting or altering your computer's communication with the remote server, which makes it a much better choice than older protocols that are not secure, such as telnet or RSH (Remote Shell).

SSH vs ssh

SSH is both the name of a protocol and the name of a Linux command line program that makes use of that protocol. When we're referring to the Secure

Shell protocol we use SSH (all uppercase); the command line program is called ssh (all lowercase).

Using the PuTTY SSH Client

PuTTY is a Windows program that you can use to connect to Linux boxes using SSH. You can download the installer from the PuTTY Website[1]—the "windows-style installer" listed on the downloads page is the file you want to grab. Once you install the program and launch it, you'll be presented with the PuTTY Configuration dialog shown in Figure 7.1. Don't be scared by the number of options available to you; for now, all you're interested in is the Host Name (or IP address) field. Enter your Linux server's name or IP address into this field, and click Open.

Figure 7.1. The PuTTY Configuration dialog.

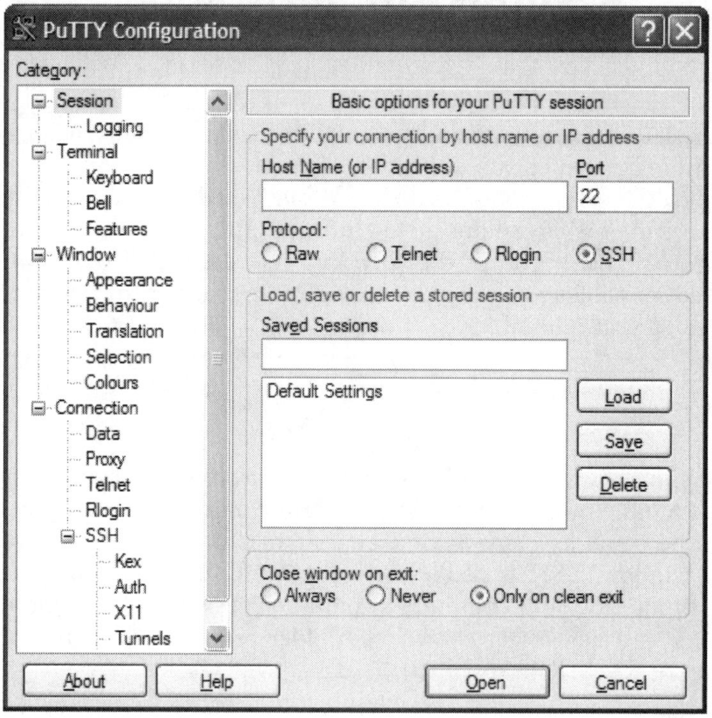

[1] http://www.chiark.greenend.org.uk/~sgtatham/putty/

Skipping Username

Tip

To avoid entering your username, enter **username@servername** in the Host Name (or IP address) field.

When you first connect to your server, you'll see the PuTTY Security Alert dialog illustrated in Figure 7.2. This is PuTTY's somewhat convoluted way of asking you to confirm that this is the server key you're expecting.

Figure 7.2. The PuTTY Security Alert.

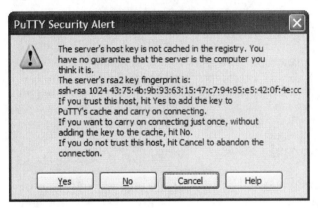

Host Keys

Each SSH server has a unique **host key**. When you attempt to connect to a machine, PuTTY (or whichever SSH client you're using) checks that the host key of that machine is the same as it was the last time you connected to it. This provides excellent protection against malicious parties pretending to be your server, but also poses a problem: how does the SSH client know what the server's host key is the first time it connects? The answer is that it doesn't. The first time you connect to a machine, the SSH client will notice that it doesn't have a host key for that machine; it will ask you (usually a little cryptically) whether it's okay to connect.

Part of this message will include a **key fingerprint**, which is an abbreviated version of the host key. To find out what a server's key fingerprint is, run the command `ssh-keygen -l -f /etc/ssh/ssh_host_rsa_key` on that server.

```
[kermit@swinetrek ~]$ ssh-keygen -l -f /etc/ssh/ssh_host_rsa_key
1024 43:75:4b:9b:93:63:15:47:c7:94:95:e5:42:0f:4e:cc
    /etc/ssh/ssh_host_rsa_key.pub
```

The part highlighted in bold is the key fingerprint. You must confirm that this key fingerprint is exactly the same as the key fingerprint that's displayed when you try to connect to the server for the first time. If the key fingerprints aren't the same, something is wrong: the machine you're trying to connect to is not the machine you're actually connecting to. If the key fingerprints agree, you can safely click Yes on this dialog. PuTTY will remember this verified host key for future connections, and will not ask again.

Avoid Changing the Host Key

You should avoid changing the SSH server's host key, which can happen if you reinstall the SSH server software, or delete files in /etc/ssh. If this happens, the key that SSH clients remember for the server will differ from the server's new key, and the SSH client will display a warning message. PuTTY's message is depicted in Figure 7.3.

Logging in with a Password

Once you've verified the host key, you'll be asked to log in: just enter your user-name and password at the prompts. After this, you'll be presented with the famil-iar command prompt:

```
login as: kermit
kermit@swinetrek's password:
Last login: Mon Oct 10 05:45:39 2005 from 192.168.69.33
[kermit@swinetrek ~]$
```

SSHing into the Server

Connecting to an SSH server is often described as "SSHing into the server."

Logging in with a Private Key

It's possible to use PuTTY (or any other SSH client) to connect to a machine without entering a username or password at all. In such cases, we connect using a public and private key pair. First, we need to generate the keys with the PuTTYgen tool, shown in Figure 7.4, which you can launch by clicking Start > All Programs > PuTTY > PuTTYgen.

Figure 7.3. The PuTTY Security Alert displaying after the host key changes.

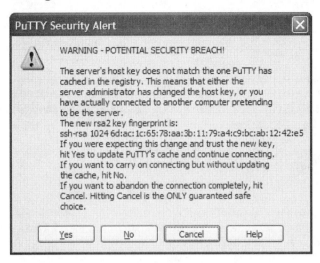

Figure 7.4. The PuTTYgen tool.

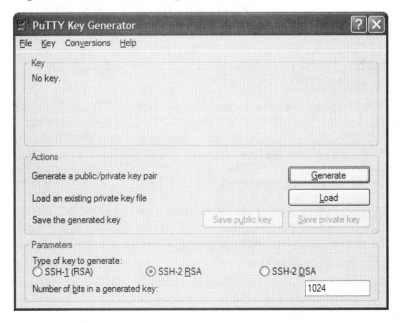

Click Generate to have PuTTYgen generate the key pair; you'll need to move your mouse about a bit, as PuTTYgen's algorithm uses your mouse movements to generate the keys. Once the keys are generated, you must save the public key on the server.

Tip

Five-minute Samba

Thereare many ways to move files from Windows to Linux, but the easiest method is probably to use Samba to gain access to part of the filesystem as a Windows file share. To quickly get Samba sharing a user's home directory, follow these steps:

1. On your Linux server, start the Samba Configuration tool (Desktop > System Settings > Server Settings > Samba).

2. Once the Samba Configuration tool has loaded, select Preferences > Samba Users..., then click Add User. Select the user you're interested in from the Unix Username drop-down list, and enter the username and password you'll use to access this share from Windows.

3. Back in the Samba Configuration tool, click Add Share, the Browse... button, and then select the user's home directory. Check the Writable and Visible checkboxes and, behind the Access tab, check the user you just created.

4. You might also find it useful to review the Samba Server Settings by selecting Preferences > Server Settings.... These settings depend largely upon your own Windows network settings.

5. Next, we'll need to allow access to Samba through the Firewall. Launch the Security Level Configuration tool (Desktop > System Settings > Security Level) and add `137:udp, 138:udp, 139:tcp, 445:tcp` to the Other Ports list. Note that you should remove these ports once you're done with Samba; leaving them open to connections from the Internet could pose a potential security problem.

6. While in the Security Level Configuration tool, click on the SELinux tab, as illustrated in Figure 7.5. Under Modify SELinux Policy, locate Samba and enable the Allow Samba to share users home directories option.

7. The last step is to start the Samba service. Open the Service Configuration tool from Desktop > System Settings > Server Settings > Services, locate the smb service, and start it.

Figure 7.5. Modifying the SELinux policy.

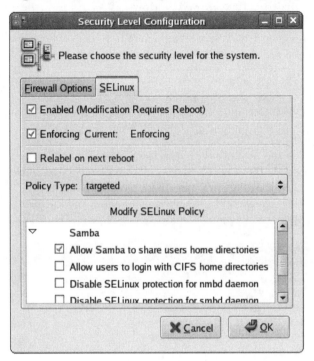

From Windows, you should now be able to access the Samba file share, as shown in Figure 7.6. Note that you should ensure that the Show hidden files and folders option is enabled in the File Explorer's Folder Options (Tools > Folder Options...).

Figure 7.6. Samba file share accessed via Windows.

On the Linux server, create a directory named `.ssh` if it doesn't already exist. We can't create this directory from Windows as Windows' file naming rules forbid directory names starting with a period. This directory also needs to have very specific permissions: read, write, and execute permissions must be disabled for everyone but the file's owner.

```
[kermit@swinetrek ~]$ mkdir .ssh
[kermit@swinetrek ~]$ chmod go-rwx .ssh
[kermit@swinetrek ~]$
```

Next, copy the text in the Public key field, open Notepad and paste the text into a new file. Save this file as `\\`*servername*`\`*sharename*`\.ssh\authorized_keys`, a shown in Figure 7.7. Be sure to surround the filename in quotation marks, otherwise Notepad will add a `.txt` extension to the filename.

Figure 7.7. Saving `\\`*servername*`\`*sharename*`\.ssh\authorized_keys`

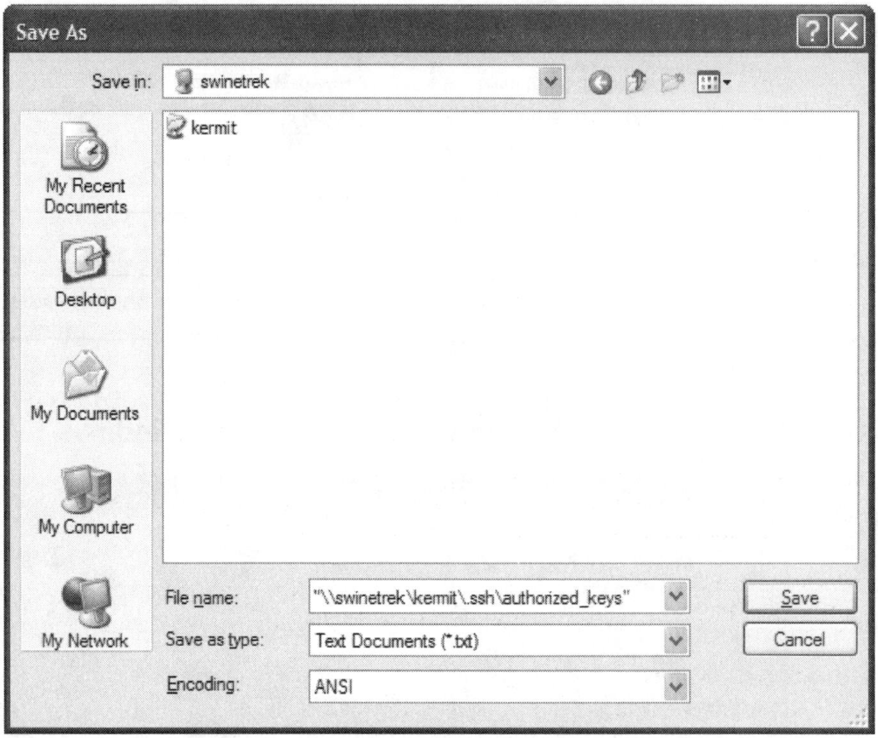

Now we need to save our private key. At this point, it's recommended that you enter a key passphrase to keep the private key secure. Click the Save private key button, and save it somewhere on your local hard disk.

To make use of this public and private key pair, launch PuTTY and enter the server name as you did previously. From the Category list on the left of the PuTTY Configuration window, select Auth. In the Private key file for authentication field, select the private key file you saved from PuTTYgen, as illustrated in Figure 7.8.

Figure 7.8. Selecting the private key.

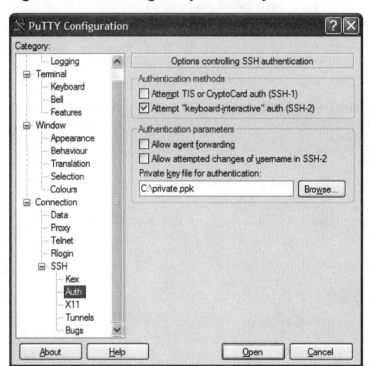

Click Open, and if you secured your private key with a password, you'll be prompted for it. Enter the password, and you're logged in.

```
Using username "kermit".
Authenticating with public key "rsa-key-20051013"
Passphrase for key "rsa-key-20051013":
Last login: Wed Oct 12 23:34:51 2005 from 192.168.69.36
[kermit@swinetrek ~]$
```

Using the ssh Client

The ssh command line client comes standard on just about every Linux distribution, and is equally prevalent on other Unix-like systems, including Mac OS X. To use it, enter **ssh *username@servername*** at the command prompt:

```
mymac:~ kfrog$ ssh kermit@swinetrek
The authenticity of host 'swinetrek (192.168.69.33)' can't be
established.
RSA key fingerprint is
43:75:4b:9b:93:63:15:47:c7:94:95:e5:42:0f:4e:cc.
Are you sure you want to continue connecting (yes/no)?
```

As with PuTTY, ssh asks you to verify that this is the key fingerprint you're expecting. Compare the listed fingerprint with the output of ssh-keygen -l -f /etc/ssh/ssh_host_rsa_key: if they match, enter **yes**:

```
Are you sure you want to continue connecting (yes/no)? yes
Warning: Permanently added 'swinetrek' (RSA) to the list of known
hosts.
kermit@swinetrek's password:
```

Once you enter your password, you'll be connected to the server.

```
kermit@swinetrek's password:
Last login: Mon Oct 10 05:45:39 2005 from 192.168.69.33
[kermit@swinetrek ~]$
```

To logout from the ssh server, enter **logout**.

```
[kermit@swinetrek ~]$ logout

Connection to swinetrek closed.
mymac:~ kfrog$
```

Remote Command Execution

A handy and powerful feature of the ssh client is that it gives us the ability to specify a command that ssh will execute, before disconnecting immediately.

```
mymac:~ kfrog$ ssh root@swinetrek passwd kermit
root@swinetrek's password:
New UNIX password: password
Retype new UNIX password: password
Changing password for user kermit.
```

```
passwd: all authentication tokens updated successfully.
mymac:~ kfrog$
```

Notice that, this time, ssh does not display the "login banner" that shows when you last connected to the server.

Logging in with a Private Key

As with PuTTY, we can use ssh to log in with a private and public key pair. To generate the keys, we use the ssh-keygen tool:

```
mymac:~ kfrog$ ssh-keygen -t rsa
Generating public/private rsa key pair.
Enter file in which to save the key (/Users/kfrog/.ssh/id_rsa):
Created directory '/Users/kfrog/.ssh'.
Enter passphrase (empty for no passphrase):
Enter same passphrase again:
Your identification has been saved in /Users/kfrog/.ssh/id_rsa.
Your public key has been saved in /Users/kfrog/.ssh/id_rsa.pub.
The key fingerprint is:
f5:4e:a6:d9:9f:42:fa:24:5e:d7:30:68:04:3f:67:60 kfrog@mymac.lan
mymac:~ kfrog$
```

After the command is run, you're prompted for a location at which you want to save the private key; hit **Enter** to accept the default. You are then prompted for a passphrase for the key; you'll need to enter the passphrase twice. The key will then be generated.

Now, we need to add the public key to the ~/.ssh/authorized_keys file on the server. The following command uses the cat command to read the key from ~/.ssh/id_rsa.pub, ssh to log in to the SSH server, and cat to add the key to ~/.ssh/authorized_keys on the server.

```
mymac:~ kfrog$ cat ~/.ssh/id_rsa.pub | ssh kermit@swinetrek \
? 'sh -c "cat - >> ~/.ssh/authorized_keys"'
kermit@swinetrek's password:
mymac:~ kfrog$
```

Now we're able to log in to our server, using the private and public key pair for authentication:

```
mymac:~ kfrog$ ssh kermit@swinetrek
Enter passphrase for key '/Users/kfrog/.ssh/id_rsa':
Last login: Wed Oct 12 23:56:16 2005 from 192.168.69.36
[kermit@swinetrek ~]$
```

VNC

What SSH is to the command line, VNC is to the desktop: VNC allows you to see and control another machine's graphical desktop remotely. It's very useful for controlling a remote server, especially since you can control that machine the way you want, rather than being restricted to the command line.

Setting up a VNC Server

Fedora Core comes with simple VNC support built-in, but this simple support should be used only for servers that are internal to your network. On its own, VNC is very insecure, but we can leverage SSH's security features to make it secure. We'll look at how this can be done a little later in the chapter.

To start the simple VNC server, launch the Remote Desktop Preferences tool shown in Figure 7.9 by selecting Desktop > Preferences > Remote Desktop.

Check Allow other users to view your desktop and Allow other users to control your desktop, and uncheck Ask you for confirmation. You can optionally provide a password that users must enter before they connect to the VNC server—tick Require the user to enter this password, and enter a password—but keep in mind that this only provides a very light level of security. It's important to note that this VNC server works only while a user is logged at the server; if the server is waiting at the login screen, VNC connections using this method are not possible using this tool.

Clients will connect to your VNC server via TCP over ports 5900–5906, so you'll need to open these ports in your firewall: add **5900:tcp, 5901:tcp, ... 5906:tcp** to the Other Ports list in the Security Level Configuration tool. Once you've done so, the server will be accessible via VNC.

Figure 7.9. The Remote Desktop Preferences tool.

VNC Viewers

Setting up a VNC server isn't much use unless you have a client with which you can access it. Here, we'll take a brief look at three VNC viewers: TightVNC for Windows, Chicken of the VNC for Mac OS X, and Fedora Core's Terminal Server Client.

TightVNC

Figure 7.10. The TightVNC Select Components screen.

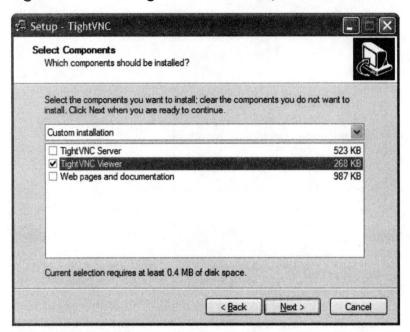

TightVNC is a popular open-source VNC server and viewer package for Linux and Windows, and is available for download from http://www.tightvnc.com/. Double-click on the installation program and proceed through the standard Windows installer wizard. When you get to the Select Components screen shown in Figure 7.10, select the TightVNC Viewer. Proceed through the rest of the wizard, and the TightVNC Viewer will be installed.

When you launch the TightVNC viewer, you're presented with three items in the All Programs menu, as shown in Figure 7.11: Best Compression, Fast Compression and Listen Mode. Best and Fast Compression are both shortcuts to the same program, but with different parameters; Listen Mode puts an icon in the system tray so the viewer can be launched quickly. Choose Best or Fast Compression to launch the viewer.

Figure 7.11. TightVNC in the All Programs menu.

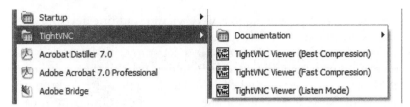

Connecting to the VNC server is a simple task: enter the name of the server and click OK. The remote server's desktop will appear in a window on your own desktop as shown in Figure 7.12. Simply move your mouse over the window to start interacting with it; you can control the remote server as if you were sitting at it. To close the VNC connection, simply click on the cross icon in the window title bar.

Figure 7.12. Using TightVNC viewer.

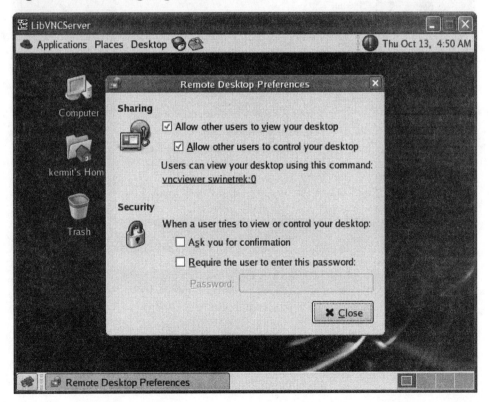

Chicken of the VNC

Chicken of the VNC is another open-source VNC viewer, but one developed for Mac OS X. You can download it from http://cotvnc.sourceforge.net/. It's distributed as a disk image, so installation is as simple as opening the disk image and copying the application into your **Applications** folder. Launch the application, enter the name of your VNC server, and click Connect. The remote desktop will appear on your own desktop; it will look similar to that shown in Figure 7.13.

Figure 7.13. Using Chicken of the VNC.

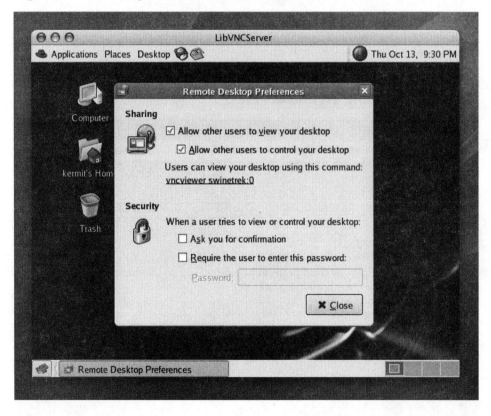

Fedora Core's Terminal Server Client

Figure 7.14. Connecting to a VNC server.

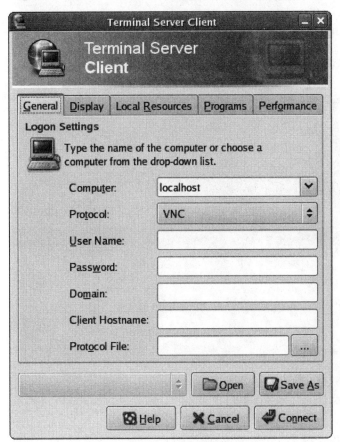

Fedora Core is supplied with a VNC client in the form of Terminal Server Client. This client can access both Windows Terminal Servers and servers running VNC. To install it, launch the Add/Remove Applications tool and, from the System Tools group, install the tsclient and vnc packages. Now, select Applications > Internet > Terminal Server Client to launch the program. This client can access both Windows Terminal Servers and servers running VNC.

Simply enter the name of the VNC server to which you want to connect, and choose VNC as the Protocol, as shown in Figure 7.14, then click Connect. The remote server's desktop will appear in a window on your own desktop, as illustrated in Figure 7.15. You can control the remote server as if you were sitting at it, and simply close the VNC connection by clicking on the cross icon in the window's title bar when you're done.

Figure 7.15. The Terminal Server client.

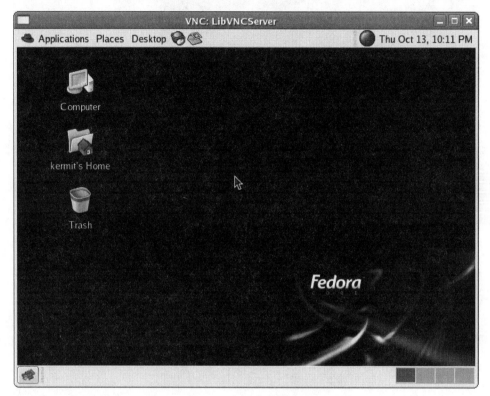

Securing VNC with SSH Tunnelling

Since the VNC protocol by itself is not secure, it's not a good idea to leave a machine that's running VNC connected to the Internet. Fortunately, SSH offers a very handy feature called SSH tunnelling or port forwarding to circumvent this problem. In essence, instead of connecting directly to the VNC server (as shown in Figure 7.16), SSH tunnelling allows you to make your VNC connection through an established SSH connection (depicted in Figure 7.17).

Figure 7.16. An unsecured VNC connection.

Figure 7.17. A secure VNC connection.

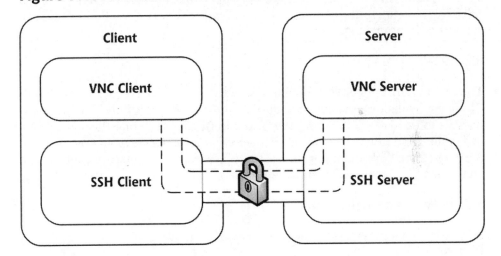

SSH tunnelling is actually quite simple to get up and running. The procedure for using VNC securely is:

1. Set up an SSH tunnel to the VNC server.

2. Start the VNC server daemon on the server.

3. Connect to the VNC server through the SSH tunnel.

4. Make use of the VNC.

5. Disconnect from the VNC server.

6. Stop the VNC server.

7. Close the SSH connection.

Setting up the VNC Server Daemon

Before we begin, we need to install the VNC server daemon; we can do so with the yum install vnc-server command, or by selecting the vnc-server package from the Network Servers package group in the Package Management tool.

Setting up the SSH Tunnel

SSH tunnelling is a technique by which we redirect communications to and from a certain port—in this case, port 5901—to a port on the local machine, through SSH, thereby encrypting communications across that port. Both PuTTY and ssh support SSH tunnelling.

Tunnelling with PuTTY

To set up PuTTY for SSH tunnelling, select the Tunnels category in the PuTTY Configuration dialog, as shown in Figure 7.18. In Source Port, enter the local port number to forward (in this case, **5901**), and in Destination, enter the server name and remote port number to forward in the format *servername:portnumber*. Click Add to add this forwarded port to the list. Once everything is set up, click Open, and your SSH session will start as normal.

Tunnelling with the ssh Client

With the command-line ssh client, tunnelling is set up using the -L option, as follows:

```
mymac:~ kfrog$ ssh -L 5901:swinetrek:5901 kermit@swinetrek
kermit@swinetrek's password:
Last login: Sun Oct 16 20:46:10 2005 from 192.168.69.36
[kermit@swinetrek ~]$
```

After the -L option, we list the local port we want to forward, the remote server name, and the port on the remote server that we want to forward to.

Figure 7.18. Setting up PuTTY for SSH tunnelling.

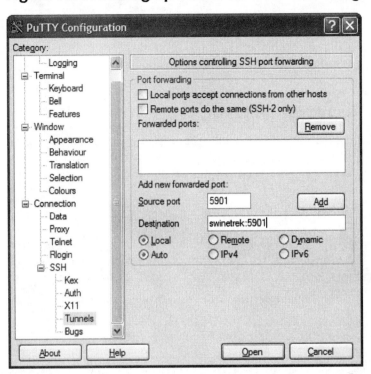

Starting the VNC Server Daemon

Now that we've opened an SSH session, we start the VNC server daemon by entering vncserver at the command prompt:

```
[kermit@swinetrek ~]$ vncserver

You will require a password to access your desktops.

Password:
Verify:

New 'swinetrek:1 (kermit)' desktop is swinetrek:1

Creating default startup script /home/kermit/.vnc/xstartup
Starting applications specified in /home/kermit/.vnc/xstartup
Log file is /home/kermit/.vnc/swinetrek:1.log
```

```
[kermit@swinetrek ~]$
```

If this is the first time you've run vncserver, it will ask for the password that is to be used for this and all future VNC connections. You can change this password later, using the vncpasswd command.

vncserver will also create configuration files for the currently logged-in user in the directory ~/.vnc. Before we make use of VNC for the first time, we need to modify one of these files to ensure that the GNOME desktop environment is started when we log in. Open the file ~/.vnc/xstartup in your text editor, locate the line that says, "Uncomment the following two lines for normal desktop," and uncomment the two lines that follow. Once you're done, the file should look like this:

File: ~/.vnc/xstartup

```
#!/bin/sh

# Uncomment the following two lines for normal desktop:
unset SESSION_MANAGER
exec /etc/X11/xinit/xinitrc

[ -x /etc/vnc/xstartup ] && exec /etc/vnc/xstartup
[ -r $HOME/.Xresources ] && xrdb $HOME/.Xresources
xsetroot -solid grey
vncconfig -iconic &
xterm -geometry 80x24+10+10 -ls -title "$VNCDESKTOP Desktop" &
twm &
```

Connecting to the VNC Server

The next step—connecting to the VNC server—is also simple. Using your VNC client, enter **localhost:1** as the server name. This may seem a little counter-intuitive, but it's correct: by connecting to localhost:1 you actually connect to port 5901 on your machine; that connection then travels down the SSH tunnel to port 5901 on the remote machine, which is where the VNC server is waiting for a connection. You now have a VNC connection that is secure, because it travels through the SSH tunnel you've set up.

Do not close the SSH session while VNC is running, or your VNC session will be abruptly cut off! Once you have finished working, disconnect from VNC by closing the window. You must then stop the VNC daemon on the server: in the SSH connection to the server, enter vncserver -kill :1 to stop the VNC server daemon. You can then log out of the SSH session, which closes the SSH tunnel.

Summary

Being able to work with your servers remotely is a thoroughly useful thing. You can work with your LAMP servers whether they're directly in front of you or on the other side of the world, using remote administration technologies such as SSH and VNC. With these tools, you can control and administer your machines as if you're sitting right next to them.

8

Occasional Administration

By comparison with daily administration—the things that need looking at and
checking all the time—there are also "occasional" administration tasks: things
that need to be done once, or infrequently. They're the tasks that you may need
to glance at from time to time, and be aware of, but aren't a focus of your con-
centration. The most important of these is setting up your backups—actually
performing the backup is a daily task, but one that should be so easy that it doesn't
qualify as an administrative chore—but there's also the question of Web traffic
reporting, and the log files you'll need to understand to set that reporting up.

Backups

Backing up the files on your servers is vitally important—but, of course, you
already know this. Since no-one actually likes performing backups, they need to
be as easy as possible to do: ideally, they should occur automatically. Traditionally,
Linux servers were backed up using a custom set of shell scripts that were created
by the system administrator; everyone rolled their own private backup solution
and tweaked it repeatedly for best results. Linux has come a long way since those
days, and more automated tools are now available. However, it's still useful to
be able to put together your own scripts for backing up a LAMP server, because
this approach gives you a very fine degree of control.

Simple Backups

The simplest way of performing a backup is to write the files to a CD or DVD, and store the backup away. Your backup strategy can be as complex as you like—and will probably need to be fairly intricate if you're integrating your new LAMP server into a larger enterprise setup—but it's better to have a simple backup process that you actually carry out than a complex strategy that never gets off the ground. Below is a simple script that can be run on a regular basis to back up your selected files to a CD.[1] The first time it runs, you'll select the files that you want to back up; thereafter, running the script (daily) will simply back up those files to a new CD. The easier it is to create the backup, the more likely it is that you'll do it.

File: **simple-cd-backup.sh**

```
#!/bin/bash
# Back up files to CD, simply.
BACKUPDIR="$HOME/.simple-cd-backup/FilesToBackUp"
ISO=/tmp/CD-Backup-$(date -Iseconds).iso
DISCNAME="Backup data, $(date +%c)"

if [ ! -f /proc/sys/dev/cdrom/info ]; then
   zenity --title "Simple CD Backup" --error --error-text \
       "Couldn't find a CD burner."
   exit
fi

BURNERINDEX=$(grep "Can write CD-R:" /proc/sys/dev/cdrom/info | \
     python -c "import sys; s=sys.stdin.readline().split(); \
     print s.count('1') and s.index('1')-1")

if [ $BURNERINDEX == '0' ]; then
   zenity --title "Simple CD Backup" --error --error-text \
       "Couldn't find a CD burner."
   exit
fi

CDDEVICE=$(grep "drive name:" /proc/sys/dev/cdrom/info | \
     python -c "import sys; s=sys.stdin.readline().split(); \
     print s[$BURNERINDEX]")

mkdir -p "$BACKUPDIR" >/dev/null 2>&1
nautilus --no-desktop --browser \
```

---

[1]This script is also available as part of this book's code archive.

```
     "$HOME/.simple-cd-backup/FilesToBackUp"

zenity --title "Simple CD Backup" --question --question-text \
    "Burn files linked in the directory?"
if [ $? == 1 ]; then exit; fi

mkisofs -f -l -o $ISO -A "$DISCNAME" "$BACKUPDIR" | \
    zenity --progress-text="Creating backup" \
    --title "Simple CD Backup" --progress --pulsate —auto-close

cdrecord -v speed=4 dev=/dev/$CDDEVICE $ISO | \
    zenity --progress-text="Burning CD" \
    --title "Simple CD Backup" --progress --pulsate —auto-close

rm $ISO

zenity --info --infotext "Backup burned to CD."
```

Save this script as ~/Desktop/simple-cd-backup.sh, then set it to be executable: either right-click on the file and set the appropriate permissions, or enter chmod +x ~/Desktop/simple-cd-backup.sh at the command line.

You can double-click on this file to see the Run or Display? dialog depicted in Figure 8.1. Click Run to run the script as-is; click Display to open the file in a text editor.

Figure 8.1. The Run or Display? dialog.

If you run the script, it will create the directory ~/.simple-cd-backup/FilesToBackUp, open that directory in Nautilus, and, finally, pop up the confirmation window shown in Figure 8.2.

Figure 8.2. The windows displayed by the `simple-cd-backup` script.

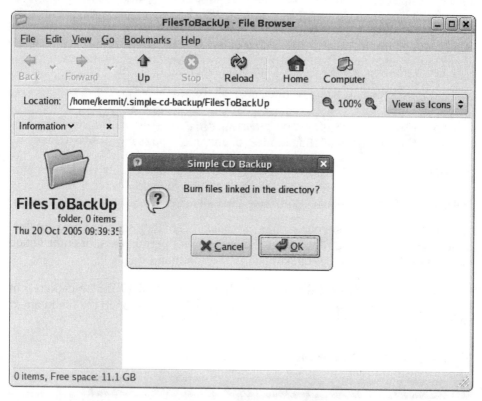

Move the confirmation dialog to the side (but don't click Cancel) and create symlinks to the files that you want to back up into this directory. It's vital that you *link* files into the directory: don't copy them. Sometimes, you can right-click on a file to create a link, but this option won't be available if you don't have permission to write to that file's directory. In these cases, use the `ln -s` command. For example, if you want to back up the `/etc` directory, which contains all your system configuration, you'd type the following:

```
[kermit@swinetrek ~]$ ln -s /etc \
> ~/.simple-cd-backup/FilesToBackUp/etc
[kermit@swinetrek ~]$
```

Alternately, if you have a three-button mouse, you could follow this procedure:

❑ Double-click the Computer icon on the desktop, or select Places > Computer.

❏ Double-click Filesystem, to show the root directory.

❏ Use the middle button to drag the etc folder into the FilesToBackUp folder.

❏ Click Link here on the menu.

Once you've established links to every file you intend to back up in the FilesTo-BackUp folder, close the FilesToBackUp window. Insert a blank CD and, where you see Burn files linked in the directory? in the dialog, click OK. The files you linked will be added to a CD image, and this image will be burned to the CD. Dialogs will appear, reporting the progress of these two steps, so you'll need to click OK when the process is complete.

The next time you run a backup (say, the following day), the links you created will still be there. This means that, to run a daily backup, you can simply click simple-cd-backup, then click OK at the Burn files linked in the directory? prompt: it will burn your files to the backup CD.

Some Explanation

Let me explain how the script works in a bit more detail. You don't need to know this information to use the script, but this is a good example of how a short shell script can act like a powerful application, requiring only a small coding effort. This explanation may also help you to debug the script if it doesn't quite work as intended on your system.

The bit of the script that actually does the work is the last couple of lines, which use mkisofs (an abbreviation of "make ISO filesystem") and cdrecord. The rest of the script focuses on setting up the backups in a user-friendly way.

First, simple-cd-backup.sh checks that the system has a CD burner by using a little Python to parse the file /proc/sys/dev/cdrom/info. This file lists all the CD-ROM drives on the system and provides an indication of the capabilities of each. On my machine, it looks like this:

```
drive name:        hdc
drive speed:       24
drive # of slots:  1
Can close tray:    1
Can open tray:     1
Can lock tray:     1
Can change speed:  1
Can select disk:   0
```

```
Can read multisession:   1
Can read MCN:            1
Reports media changed:   1
Can play audio:          1
Can write CD-R:          1
Can write CD-RW:         1
Can read DVD:            1
Can write DVD-R:         1
Can write DVD-RAM:       0
Can read MRW:            1
Can write MRW:           1
Can write RAM:           1
```

The file above lists one CD drive, called "hdc," which can be addressed as /dev/hdc. The presence of more CD drives would add columns to the file. Our script uses a single line of Python to look into this file for the line "Can write CD-R" followed by a 1. If it doesn't find such a column, it displays an error (using zenity, which is discussed below) and exits.

The FilesToBackUp window is a Nautilus window that shows the directory ~/.simple-cd-backup/FilesToBackUp, which the script creates (if it doesn't already exist). To view it, run Nautilus directly using this command:

```
[kermit@swinetrek ~]$ nautilus --no-desktop --browser \
> "$HOME/.simple-cd-backup/FilesToBackUp"
```

The script makes extensive use of zenity, a command which is used to pop up various types of GNOME alert boxes and dialog windows from shell scripts. For example, the script uses the following code to display a dialog that contains OK and Cancel buttons:

```
[kermit@swinetrek ~]$ zenity --title "Simple CD Backup" \
> --question --question-text "Burn files linked in the directory?"
```

This displays the dialog shown in Figure 8.3.

Once you've confirmed that you'd like to burn the CD, the real work begins. The script uses mkisofs to create an ISO CD image that contains all the files linked in the directory. It does so using the following mkisofs command:

File: **simple-cd-backup.sh (excerpt)**
```
mkisofs -f -l -o $ISO -A "$DISCNAME" "$BACKUPDIR"
```

Figure 8.3. A question dialog displayed using zenity.

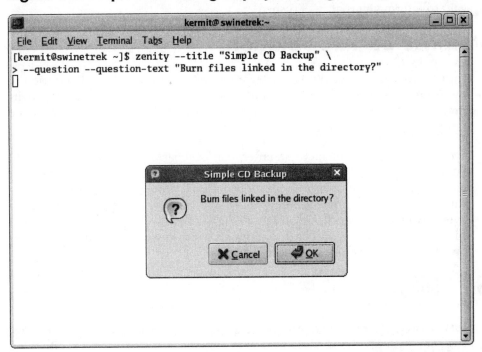

$ISO has previously been defined as the name under which the generated ISO file should be saved; $DISCNAME identifies a useful name for the disk (containing the date); $BACKUPDIR is the ~/.simple-cd-backup/FilesToBackUp directory. The options -f and -l control minor aspects of the way mkisofs works: -f means "follow symbolic links in the directory", and -l saves the files with full names (rather than abbreviated Windows 95 FILENA~1.EXT names).

Once the CD image has been created, the cdrecord command is used to burn it to the disc:

File: **simple-cd-backup.sh (excerpt)**

```
cdrecord -v speed=4 dev=/dev/$CDDEVICE $ISO
```

This simply burns the ISO image ($ISO) to the specified CDROM drive (/dev/$CDDEVICE, which we determined earlier) at four-speed (a low speed like this reduces the risk of errors on some drives).

Finally, the created ISO image is deleted with `rm`, and the script uses `zenity` again to inform you that it's finished.

Enterprise Backup Solutions

Linux is very well supplied with "enterprise level" backup tools. A description of how to create a backup strategy in a multi-operating-system, multi-server environment would constitute a book in itself, so here I'll simply provide some pointers for further reading.

If you're looking to implement an enterprise level backup strategy from scratch, you should investigate Bacula[2] or AMANDA.[3] Both these tools are capable of being the centerpiece of a full enterprise backup strategy, and both are open-source. A number of commercial tools that may already be in use in your enterprise environment are also available on Linux. Veritas Backup,[4] a commonly used tool in industry, can run on and back up Linux servers as well as Windows; another powerful commercial tool is Arkeia.[5]

Log Files

Most of the services running on your LAMP server will keep logs of their activities, usually in the form of text files in the `/var/log` directory. Services can either log their outputs in the system log `/var/log/messages`, or in specific logs kept for individual services. Some of the logs that you may find useful include:

`/var/log/messages`
> This is the system log, which contains log messages from the kernel itself, as well as those from a number of system daemons.
>
> The system log is a useful place to look if you suspect that your machine has low-level issues: that Linux itself is causing the problem, rather than one of the programs you have running on it. Lots of programs write to the system log, making it a constant stream of "chatter" about low-level processes that occur on the machine. It's often incomprehensible, but it's worth looking into, because the system log may provide clues about what the machine was doing when the problem occurred.

---

[2] http://www.bacula.org/
[3] http://www.amanda.org/
[4] http://www.veritas.com/linux/
[5] http://www.arkeia.com/

/var/log/httpd/access_log
/var/log/httpd/ssl_access_log

These are the Apache access logs, which list the details of each Website hit as it occurs. The logged details of a single request are shown below.

File: **/var/log/httpd/access_log** (excerpt)
```
192.168.69.36 - - [17/Oct/2005:23:07:59 -0400]
   "GET /about.html HTTP/1.1" 200 - "-"
   "Mozilla/5.0 (Windows; U; Windows NT 5.1; en-US; rv:1.8b5)
      Gecko/20051006 Firefox/1.4.1"
```

/var/log/httpd/error_log
/var/log/httpd/ssl_error_log

This comprises a log of errors occurring in Web pages or in Apache itself.

The Apache error log is extremely useful to Web developers deploying applications on the LAMP server, because more detail about an error in a Web application will normally be displayed in the log.

File: **/var/log/httpd/error_log** (excerpt)
```
[client 192.168.69.36] PHP Warning:  Division by zero in
   /var/www/html/div-zero-test.php on line 2
```

This file also logs errors in the Apache configuration, and errors caused by Apache itself. For example, if the server doesn't seem to be serving Web pages, your examination of the log might show the following line:

File: **/var/log/httpd/error_log** (excerpt)
```
[Mon Oct 10 04:10:49 2005] [error] (12)Cannot allocate memory:
   fork: Unable to fork new process
```

This is a good indication that the machine has, for some reason, run out of memory. While this doesn't help you work out *why* it ran out of memory, it does, at least, alert you that the problem has occurred; you can now concentrate on finding out what's eating all the memory, and fixing it before you restart Apache.

/var/log/samba/*client*.log

This is Samba's access log from *client*.

/var/log/yum.log

This comprises a log of packages that were updated or installed via yum.

All of these logs are presented as plain text files. You don't need to use the GUI tool to view them: use the following simple command to view the logs in a terminal.

```
[root@swinetrek kermit]# cat /var/log/messages
Oct 11 06:14:59 swinetrek syslogd 1.4.1: restart.
Oct 11 06:14:59 swinetrek kernel: klogd 1.4.1,
    log source = /proc/kmsg started.
Oct 11 06:14:59 swinetrek kernel: Linux version 2.6.11-1.1369_FC4
    (bhcompile@decompose.build.redhat.com)
    (gcc version 4.0.0 20050525 (Red Hat 4.0.0-9))
    #1 Thu Jun 2 22:55:56 EDT 2005
Oct 11 06:14:59 swinetrek kernel: BIOS-provided physical RAM map:
Oct 11 06:14:59 swinetrek kernel:
    BIOS-e820: 0000000000000000 - 000000000009fc00 (usable)
Oct 11 06:14:59 swinetrek kernel:
    BIOS-e820: 000000000009fc00 - 00000000000a0000 (reserved)
...
Oct 17 21:01:10 swinetrek sshd(pam_unix)[2898]: session closed for
    user kermit
Oct 17 21:16:15 swinetrek su(pam_unix)[2605]: session closed for
    user root
Oct 17 21:16:21 swinetrek su(pam_unix)[3060]: session opened for
    user root by (uid=500)
[root@swinetrek kermit]#
```

The text-based nature of logs is very useful when you're using SSH connections to other machines; you can view their log files from the command line without needing to use VNC or similar graphical tools.

A useful command to know when you're investigating log files from the command line is `tail`. This lists the last ten lines of any file.

```
[root@swinetrek kermit]# tail /var/log/httpd/error_log
[client 192.168.69.36] PHP Warning:  Division by zero in
    /var/www/html/div-zero-test.php on line 2
[Mon Oct 17 23:07:59 2005] [error] [client 192.168.69.36] File
    does not exist: /var/www/html/favicon.ico
[Mon Oct 17 23:08:05 2005] [error] [client 192.168.69.36] File
    does not exist: /var/www/html/favicon.ico
[Tue Oct 17 01:27:22 2005] [error] [client 69.20.16.232] File
    does not exist: /var/www/html/favicon.ico
[Tue Oct 17 03:50:12 2005] [error] [client 192.168.69.36] File
    does not exist: /var/www/html/favicon.ico
[client 192.168.69.36] PHP Fatal error:  Call to undefined
    function blowup() in /var/www/html/blowup-test.php on line 2
```

```
[Tue Oct 17 03:52:47 2005] [error] [client 192.168.69.36] File
    does not exist: /var/www/html/favicon.ico
[Tue Oct 17 03:53:01 2005] [error] [client 192.168.69.36] File
    does not exist: /var/www/html/favicon.ico
[client 192.168.69.36] PHP Warning:  Division by zero in
    /var/www/html/div-zero-test.php on line 2
[Tue Oct 17 03:57:26 2005] [error] [client 192.168.69.36] File
    does not exist: /var/www/html/favicon.ico
[root@swinetrek kermit]#
```

If you're investigating an error that's just occurred, tail can be very handy: it lets you avoid having to skip through the whole log. If you want to view more (or less) of the file, you can use tail -n filename to show the last n lines of filename. The -f option will instruct tail to display new lines as they're added to the file. This is exceptionally helpful for "watching" a log file. As an experiment, run tail -f /var/log/httpd/error_log, then try to load a URL pointing to a file that doesn't exist on your server (e.g. **http://localhost/foo.txt**). You'll see that tail outputs the error immediately. Hit **Ctrl-C** to exit tail -f.

Log Rotation

You may notice that, over time, copies of your log files start to appear. For example:

```
[root@swinetrek kermit]# cd /var/log/httpd/
[root@swinetrek httpd]# ls error_log*
error_log  error_log.1  error_log.2  error_log.3  error_log.4
```

Not only do we have the error_log file itself, but also an error_log.1, an error_log.2, right through to an error_log.4. These copies are being made by the **log rotator**, a cron job that works to keep the size of your log files under control.

error_log (in this example) is the current log; error_log.1 is an older log, error_log.2 is older still, and so on. When the log rotator cron job is triggered, error_log is moved to error_log.1, the old error_log.1 is moved to error_log.2, and so on. This ensures that your saved logs cover more than just the immediate past, but avoids their being saved as one enormous, unmanageable file.

Traffic Reporting with Webalizer

If you're running a Website, you're likely to be interested in the amount of traffic it receives, where it's coming from, and where it's going. The analysis of Web traffic enables developers to assess whether or not the Websites hosted on your server are being used as expected. It allows those developers to make the changes required to deal with unexpected loads, or to direct visitors towards particular Web pages of which they may not be aware.

Traffic reporting for Web pages is a two-stage process. First, there needs to be a log of each request made for each Web page; fortunately, that's exactly what Apache's `/var/log/httpd/access_log` log file contains. Second, the raw data in that log file needs to be turned into a useful report. This is where Webalizer, an open source Web server log analysis program, comes in handy. Webalizer periodically goes through Apache's access logs and produces an HTML report, complete with charts, so that we can quickly and easily identify any trends in site traffic.

If Webalizer is not installed, install it from the Package Management tool by selecting the Webalizer package from the Web Server package group, or by entering `yum install webalizer` at the command prompt.

Fedora's Webalizer package is already configured to read `/var/log/httpd/access_log` once daily to regenerate its reports, so there's no need to configure Webalizer. The default configuration writes its reports to the directory `/var/www/usage`, which can be accessed via the browser at `http://localhost/usage/`, as shown in Figure 8.4. Note that if Webalizer's cron job has not been run, nothing will be available at this address: you'll see an error message. To force Webalizer to generate reports, run `webalizer` from the command line as root.

The reports are very detailed, showing not only tables that indicate the "number of hits" the site has received, but graphs of changing hit counts over time, traffic statistics broken up by month, week, day, and hour, and details of which "user agents" (Web browsers) were used to access the sites.

There are many, many Web traffic analysis tools like Webalizer. You may already have experience with another and, if so, you may prefer to use that. I'd recommend Webalizer because it provides comprehensive statistics in a clearly understandable format, and requires no configuration to set up and get working.

Figure 8.4. A Webalizer report.

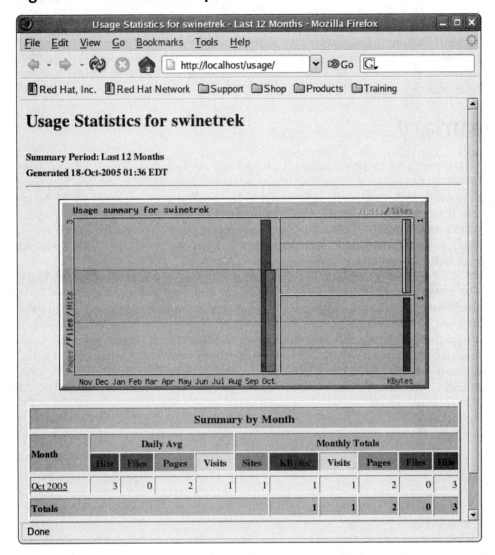

While Web traffic analysis reports are useful to Web application developers, they can also be useful to you, the system administrator. A traffic report can give you an idea of when site traffic typically spikes to higher levels, and which parts of your Website attract the greatest numbers of users, which will help you make decisions about network bandwidth. For example, if you find that your server is serving a lot of images, and that, consequently, those requests are slowing down the other processes on the machine, you might think about setting up a second LAMP server purely to serve the images, thereby reducing the load on your first server. You might also decide to use traffic shaping tools to alter your network bandwidth to route more (or less) traffic to particular servers or services. This can be particularly handy if you're seeing bandwidth spikes to particular services, or at particular times.

Summary

Occasional system administration procedures address the things that you have to set up or tweak infrequently, but may be used regularly. Backups are a good example of this; you should only have to identify *what* you'll back up once, though you'll run backups regularly. Web traffic analysis is another good example: spend a little time setting up the traffic reports so that they display what you (or your Web development team) need to see, then leave them running. You'll receive new reports every day without any more work.

Automate these tasks as much as possible; the less you have to do, the fewer tasks you'll forget or delay. For this reason, scripting is a vital tool in every sysadmin's toolbox. Often, a short bash script can take the place of an expensive third-party application, and you can put it together yourself! Most Linux sysadmins will gradually build up a small library of little scripts that do the work they want to do, and revel in the fact that they can control the machine with just a few lines of code.

Server Security

When you run a publicly available Web server, nothing's more important than security. Web server compromises are common, and can result in anything from a defaced Website to a cracker taking full ownership of the server.

IMPORTANT

A Long Road

It must be stressed that security is an ongoing process; you can't just set up a server as "secure" and never think about security again. You must keep the software that you use up-to-date, and regularly check for and apply security updates. Nevertheless, you can take steps both to decrease the chance that your server will be compromised and, in the worst case scenario, to limit the damage that can be done by a cracker who manages to breach the server's security.

Overview: Making your System Secure

Server security should be instituted on many levels. Taking a layered approach to security makes it much more difficult for crackers to do serious damage to your machine, because, even if they do manage to break through one layer, they won't necessarily have access to the whole machine. Make sure you implement the following layers of security to help ensure that a cracker who manages to break through the first layer of security is prevented from progressing any further:

1. Turn off any services that you don't need on the machine, so that they can't be compromised.

2. Implement a firewall that allows only users from specified locations to access services. For example, ensure that services that should be accessible only from your internal network *are* accessible only from your internal network.

3. Implement an intrusion detection system to check for suspicious-looking network traffic.

4. Ensure that all services are unable to do things they don't need to do. This measure helps to ensure that, if your server is compromised, the cracker will be unable to use any of your services to penetrate the server further.

Another important part of your security setup is audit, which will enable you to detect whether or not a compromise has occurred, and take steps to fix any problems. In the first case, this requires that, when your server alerts you to potential compromises, you pay attention to those warnings. In this chapter, we'll look at software that's designed to address all these areas of security: how to stop your server from being compromised in the first place, how to limit the damage that can be done if a compromise occurs, and how to detect any compromises and fix the associated problems.

Security is one of those things that everyone knows they should do, but an awful lot of people neglect. It's not difficult to implement security measures around your server. Remember that security is always a question of balance: balance the work that you need to do to secure the server against the work and trouble that would be caused by a compromise. A server containing client data should be secured much more heavily than one that contains no sensitive data, which could be rebuilt or recreated from an image at the touch of a button. Look at it this way: an ounce of prevention is worth a hundred pounds of running about like a headless chicken after you discover a security breach.

Staying Up to Date

One important aspect of server security that outranks the choice of programs you use to secure your network is the absolute necessity of keeping those programs up to date. While security software—a firewall, for example—can help you avoid situations in which unanticipated security holes are discovered in network software, such as Apache, a security hole within the security software itself opens your network to serious compromise.

It's very important to stay up to date with the latest software patches; most Linux distributions maintain an archive of security-patched software, and roll updated versions of software with security patches into that archive as each new patch is released. In Fedora Core, you can check for updates to the packages you've installed by running `yum update`. This displays a report of the available updates, then asks if you want `yum` to download and install the updates.

Checking for, and applying patches on an ongoing basis is part of the layered approach to security described above: it allows you to achieve "defense in depth." If, for example, you were simply to rely on your firewall to prevent unauthorized access to your network, and decided not to bother with security behind the firewall, then that firewall would become a single point of failure; a compromise in the firewall would automatically mean the compromise of your entire network. If you take a layered approach to security, compromising the firewall merely gives crackers the opportunity to further attempt to compromise the machine or network; however, they should not be able to achieve their ends, because you'll have put more layers of security in place to prevent that. In the worst case, where a compromise is achieved, audit tools such as Snort should at least alert you to the compromise, enabling you to put a stop to it.

Tripwire

Tripwire is a tool that helps detect compromises. It stores the state of the system and all the programs stored on it, and then, at regular intervals, compares the current state with the stored state. If it detects any changes, Tripwire can indicate that the server has been compromised and that a cracker has installed some other program (for example, a Trojan horse that pretends to be the "login" program but actually stores entered usernames/passwords for later retrieval).

Tripwire should be installed and configured as soon as possible after you build the machine; you need to be sure that the machine has not already been compromised! To install it, use the `yum install tripwire` command, which requires access to the Internet in order to download the Tripwire package.

Initial Setup

Once you've installed Tripwire, you'll need to set it up. Tripwire works by building a database of the files installed on your system. At regular intervals, you can then check the system against the Tripwire database, and be alerted if anything has changed.

IMPORTANT

Beware the Early Invader!

It's important that you know that your system has not been compromised before you set up Tripwire! Tripwire only detects changes from your "initial setup," so, if your initial setup is already compromised, Tripwire can't help you. This is why it's important to install and configure Tripwire as soon as possible after you build the machine. If you're working on a machine that has been connected to the Internet for a while, you may want to consider backing up the data on it, erasing the data from the hard drive, reinstalling the operating system, restoring the data, then configuring Tripwire before you reconnect it to the 'net. Yes, that process is as tedious as it sounds, but security is about preventing potential issues and identifying problems; if crackers have already compromised your machine, and you don't take the necessary steps to remove their access before you install Tripwire, the software won't be able to do its job properly.

The first step involved in setting up Tripwire is to generate the public and private keys the software uses to encrypt its reports and policy (or configuration) files. To do this, we use the `tripwire-setup-keyfiles` tool:

```
[root@swinetrek kermit]# /usr/sbin/tripwire-setup-keyfiles

----------------------------------------------------
The Tripwire site and local passphrases are used to sign a
variety of files, such as the configuration, policy, and database
files.

Passphrases should be at least 8 characters in length and contain
both letters and numbers.

See the Tripwire manual for more information.

----------------------------------------------------
Creating key files...

(When selecting a passphrase, keep in mind that good passphrases
typically have upper and lower case letters, digits and
punctuation marks, and are at least 8 characters in length.)

Enter the site keyfile passphrase:
```

Here, you're asked to enter a site keyfile passphrase, which will be used to encrypt Tripwire's policy files. This passphrase should really be a sentence—maybe two—and, as it cannot be recovered, be careful not to forget it! This particular step may be onerous, but it's critical to your system's security.

Do Not Use Your Main Password

If you decide to ignore this advice and just choose a word, do *not* choose
your main password. Doing that will allow anyone who compromises the
machine to compromise the Tripwire database, which would defeat the point
of running Tripwire. Enter the passphrase at the prompt, and enter it again
when you're asked to verify the passphrase.

```
Enter the site keyfile passphrase:
Verify the site keyfile passphrase:
Generating key (this may take several minutes)...Key generation
complete.

(When selecting a passphrase, keep in mind that good passphrases
typically have upper and lower case letters, digits and
punctuation marks, and are at least 8 characters in length.)

Enter the local keyfile passphrase:
```

After you confirm the site keyfile passphrase, you will be prompted for a local
keyfile passphrase, which will be used to encrypt the reports Tripwire generates.
Tripwire uses two different passphrases, which allows you to give users the local
passphrase, so they can read and work with the reports, without giving them the
ability to change the way Tripwire works by altering its configuration. Be sure
to pick another passphrase for the local keyfile passphrase; don't enter the one
that you used for the site keyfile passphrase.

```
Enter the local keyfile passphrase:
Verify the local keyfile passphrase:
Generating key (this may take several minutes)...Key generation
complete.

--------------------------------------------------
Signing configuration file...
Please enter your site passphrase:
```

Tripwire will generate a key to go with each passphrase, then use those keys to
sign files. To do this, it will ask you for the passphrases once again:

```
Please enter your site passphrase:
Wrote configuration file: /etc/tripwire/tw.cfg

A clear-text version of the Tripwire configuration file:
/etc/tripwire/twcfg.txt
has been preserved for your inspection. It is recommended that you
move this file to a secure location and/or encrypt it in place
```

```
(using a tool such as GPG, for example) after you have examined
it.


- - - - - - - - - - - - - - - - - - - - - - - - - - - - - - - - - - - - - - - - - - - -
Signing policy file...
Please enter your site passphrase:
Wrote policy file: /etc/tripwire/tw.pol

A clear-text version of the Tripwire policy file:
/etc/tripwire/twpol.txt
has been preserved for your inspection. This implements a minimal
policy, intended only to test essential Tripwire functionality.
You should edit the policy file to describe your system, and then
use twadmin to generate a new signed copy of the Tripwire policy.

Once you have a satisfactory Tripwire policy file, you should move
the clear-text version to a secure location and/or encrypt it in
place (using a tool such as GPG, for example).

Now run "tripwire --init" to enter Database Initialization Mode.
This reads the policy file, generates a database based on its
contents, and then cryptographically signs the resulting database.
Options  can  be entered on the command line to specify which
policy, configuration, and key files are used to create the
database. The filename for the database can be specified as well.
If no options are specified, the default values from the current
configuration file are used.

[root@swinetrek kermit]#
```

As you can see, Tripwire has generated and encrypted the configuration file,
/etc/tripwire/tw.cfg, and the policy file, /etc/tripwire/tw.pol, and has
also saved plain text versions of these files. As suggested, move these files from
/etc/tripwire to a more secure location, such as a floppy disk. Even if crackers
do compromise your system, they'll have a very difficult time gaining access to
files stored on a floppy disk that's sitting in your desk drawer.

```
[root@swinetrek kermit]# mount /media/floppy
[root@swinetrek kermit]# mv /etc/tripwire/twcfg.txt \
> /media/floppy
[root@swinetrek kermit]# mv /etc/tripwire/twpol.txt \
> /media/floppy
[root@swinetrek kermit]# umount /media/floppy
[root@swinetrek kermit]#
```

Now, as `tripwire-setup-keyfiles` suggests, run `tripwire --init` to build the database. This may take a while.

```
[root@swinetrek kermit]# /usr/sbin/tripwire --init
Please enter your local passphrase:
Parsing policy file: /etc/tripwire/tw.pol
Generating the database...
*** Processing Unix File System ***
### Warning: File system error.
### Filename: /usr/sbin/fixrmtab
### No such file or directory
### Continuing...
...
### Warning: File system error.
### Filename: /proc/scsi
### No such file or directory
### Continuing...
Wrote database file: /var/lib/tripwire/swinetrek.twd
The database was successfully generated.
[root@swinetrek kermit]#
```

Tripwire is likely to complain about missing files with a series of "No such file or directory" errors. This isn't a problem; Tripwire's default configuration includes some files that aren't installed in a normal Fedora system. These errors can be ignored.

Now that Tripwire has created its database, you should perform your first Tripwire system check.

Using Tripwire

Use Tripwire to check your system on a regular basis (monthly should be sufficient, unless you have reason to suspect a compromise, which would make you check more frequently) and ensure that no part of the setup has changed without your knowledge. You can check your system using the `tripwire --check` command.

```
[root@swinetrek kermit]# /usr/sbin/tripwire --check
Parsing policy file: /etc/tripwire/tw.pol
*** Processing Unix File System ***
Performing integrity check...
### Warning: File system error.
### Filename: /usr/sbin/fixrmtab
```

```
### No such file or directory
### Continuing...
```

Tripwire will whir for a little while (and possibly display missing file errors, as it did when it built the database), but eventually it will display a long report, like the one shown here:

```
### Warning: File system error.
### Filename: /proc/scsi
### No such file or directory
### Continuing...
Wrote report file:
/var/lib/tripwire/report/swinetrek-20051019-023039.twr


Tripwire(R) 2.3.0 Integrity Check Report

Report generated by:        root
Report created on:          Wed 19 Oct 2005 02:30:39 AM EDT
Database last updated on:   Never


===================================================================
Report Summary:
===================================================================

Host name:              swinetrek
Host IP address:        127.0.0.1
Host ID:                None
Policy file used:       /etc/tripwire/tw.pol
Configuration file used: /etc/tripwire/tw.cfg
Database file used:     /var/lib/tripwire/swinetrek.twd
Command line used:      /usr/sbin/tripwire --check
```

The important part of this report is the Rule Summary section, which shows whether any violations are apparent:

```
===================================================================
Rule Summary:
===================================================================

-------------------------------------------------------------------
  Section: Unix File System
-------------------------------------------------------------------

  Rule Name            Severity Level     Added   Removed  Modified
  ---------            --------------     -----   -------  --------
```

User binaries	66	0	0	0
Tripwire Binaries	100	0	0	0
Critical configuration files				
	100	0	0	0
Libraries	66	0	0	0
Operating System Utilities				
	100	0	0	0
Critical system boot files				
	100	0	0	0
File System and Disk Administraton Programs				
	100	0	0	0
Kernel Administration Programs				
	100	0	0	0
Networking Programs	100	0	0	0
System Administration Programs				
	100	0	0	0
Hardware and Device Control Programs				
	100	0	0	0
System Information Programs				
	100	0	0	0
Application Information Programs				
	100	0	0	0
Shell Related Programs				
	100	0	0	0
Critical Utility Sym-Links				
	100	0	0	0
Shell Binaries	100	0	0	0
* Tripwire Data Files	100	1	0	0
System boot changes	100	0	0	0
OS executables and libraries				
	100	0	0	0
Security Control	100	0	0	0
Login Scripts	100	0	0	0
Root config files	100	0	0	0
Invariant Directories				
	66	0	0	0
Temporary directories				
	33	0	0	0
Critical devices	100	0	0	0

```
Total objects scanned:  21750
Total violations found:  1
```

The last line of this section shows that one violation has been found: a file was added to the Tripwire Data Files section. If the Tripwire check shows a violation,

you need to identify why that violation arose, and whether it indicates a compromise. The details of any violations are listed in the Object Summary section:

```
================================================================
Object Summary:
================================================================


----------------------------------------------------------------
# Section: Unix File System
----------------------------------------------------------------


----------------------------------------------------------------
Rule Name: Tripwire Data Files (/var/lib/tripwire)
Severity Level: 100
----------------------------------------------------------------

Added:
"/var/lib/tripwire/swinetrek.twd"
```

The first time you run `tripwire --check`, you should find that one file has been
added to the Tripwire Data Files section: `/var/lib/tripwire/swinetrek.twd`
is the database file created by Tripwire as part of its initialization. You can be
confident that it is a safe addition.

Tip

Severity Levels

The change depicted in the above output is indicated as "Severity Level:
100." Higher numbers reflect the increasing seriousness of the errors; 100
is as high as the scale goes. The above error was flagged as potentially being
very severe because it identified a change to one of Tripwire's own files,
which is considered possible evidence of tampering. You should assess all
potential violations and satisfy yourself as to the reasons for them, though:
do not ignore those with lower severity levels! The severity level exists
primarily for system administrators who run very large networks, allowing
them to generate reports of potential compromises at different levels of
severity.

After the Object Summary section, Tripwire lists all of the errors it encountered.
The first time around, this report should only include the Unix File System errors
displayed while Tripwire was running, as well as its copyright notice:

```
================================================================
Error Report:
================================================================

----------------------------------------------------------------
```

```
   Section: Unix File System
------------------------------------------------------------------

1.    File system error.
      Filename: /usr/sbin/fixrmtab
      No such file or directory
...
72.   File system error.
      Filename: /proc/scsi
      No such file or directory


------------------------------------------------------------------
*** End of report ***

Tripwire 2.3 Portions copyright 2000 Tripwire, Inc. Tripwire is a
registered trademark of Tripwire, Inc. This software comes with
ABSOLUTELY NO WARRANTY; for details use --version. This is free
software which may be redistributed or modified only under certain
conditions; see COPYING for details.
All rights reserved.
Integrity check complete.
[root@swinetrek kermit]#
```

If a file changed, and that change did not show up in the last Tripwire check, you need to work out why the change occurred, and whether that change could be evidence of a compromise.

Once a file has changed, Tripwire will warn you about that change in every subsequent report until you update the database. To update the Tripwire database, and stop those violations being reported, use the `tripwire --update --accept-all --twrfile` *reportfile* command:

```
[root@swinetrek kermit]# /usr/sbin/tripwire --update \
> --accept-all --twrfile \
> /var/lib/tripwire/report/swinetrek-20051019-221705.twr
Please enter your local passphrase:
Wrote database file: /var/lib/tripwire/swinetrek.twd
[root@swinetrek kermit]#
```

Database Updates Absorb Violations

When you update the database, any violations that were listed in the report will no longer be considered violations. Be sure that you're satisfied with the reasons why those violations occurred before you update the database to incorporate them.

note

The Database Backup

Updating the database will produce a backup of the old database as `/var/lib/tripwire/report/`*servername*`.twd.bak`. The addition of this file will cause yet another violation, just as the addition of the database file itself did.

Generally speaking, your day-to-day usage of the machine will not cause violations. However, if you install new versions of software packages, the files within those packages will, obviously, change. Tripwire can't tell whether those files were changed by you, or by a cracker, so it will alert you to a violation. It's a good policy to run a Tripwire check before you run `yum upgrade` or `yum install`, and before you install any other RPM packages. Resolve any indicated violations to your own satisfaction before upgrading. You can then be reasonably confident that any changes came about because of the upgrade, and as you're happy with the state of the machine, you can go ahead and recompute the Tripwire database.

iptables

`iptables` is the name of the standard Linux firewall. A firewall limits incoming network connections to your machine by blocking or limiting traffic to certain network ports; this makes it impossible for a cracker to connect to a port that a system administrator hasn't left open. Firewall configuration can be very complex, but fortunately there are some graphical tools that make the process considerably simpler.

You're already familiar with the Security Level Configuration tool, which includes a simple GUI for editing the `iptables` configuration, but it's not really appropriate for setting up complex firewall rules. Here, we'll take a look at Firestarter, a more advanced `iptables` configuration tool.

Firestarter

Firestarter is available for download with `yum` in Fedora Core 4; just enter `yum install firestarter` at the command line.

Setting Up Firestarter

Once Firestarter is installed, you can run the program by accessing Applications > System Tools > Firestarter. When you launch Firestarter, you'll be asked if you want to run the program with administrative privileges (that is, run it as root), or run it without privileges, as the dialog in Figure 9.1 shows. Firestarter will not run correctly without root permission, so you'll need to run it with administrative privileges.

Figure 9.1. The Firestarter Query dialog.

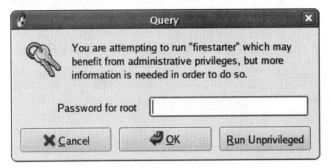

Firestarter's initial configuration is achieved using the wizard shown in Figure 9.2.

Figure 9.2. The first screen of the Firestarter Firewall Wizard.

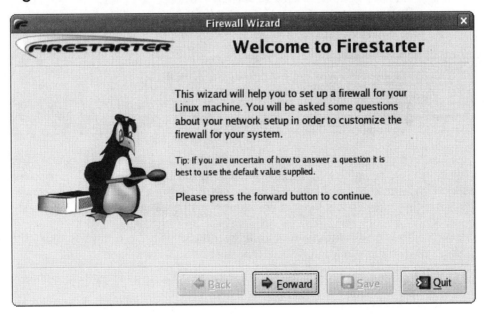

The wizard is very helpfully put together, and explains exactly what it is you're configuring at each step. Options and checkboxes are accompanied by explanatory tooltips that appear when you hover your cursor over them.

In the next configuration screen of the wizard, shown in Figure 9.3, the network card has been correctly detected. Firestarter now needs to be told whether or not it should get the network card's IP address from DHCP.

Figure 9.3. The second screen of the Firestarter Firewall Wizard.

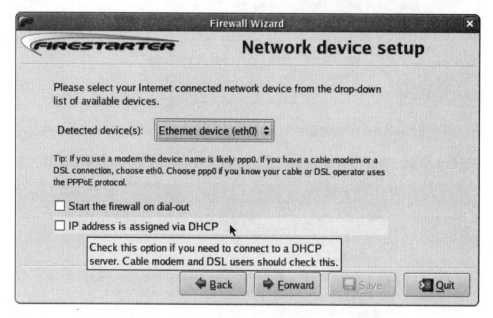

The next screen of the wizard, depicted in Figure 9.4, allows you to share your connection to the Internet. Since this machine is a LAMP server, it's not acting as a gateway (you may well have a gateway machine, but this LAMP server should not be it), so leave Enable Internet connection sharing unchecked and move on.

The configuration wizard then completes, giving you the option to start the firewall now, shown in Figure 9.5; check the box and click Save.

Figure 9.4. The third screen of the Firestarter Firewall Wizard.

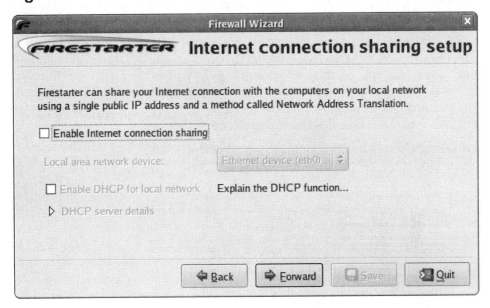

Figure 9.5. The final screen of the Firestarter Firewall Wizard.

Using Firestarter

Firestarter's main window has three tabs: Status, Events, and Policy. Status and Events are for monitoring the firewall; they show whether it is currently enabled, which network traffic it has blocked, and so on. Policy displays the existing firewall rules, and allows you to configure new ones. By looking at the policy screen shown in Figure 9.6, we can see that no rules are currently defined—all traffic is blocked.

Figure 9.6. The Firestarter Policy screen.

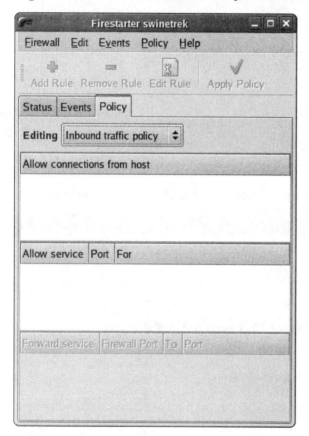

If you try to log into the computer via SSH or load up the Website hosted on this computer, the blocked requests will be listed in the Events screen, as shown in Figure 9.7.

Figure 9.7. The Firestarter Events screen.

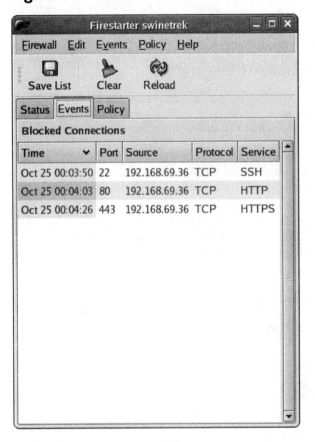

Blocking Requests, Not Connections

Firestarter will only display connection requests, not existing connections. This means that existing SSH connections won't be terminated, but new SSH sessions won't be allowed until you explicitly allow them.

The easiest way to allow these blocked connections is to right-click on the blocked connection and select either Allow Connections From Source, Allow Inbound Service for Everyone, or Allow Inbound Service for Source.

For example, you may only want to allow SSH connections from a particular IP address. To allow this, locate a blocked SSH connection from this IP address, right click and select Allow Inbound Service for Source. Similarly, you'll probably want to allow HTTP requests from any address; locate an HTTP request, right click on it and select Allow Inbound Service for Everyone. As you define rules using this method, they will appear in the Policy screen, which you can use to manage your rules.

Remote Configuration? Be careful!

Be very careful if you're configuring the firewall on a machine remotely from a different computer, since a mistake in firewall configuration can lock out the remote connection, leaving you unable to connect back to the server to correct the mistake!

There are two types of rules that apply to incoming connections: those that allow connections only from certain machines—allow all connections from your main desktop machine, for example—which are displayed in the top half of the window, and those that allow connections only to certain ports—such as port 80 for Web servers—which are displayed in the bottom half of the window. This second type can be restricted to allow connections to a certain port from a certain address, too.

Figure 9.8. The Add new inbound rule dialog.

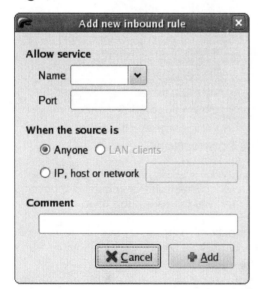

Let's add a rule to allow all connections to port 80. Click the bottom white area, and then click the Add Rule button to bring up the Add new inbound rule dialog shown in Figure 9.8.

Enter the port number, **80**, in the Port box. Firestarter will then attempt to guess which service you mean; in this case, it will correctly write HTTP in the Name box. You could change the name of this port, but that's not recommended for standard ports. You want to allow connections to this newly opened port from anywhere, so leave Anyone selected. Add a comment if you feel one is required, and click Add.Figure 9.9 shows that the rule has been added.

Figure 9.9. The new rule has been added.

Now, imagine you want to set a second required rule, because you want to be able to connect to this machine from your home computer in order to administer it. Your home computer has the address mymac.yourisp.net. Click the white area in the top half of the window and click Add Rule again, which will bring up the Add new inbound rule dialog.

Once you have successfully added all the rules you require, as shown in Figure 9.10, you must remember to click Apply Policy to put the rules into effect.

Figure 9.10. Adding a new rule to the new inbound rule dialog.

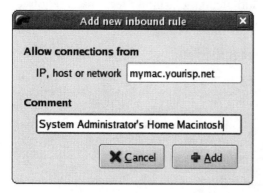

Turning off Nonessential Services

One step beyond using your firewall to restrict access to services is to turn off services themselves if they don't need to be running: a service can't be compromised if it isn't turned on! In this section, you'll see which network services are running in a default Fedora Core installation, and how to turn them off if you don't need to use them.

To configure the services that start automatically when the server is booted, open the Service Configuration tool (Applications > System Settings > Server Settings > Services) and make sure the tool displays the configuration for runlevels 3, 4, and 5 by selecting Edit Runlevel > Runlevel All. All the services running on the machine are displayed; note that not all of these are network services. Click on a service to see a brief description of it. Fedora Core ships with a lot of services that, for security reasons, are disabled by default, which makes your job here an easier one.

For example, if you're not using NFS to make files available over the network (if you're not sure what this means, then you're probably not using NFS!), you can safely disable the NFS services `portmap`, `rpcgssd`, `rpcidmapd`, and `rpcsvcgssd`.

NFS is used to share files between Linux and other UNIX-like machines. Similarly, if you're not using Samba to share files (usually with Windows machines), you should disable Samba's `smb` service.

If you prefer, you can also disable and enable services from the command line using the `chkconfig` command. For instance, to disable the `smb` service, enter:

```
[root@swinetrek kermit]# /sbin/chkconfig smb off
[root@swinetrek kermit]#
```

To enable the service, use:

```
[root@swinetrek kermit]# /sbin/chkconfig smb on
[root@swinetrek kermit]#
```

The `chkconfig --list` command displays a list of all the services on the machine, showing whether each is enabled or disabled.

Snort

Snort is an Intrusion Detection System, or IDS. An IDS monitors incoming network traffic and looks for things that seem suspicious. For example, Snort will watch incoming Web requests and match those requests against its database of known vulnerabilities; if a request looks suspicious, it will record specific details in its log files. This can help you to detect a compromise quickly after it happens, and take immediate steps to fix the problem.

Installing Snort

Snort isn't part of the Fedora archive, but it's available from the Snort project's Website.[1] Follow the Download link, and look for the pre-compiled binary packages. At the time of writing, Snort is only available as an RPM package for Fedora Core 3, but this package installs fine on Fedora Core 4.

While you're at the Snort Website, you should also download a set of Snort rules; there's a big orange link on the right-hand side of the download page. Snort rules are configuration files that tell Snort what to look for when it searches for evidence of intrusions. Three official rule sets are provided by Sourcefire, the company that maintains Snort: the subscription release, which contains the very latest rules, but requires a paid subscription; the registered user release, which contains

---

[1] http://www.snort.org/

the latest rules five working days after they appear in the subscription release, and only requires a free registration; and the unregistered user release, which is updated with every major release of Snort. There is also the "community rules" release, which contains rules that are contributed by the Snort user community, and have been only briefly tested by Sourcefire. Download the set of rules that you're most comfortable with. I'd recommend the registered user release.

Keeping Snort Up to Date

Snort rules are being constantly updated by Sourcefire; you should check for new rules at least once a week.

Setting Up Snort

The Snort RPM installs Snort with a good initial configuration: you shouldn't need to change too much to have the program running usefully. It's possible to configure Snort in many different and complicated ways; the Snort manual and FAQ, available from the Snort project's Website,[2] will help here. For the moment, we'll work with the default configuration, except for a couple of things. First, Snort needs to know where your local network is, so that it doesn't alert you to "suspicious" traffic originating from the local network. Also, we should set up Snort so that it uses its full logging mode to provide you with the most useful information it can.

Open the file /etc/snort/snort.conf in a text editor and locate the following section:

File: **/etc/snort/snort.conf (excerpt)**

```
#####################################################
# Step #1: Set the network variables:
#
# You must change the following variables to reflect your local
# network. The variable is currently setup for an RFC 1918 address
# space.
#
# You can specify it explicitly as:
#
# var HOME_NET 10.1.1.0/24
#
# or use global variable $<interfacename>_ADDRESS which will be
# always initialized to IP address and netmask of the network
```

---

[2] http://www.snort.org/

```
# interface which you run snort at.  Under Windows, this must be
# specified as $(<interfacename>_ADDRESS), such as:
# $(\Device\Packet_{12345678-90AB-CDEF-1234567890AB}_ADDRESS)
#
# var HOME_NET $eth0_ADDRESS
#
# You can specify lists of IP addresses for HOME_NET by separating
# the IPs with commas like this:
#
# var HOME_NET [10.1.1.0/24,192.168.1.0/24]
#
# MAKE SURE YOU DON'T PLACE ANY SPACES IN YOUR LIST!
#
# or you can specify the variable to be any IP address like this:

var HOME_NET any
```

This section of snort.conf defines your server's home network. Comment out the var HOME_NET any line, uncomment the var HOME_NET 10.1.1.0/24 line, and enter your local network's subnet, or the machine's IP address if it's not part of a local network. (A network administrator should be able to help here if you're not sure.) For example, if your subnet was 192.168.1.0/24, snort.conf should be edited as shown below.

File: **/etc/snort/snort.conf** (excerpt)

```
###################################################
# Step #1: Set the network variables:
#
# You must change the following variables to reflect your local
# network. The variable is currently setup for an RFC 1918 address
# space.#
# You can specify it explicitly as:

var HOME_NET 192.168.1.0/24

# or use global variable $<interfacename>_ADDRESS which will be
# always initialized to IP address and netmask of the network
# interface which you run snort at.  Under Windows, this must be
# specified as $(<interfacename>_ADDRESS), such as:
# $(\Device\Packet_{12345678-90AB-CDEF-1234567890AB}_ADDRESS)
#
# var HOME_NET $eth0_ADDRESS
#
# You can specify lists of IP addresses for HOME_NET by separating
# the IPs with commas like this:
```

```
#
# var HOME_NET [10.1.1.0/24,192.168.1.0/24]
#
# MAKE SURE YOU DON'T PLACE ANY SPACES IN YOUR LIST!
#
# or you can specify the variable to be any IP address like this:
#
# var HOME_NET any
```

Next, open the file /etc/sysconfig/snort and locate the following section:

File: **/etc/sysconfig/snort (excerpt)**

```
# How should Snort alert? Valid alert modes include fast, full,
# none, and unsock.  Fast writes alerts to the default "alert"
# file in a single-line, syslog style alert message.  Full writes
# the alert to the "alert" file with the full decoded header as
# well as the alert message.  None turns off alerting. Unsock is
# an experimental mode that sends the alert information out over a
# UNIX socket to another process that attaches to that socket.
# -A {alert-mode}
# output alert_{type}: {options}
ALERTMODE=fast
```

After making a backup of the file, change ALERTMODE=fast to ALERTMODE=full. This will set up Snort to produce more output, which will adversely affect its performance. If you find that your server is running slowly, consider changing this setting back to ALERTMODE=fast.

Finally, you'll need to extract the rules you've downloaded using the tar command:

```
[root@swinetrek kermit]# tar -x -z -f \
> /home/kermit/Desktop/snortrules-snapshot-CURRENT.tar.gz \
> -C /etc/snort
[root@swinetrek kermit]#
```

Once you've configured Snort correctly, you can start the snortd daemon.

Using Snort

Snort stores its logs in the /var/log/snort directory. Snort's default setup will log alerts in the file /var/log/snort/alert. Whenever Snort detects suspicious traffic, it writes a description of the traffic into the alert file. To perform a simple test of this, try to access http://*servername*/wwwboard/passwd.txt from a machine outside of your network. This should return a standard 404 Page Not Found error (assuming that you don't have wwwboard installed, that is!), but will cause Snort to log an alert. Now, return to your server, and look in /var/log/snort/alert. You should see a block of text that looks something like this:

File: **/var/log/snort/alert** (excerpt)
```
[**] [1:807:11] WEB-CGI /wwwboard/passwd.txt access [**]
[Classification: Attempted Information Leak] [Priority: 2]
10/26-02:47:33.815036 192.168.69.36:5335 -> 192.168.69.28:80
TCP TTL:128 TOS:0x0 ID:2463 IpLen:20 DgmLen:564 DF
***AP*** Seq: 0x7DC78CE4 Ack: 0xAC48865C Win: 0xFFFF TcpLen: 20
[Xref => http://cgi.nessus.org/plugins/dump.php3?id=10321]
 [Xref => http://cve.mitre.org/cgi-bin/cvename.cgi?name=1999-0954]
 [Xref => http://cve.mitre.org/cgi-bin/cvename.cgi?name=1999-0953]
 [Xref => http://www.securityfocus.com/bid/649]
 [Xref => http://www.whitehats.com/info/IDS463]
```

This is all rather overwhelming, so let's take a closer look, line by line.

File: **/var/log/snort/alert** (excerpt)
```
[**] [1:807:11] WEB-CGI /wwwboard/passwd.txt access [**]
```

The first line is the key: it tells you what the suspicious activity involved. Snort has a rule that watches for HTTP requests for the file /wwwboard/passwd.txt, because a software package called WWWBoard contains a security hole that makes the password file publicly accessible. Since you tried to access that file, Snort logged the access attempt. You can see from the above line that the alert was triggered by a rule which is part of the WEB-CGI set of rules, which means that it was a potential attack on the Web server, or an application installed on the Web server. In this case, the attack was made on WWWBoard. If you don't have WWWBoard installed, you can rest easy: someone was trying to exploit a vulnerability in WWWBoard, but you are not vulnerable.

File: **/var/log/snort/alert** (excerpt)
```
[Classification: Attempted Information Leak] [Priority: 2]
```

The second line of the alert explains what sort of alert it is; in this case, it is an "attempted information leak." Each Snort rule defines suspicious activity, then categorizes that activity. This was a "priority 2" alert, meaning "fairly serious." Priority levels range from 1 (potentially very serious) to 5 (not very serious at all). Again, though, it's only fairly serious if you have WWWBoard installed; Snort doesn't know whether you do or not, so it flags this as being, potentially, a fairly serious vulnerability.

File: /var/log/snort/alert (excerpt)
```
10/26-02:47:33.815036 192.168.69.36:5335 -> 192.168.69.28:80
```

The third line tells you when the attack happened, and where it came from. In this case, the attack happened on the 26th October (10/26) at 2:47 a.m. (02:47:33.815036), and it was made from IP address 192.168.0.100 (the first one listed), which should be the IP of the machine you used to make the test. This will allow you to work out whether you're being attacked repeatedly from one IP address; if you are, it might be worth using your firewall (see above) to block all connections from that IP address by adding a new rule that denies access to the service from that IP address. Since this example is an attack on your Web server, you could block access to port 80 from the IP address flagged in the alert (192.168.0.100) using Firestarter.

File: /var/log/snort/alert (excerpt)
```
TCP TTL:128 TOS:0x0 ID:2463 IpLen:20 DgmLen:564 DF
***AP*** Seq: 0x7DC78CE4  Ack: 0xAC48865C  Win: 0xFFFF  TcpLen: 20
```

The fourth and fifth lines contain detailed network information, which may be useful to a network administrator. If you already understand that line, you'll know whether the information in it is useful in diagnosing the attack; if you don't understand this information, you may want to call in some network technicians in the event of an attack. These details are not usually all that useful, so it's not something that warrants too much worry.

File: /var/log/snort/alert (excerpt)
```
[Xref => http://cgi.nessus.org/plugins/dump.php3?id=10321]
[Xref => http://cve.mitre.org/cgi-bin/cvename.cgi?name=1999-0954]
[Xref => http://cve.mitre.org/cgi-bin/cvename.cgi?name=1999-0953]
[Xref => http://www.securityfocus.com/bid/649]
[Xref => http://www.whitehats.com/info/IDS463]
```

Line 5 provides links to references to help you find out the details of the attack. Each URL that's listed explains the WWWBoard passwd.txt vulnerability, as you can see in Figure 9.11.

Figure 9.11. The WWWBoard passwd.txt vulnerability explained.

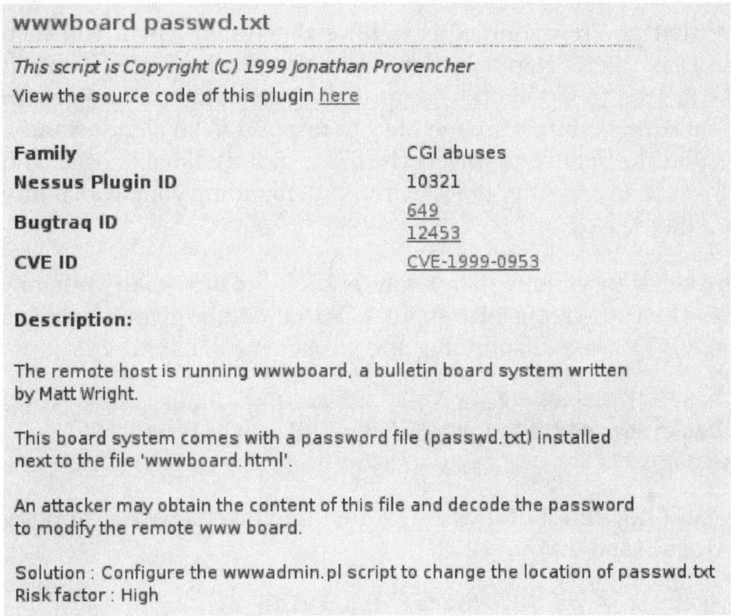

wwwboard passwd.txt

This script is Copyright (C) 1999 Jonathan Provencher
View the source code of this plugin here

Family	CGI abuses
Nessus Plugin ID	10321
Bugtraq ID	649
	12453
CVE ID	CVE-1999-0953

Description:

The remote host is running wwwboard, a bulletin board system written by Matt Wright.

This board system comes with a password file (passwd.txt) installed next to the file 'wwwboard.html'.

An attacker may obtain the content of this file and decode the password to modify the remote www board.

Solution : Configure the wwwadmin.pl script to change the location of passwd.txt
Risk factor : High

These descriptions should allow you to understand the nature of the vulnerability, and identify whether you are vulnerable to compromise. They'll also explain workarounds or solutions to prevent your continuing vulnerability. For example, the description of the WWWBoard vulnerability explains how it can be fixed: edit the wwwadmin.pl script to change the location of the passwd.txt file.

Now that you understand what Snort stores in its alert file, you need to remember to check that alert file. The best Intrusion Detection System in the world is completely useless if, even though it detects intrusions, no-one notices that it's doing so. The primary way to check is simply to do what we did above: manually look in the file on a regular basis, and examine each alert to see if it represents a potential vulnerability. However, having to remember regularly to look at the file is boring, and boring tasks get forgotten. It's much better to set up a system explicitly to notify you of Snort alerts, rather than having to remember them yourself.

Setting up a Nightly Email

One way to ensure that you're reminded is to have the system email you each night with details of any alerts that were logged in the previous day. While it would be nice to be alerted to a potential compromise the instant it happens, in practice, most system administrators are too busy to respond to an alert instantly. A daily email gives you the chance to review the alerts at a reasonable pace, and to take action to close off any security holes, without demanding your availability twenty-four hours a day.

The Snort Website links to various data analysis tools.[3] These take your raw Snort logs and uses them to create nice reports. For a simple nightly email, a good tool is snortalog.[4] Download snortalog and extract it to /usr/local:

```
[root@swinetrek kermit]# tar -x -p -f \
> /home/kermit/Desktop/snortalog_v2.3.0.tgz -C /usr/local
[root@swinetrek kermit]#
```

Running snortalog isn't difficult, but it does require that you change the working directory to /usr/local/snortalog_v2.3/.

```
[root@swinetrek kermit]# cd /usr/local/snortalog_v2.3/
[root@swinetrek snortalog_v2.3]# ./snortalog.pl < \
> /var/log/snort/alert
subject: IDS Statistics generated on Wed Oct 26 23:13:53 2005
The log begins at : Wed 26 09:58:27
The log ends at : Wed 26 22:58:42

Total of Lines in log file : 2330
Total of Logs Dropped : 0 ( 0.00%)


Total events in table : 372
Source IP recorded : 5
Destination IP recorded : 21

Host logger recorded : 1 with 1 interface(s)
Signatures recorded : 21
Classification recorded : 5
Severity recorded : 3
Portscan detected : 0
```

---

[3] http://snort.org/dl/contrib/data_analysis
[4] http://www.snort.org/dl/contrib/data_analysis/snortalog/

```
Version: 2.3.0
Jeremy CHARTIER, <jeremy.chartier@free.fr>
Date: 2004/12/02 11:31:03
[root@swinetrek snortalog_v2.3]#
```

This brief summary shows that 21 different types of suspicious traffic were identified by Snort between October 26th at 9.58 a.m. and October 26th at 10.58 p.m. The summary can then prompt you to dig further into the alert file itself, to identify what those different types of suspicious traffic were, and whether you need to do anything about them.

To set the system up so that the report is mailed to you nightly, simply add an entry to /etc/crontab, as shown below.

File: **/etc/crontab**

```
SHELL=/bin/bash
PATH=/sbin:/bin:/usr/sbin:/usr/bin
MAILTO=root
HOME=/

# run-parts
01 * * * * root run-parts /etc/cron.hourly
02 4 * * * root run-parts /etc/cron.daily
22 4 * * 0 root run-parts /etc/cron.weekly
42 4 1 * * root run-parts /etc/cron.monthly

32 3 * * * cd /usr/local/snortalog_v2.3/ && ./snortalog.pl
    < /var/log/snort/alert | sendmail root@localhost
```

That line simply schedules the command above—which generated the summary—to run daily, and to email the results to the root user, whose mail is readable by you. Now you have a daily nudge to check the Snort logs if there seems to be a problem.

Further Reporting

Some Snort data analysis tools provide much (much!) more comprehensive and detailed reports, and you may want to investigate these tools if you need to get further into this area. One of the best is SnortSnarf,[5] which produces a detailed HTML report that considers the alerts in your Snort alert file from a variety of different angles, and makes it very easy to pore through your files and understand what the alerts indicate. Again, to expand SnortSnarf, use the tar command:

---

[5] http://www.snort.org/dl/contrib/data_analysis/snortsnarf/

```
[root@swinetrek kermit]# tar -x -z -f
> /home/kermit/Desktop/SnortSnarf-050314.1.tar.gz -C /usr/local
[root@swinetrek kermit]#
```

Before you can generate a report, you need to install the Time::ParseDate Perl module. A Perl module is nothing more than a piece of code that can be used by many different Perl scripts. The most popular modules are hosted at the Comprehensive Perl Archive Network (CPAN). Mercifully, the CPAN Perl module makes installing the Time::ParseDate module easy.

```
[root@swinetrek kermit]# perl -MCPAN -e 'install Time::ParseDate'

/usr/lib/perl5/5.8.6/CPAN/Config.pm initialized.


CPAN is the world-wide archive of perl resources. It consists of
about 100 sites that all replicate the same contents all around
the globe. Many countries have at least one CPAN site already. The
resources found on CPAN are easily accessible with the CPAN.pm
module. If you want to use CPAN.pm, you have to configure it
properly.

If you do not want to enter a dialog now, you can answer 'no' to
this question and I'll try to autoconfigure. (Note: you can
revisit this dialog anytime later by typing 'o conf init' at the
cpan prompt.)

Are you ready for manual configuration? [yes]
```

The first time you run CPAN, you'll be asked if you want to configure CPAN manually, or if you'd rather let it configure itself. Most of the time, CPAN's automatic configuration will work fine, so enter **no**:

```
Are you ready for manual configuration? [yes] no


The following questions are intended to help you with the
configuration. The CPAN module needs a directory of its own to
cache
…
Installing /usr/share/man/man3/Time::Timezone.3pm
Installing /usr/share/man/man3/Time::DaysInMonth.3pm
Writing /usr/lib/perl5/site_perl/5.8.6/i386-linux-thread-multi
    /auto/Time-modules/.packlist
Appending installation info to /usr/lib/perl5/5.8.6
    /i386-linux-thread-multi/perllocal.pod
```

```
  /usr/bin/make install  -- OK
[root@swinetrek kermit]#
```

If you need to configure CPAN to use HTTP or FTP proxies, you can enter **yes** and go through the configuration process step by step.

Generating a report is very similar to running snortalog. The Perl script will return some warnings, but these can safely be ignored:

```
[root@swinetrek kermit]# cd /usr/local/SnortSnarf-050314.1
[root@swinetrek SnortSnarf-050314.1]# ./snortsnarf.pl \
> /var/log/snort/alert
Using an array as a reference is deprecated at
    include/SnortSnarf/HTMLMemStorage.pm line 290.
Using an array as a reference is deprecated at
    include/SnortSnarf/HTMLAnomMemStorage.pm line 266.
[root@swinetrek SnortSnarf-050314.1]#
```

Load /usr/local/SnortSnarf-050314.1/snfout.alert/index.html in your Web browser to see the full report, as shown in Figure 9.12.

Figure 9.12. A SnortSnarf report.

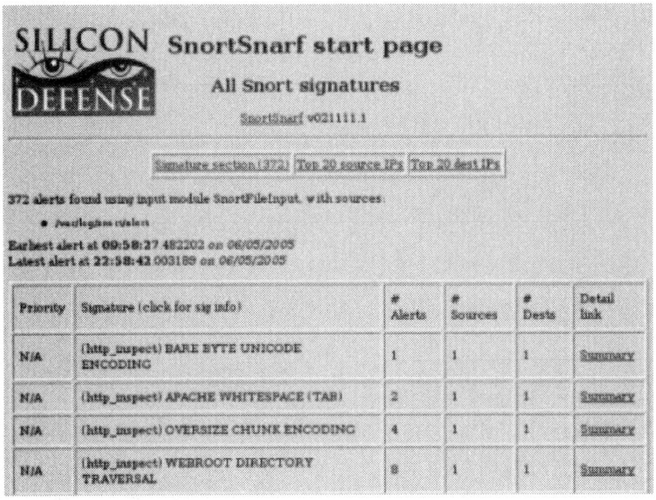

Summary

Security is critically important. In this chapter, you've been introduced to the idea of establishing "defence in depth" by setting up layers of security to prevent crackers from turning a little security hole into a full compromise of the machine. Those security layers are built using tools such as firewalls like Firestarter, intrusion detection systems like Snort, and integrity checkers like Tripwire. The most important lesson about security, however, is that you need to actually implement and manage it. Don't read this and agree... but then decide to implement "all that security stuff" later, when you get time. Far too many people are taught the value of security by being a victim first, then growing wise after the event. Make sure that's not you!

Appendix A: Command Line Reference

This appendix contains brief summaries of most of the command line tools mentioned throughout this book, and others that might be helpful, listed in alphabetical order. This reference is by no means comprehensive, but should serve as a helpful reminder of what the various commands and command line options do. For more information on any command, the Linux online manual, accessible via man *commandname*, is a great place to start.

 Tip

Case Sensitivity

Keep in mind that the Linux command line is case sensitive; the options -a and -A are not the same thing.

apachectl *command*

Control the Apache Web server's HTTPd daemon. Note that in Fedora Core 4, this tool is located in /usr/sbin, which is not part of the default PATH.

start

Start the daemon.

stop

Stop the daemon.

restart

Stop and then start the daemon, killing all current sessions. This command is useful for making changes to httpd.conf take effect.

fullstatus
status

Display Apache's current status. fullstatus includes a list of the current requests being serviced; status does not.

graceful

Wait until all current requests are serviced, then restart the daemon.

configtest

Test the Apache configuration files to make sure they're syntactically correct.

at *time*

Schedule a once-off job at *time*. Hit **Ctrl-D** to exit at.

atq

Display the queue of jobs scheduled with at. Run as root to see all users' scheduled jobs.

atrm *job*

Remove a job scheduled with at. *job* is the job ID, as displayed by atq.

cat *options file*

Print *file* to the screen.

-n

Print line numbers.

cd *directory*

Change the working directory to *directory*; if *directory* is omitted, the user's home directory is assumed.

cdrecord *options* **dev=***device file*

Burn data from *file* to the CD burner or DVD burner specified by *device*. If *file* is an ISO image, the files in the image's filesystem will be burnt onto the disk.

-sao

Write the disk in session-at-once (or disk-at-once) mode.

-tao

Write the disk in track-at-once mode.

-multi

Burn a multi-session disk; this allows you to add to the filesystem at a later date.

-eject

Automatically eject the disk once burning is complete.

speed=*n*

Burn the disk at *n*-speed.

cp *options source destination*

Copy a file or directory.

-f

If the copy tries to overwrite a file, force the overwrite, suppressing any prompts for confirmation. The opposite of this is -i, which will confirm every overwrite.

-p

Preserve all information, including file ownership.

-r

Copy files and directories recursively.

-u

Update: don't overwrite an existing file if it has the same or a more recent creation time.

chgrp *group file*

Change the group ownership of a file.

-R

Change the group ownership recursively.

-v

Be verbose in describing the ownership changes.

chkconfig *option service*

Control which services are started and stopped at given runlevels when the computer is booted.

Note that in Fedora Core 4, this tool is located in /sbin, which is not part of the default PATH.

--list

List the services installed on this system, and when they're configured to start.

--add

Add a daemon to be managed by chkconfig.

--del

Remove a daemon from chkconfig's management.

--level *level*

Configure which services start at given runlevels; *level* specifies which levels the service starts at. You'll also need to include on or off at the end of the command line. For example, `service --level 345 httpd on` sets up Apache to start at runlevels 3, 4, and 5.

chmod *options mode file*

Change file permissions (or mode).

mode comprises the following information:

❏ who these permissions apply to: group (g), owner (u), or others (o)

❏ whether the permissions are being granted (+) or denied (-)

❏ which permissions are being dealt with: write (w), read (r), and/or execute (x)

For example, u+x grants executable permission to the file's owner; g-rw denies users in the file's group read or write access.

-R

Change permissions recursively.

chown *user file*

Change file ownership.

user can be either a user name, or a user name and a group name in the form *user:group*. This will cause the owning user and group to be changed.

-R

Change ownership recursively.

-v

Print information about each file regardless of whether or not the ownership has changed.

cp *options source destination*

Copy *source* to *destination*.

-r

Copy the directory and everything it contains.

-b

When you copy a file to a location at which a file with the same name exists, -b creates a backup of the old file.

-i

Prompt the user before overwriting any files.

-u

Only replace files if the modification date of the file being copied is more recent than that of the file in the destination directory. This will ensure that you have the most up-to-date files in the destination directory.

df *options*
Produce a report of disk usage across filesystems.

-h

Display numbers in a more user-friendly form. For example, 1024 bytes would be displayed as 1k if the -h option were enabled.

-T

Include the type of filesystem in the report.

echo *text*
Print *text* to the screen.

exit
Exit from the current shell session. Run this after su to return to the original user, or, in a terminal session, to close the terminal application.

find *options expression*
Find files.

-L

Follow symbolic links.

-atime *±n*

Find files that were accessed more or less than *n* days ago. -atime +5 finds files that were accessed more than five days ago; -atime -5 finds files that were accessed less than five days ago.

-ctime *±n*

Find files that were created more or less than *n* days ago.

-mtime *±n*

Find files that were modified more or less than *n* days ago.

-name *pattern*

Find files with names that match *pattern*.

grep *options pattern file(s)*

Search files for a regular expression pattern.

-r

Read all files under this directory recursively.

-w

Match on whole words only.

groupadd *groupname*

Create a group called *groupname*.

groupdel *groupname*

Delete the specified group.

htpasswd *options filename username password*

Add users to an Apache user file. You can specify the password on the command line, or omit it to be prompted for the password.

-c

Create a new password file.

-D

Delete the specified user.

ll *options directory*

Synonymous with ls -l. See ls for more information.

ln *options linktarget link*

Create a link to *linktarget* at *link*.

-s

Create a symbolic link.

ls *options directory*

Display a list of files in the specified directory or, if no directory is specified, the working directory.

-a

Show all files, including hidden files.

-l

Show listing in long format. In Fedora Core, ll is a synonym for ls -l.

man *command*

Read the online manual for *command*. Use the up and down arrows to move through the manual, and press **Q** to quit.

mkdir *options directory*

Create a directory.

-p

Make any required parent directories. For example, `mkdir -p ~/foo/bar` would create the directories `foo` and `bar`. Without the `-p` option, this would fail.

-m *mode*

Set permissions for the new directories. *mode* is defined as for `chmod`.

mkisofs *options directory*

Create an ISO disk image containing the files from *directory*.

-f

Follow symbolic links when creating the image.

-l

Use full-length 31-character file names.

-o *filename*

Specify the location to which the disk image will be written.

-A *name*

Name the filesystem. If you burn this ISO image to a CD, this will be the disk's volume label.

mount *options device mountpoint*

Mount the specified device at the specified mount point. If *device* is omitted, `/etc/fstab` will be searched for a device with the specified mount point.

-t *type*

Specify the filesystem type (`ntfs`, `hfs`, `ext3`, etc.).

-r

Mount the file system in read-only mode.

mv *options source destination*

Move or rename a file from *source* to *destination*. mv foo /var/backup moves the file foo into the directory /var/backup; mv foo bar renames the file foo to bar.

-b

When you're moving a file to a location at which a file with the same name exists, -b will create a backup of the old file.

-i

Prompt the user before overwriting any files.

-u

Only replace files if the modification date of the file being moved is more recent than the file in the destination directory. This will give you the most up-to-date files in the destination directory.

newaliases

Inform the Sendmail daemon that its aliases file has changed.

passwd *options username*

Set the password for the user *username*. If *username* is omitted, the current user is assumed.

-u

Unlock the user's account.

-n *days*

Set the password's minimum lifetime to *days* days.

-x *days*

Set the password's maximum lifetime to *days* days.

-w *days*

Specify the number of days in advance of password expiration that the user will start to receive warnings that their password is about to expire.

pwd

Print the current working directory.

rm *options filename*

Remove a file or directory.

-f

Force the removal of the file, suppressing any prompts for confirmation. The opposite of this is -i, which will confirm the deletion of every file.

-r

Remove a directory recursively.

service *name action*

Control services or daemons installed on the system. *name* is the name of the daemon, and *action* is one of start, stop, restart, or status.

Note that in Fedora Core 4, this tool is located in /sbin, which is not part of the default PATH.

sleep *seconds*

Pause for *seconds* seconds.

shutdown *options* time

Shut down the computer safely. The time argument can be specified in hh:mm format, as a + character followed by a number of minutes, or as the word now.

Note that in Fedora Core 4, this tool is located in /sbin, which is not part of the default PATH.

-r

Reboot the computer after shutdown.

-c

Cancel a shut down. When used, shutdown does not require a time.

ssh *options username@servername command*

Connect to *servername* as *username* via SSH. If *command* is specified, it will be executed and your SSH session will be ended. If *command* is omitted, a shell session will be opened to the server.

-L *localport:servername:serverport*

Set up port forwarding over the SSH connection between *localport* and *serverport* on *servername*.

su *user*

Switch to *user* at the command line. If *user* is omitted, root is assumed.

tail *options filename*

Display the last few lines of *filename*.

-n

Display the last *n* lines. For example, `tail -7 filename` would display the last seven lines in *filename*.

-f

Display lines as they're added to the file. Press **Ctrl-C** to exit.

umount *mountpoint*

Unmount the filesystem mounted at *mountpoint*.

useradd *options username*

Create a user called *username*.

-G *groupname*

Add the new user to the group *groupname*.

-c *fullname*

Create the user with the full name *fullname*. If this name contains spaces, it should be surrounded by quotation marks; for example, `useradd -c "Robert Jones" rj` would create the user "rj" with the full name "Robert Jones."

userdel *options username*

Delete the specified user.

-r

Delete the user's home directory and any local email for that user.

vncpasswd

Set the password required to connect to a VNC server.

vncserver

Start the VNC server daemon.

wget *options url*

Download a file from a URL via HTTP, HTTPS, or FTP.

-c

Resume the download of a partially downloaded file.

`--http-user=`*user*`
`--http-password=`*password*`
> This command allows you to specify a username and password for basic HTTP authentication.

`yum` *`options command`*
> Manage installed RPM packages.

`-y`
> Automatically answer "yes" to all questions.

`install` *`package`*
> Install the latest available version of *package*.

`update` *`package`*
> Install any available updates to *package*. If *package* isn't specified, yum will update all the packages installed and managed by yum.

`check-update` *`package`*
> Check for an update to *package*. If *package* isn't specified, yum will check for updates to all packages installed and managed by yum.

`remove` *`package`*
> Remove the installation of *package* and the packages that depend on it.

`info` *`package`*
> Display a description of *package*.

`clean`
> Clean yum's cache of RPM headers.

`search` *`text`*
> Search the packages managed by yum for the string *text*.

Appendix B: Troubleshooting

This appendix lists solutions to a range of the more common problems you may experience as you work with Linux and Apache.

How can I list all the programs that are running, and kill a troublesome one?

Just as Windows users hit **Ctrl-Alt-Del** to show the Task Manager, Fedora users can access Applications > System Tools > System Monitor to start the System Monitor. This tool allows you very simply to select a process; hit End Process to kill it.

If you prefer to work from the command line, you can list all the processes running on the machine using the ps command:

```
[kermit@swinetrek ~]$ ps axu
USER       PID %CPU %MEM    VSZ    RSS TTY    STAT START TIME COMMAND
root         1  0.0  0.4   1744    544 ?      S    Nov01 0:04 init [5]
root         2  0.0  0.0      0      0 ?      SN   Nov01 0:00 [ksofirq]
root         3  0.0  0.0      0      0 ?      S    Nov01 0:00 [watcdog]
root         4  0.0  0.0      0      0 ?      S<   Nov01 0:00 [evens/0]
root         5  0.0  0.0      0      0 ?      S<   Nov01 0:00 [khelper]
...
kermit    2447  0.0  3.4  22196   4300 ?      S    Nov01 0:10 /usr/libe
snort     2516  0.2  9.2  50544  11624 ?      Ss   Nov01 0:48 /usr/sbin
root     28872  0.0  2.2  10864   2868 ?      S    Nov01 0:01 smbd -D
root     29809  0.0  1.7   7248   2260 ?      Ss   Nov01 0:00 sshd: ker
kermit   29812  0.0  1.8   7248   2332 ?      S    Nov01 0:00 sshd: ker
kermit   29813  0.0  1.1   4384   1408 pts/1  Ss   Nov01 0:00 -bash
kermit   30227  0.0  0.7   4488    936 pts/1  R+   00:46 0:00 ps axu
[kermit@swinetrek ~]$
```

To search for a particular process, use grep on the output of ps:

```
[kermit@swinetrek ~]$ ps axu | grep snort
snort     2516  0.2  9.2  50544 9636 ?       Ss   Nov01 0:48
    /usr/sbin/snort -A fast -b -d -D -i eth0 -u snort -g snort
    -c /etc/snort/snort.conf -l /var/log/snort
kermit   30403  0.0  0.3   3732  384 pts/1   R+   01:01 0:00
```

```
    grep snort
[kermit@swinetrek ~]$
```

The second column—2516 in the above example—identifies the process ID. Kill the process by passing that process ID to the kill command:

```
[root@swinetrek kermit]# kill 2516
[root@swinetrek kermit]#
```

My machine won't boot! How do I fix it?

If your machine won't boot at all, you need to use a rescue disk. Linux is available in Live CD form, which is a full Linux installation that runs entirely from a CD without touching the machine's hard disks. Fortunately, you can boot a Live CD and then look at the hard disks from the Live CD environment.

Before you boot from a Live CD, watch the failing boot process. Linux tries to be verbose about errors that occur while the system is booting; make a note of anything that fails. Often, the best way to find a remedy for this kind of problem is to search the Web for the error message that the system displays. Of course, once you've identified what the error is, you'll need to be able to get at Linux in order to fix it; this is where the Live CD becomes useful.

There is no "official" Fedora Live CD, but many other Linux distributions offer Live CDs that will work similarly to a Fedora installation. The Berry Linux CD, which is based on Fedora Core, can be obtained from http://yui.mine.nu/linux/eberry.html, and the Ubuntu Linux CD can be downloaded from http://www.ubuntulinux.org/download/. Download the CD image from the Website, burn it to a CD, and boot your LAMP server from it.

Once the server has booted, open a Terminal. You will need to know which device is your root partition (a decision that was made when the system was installed); if the machine runs only Fedora Core, it's likely to be /dev/VolGroup00/LogVol00. Execute the following commands:

```
$ su
Password:
# mkdir /tmp/hd
# mount /dev/VolGroup00/LogVol00 /tmp/hd
#
```

The files in your root partition will now be available in the directory /tmp/hd, and you can make alterations to them as necessary.

I've forgotten my root password. How can I reset it?

Boot from your Fedora CD, and type **linux rescue** at the boot prompt. This will boot you into "single-user mode" in your Linux installation, and log you in as root. Enter passwd, and you'll be able to change your root password. After you do so, remove the CD from the machine and reboot (enter **reboot**). Your root password will be changed.

Programs are failing oddly. What's going on?

Programs can fail oddly for a number of possible reasons, but a common explanation is that you're out of disk space. Check the disk usage in a Terminal with the **df** command:

```
[kermit@swinetrek ~]$ df -h
Filesystem            Size  Used Avail Use% Mounted on
/dev/mapper/VolGroup00-LogVol00
                       12G  1.8G  8.8G  17% /
/dev/hda2              99M  9.8M   84M  11% /boot
/dev/shm               62M     0   62M   0% /dev/shm
[kermit@swinetrek ~]$
```

The Used and Avail columns show how much space is used and available on each partition on your machine. If a partition is nearly or completely full, it may be the cause of your problem; find some files to delete from that partition to see if it helps. Good candidates are log files, which are stored in the /var/log directory.

A service isn't running. What's the problem?

You can stop and start services using the Service Configuration tool (Desktop > System Settings > Server Settings > Services), but if a service keeps stopping, you may want to try restarting it from the command line: if an error occurs while running the service from the command line, the error may be displayed. Restart the service using /sbin/service *daemonname* start, and watch to see whether any errors are displayed.

If restarting the service doesn't show errors, then it's worth investigating any log files that the service creates. You already know about the log files Apache stores in /var/log/apache; look in /var/log to see if a log file exists for your failing service, and check the system logs.

I can't see the network. What should I do?

You already know most of the steps to take if your LAMP server can't see the network: check that the cable's plugged in, that the machine next to it can see the network, and that the light on the network card is flashing. All of the common command line network tools, like ping and traceroute, are available on Linux. It may also be worth checking the output of ifconfig:

```
[kermit@swinetrek ~]$ /sbin/ifconfig -a
[kermit@swinetrek ~]$ /sbin/ifconfig -a
eth0 Link encap:Ethernet  HWaddr 00:03:FF:42:1E:92
     inet addr:192.168.69.3 Bcast:192.168.255.255 Mask:255.255.0.0
     inet6 addr: fe80::203:ffff:fe42:1e92/64 Scope:Link
     UP BROADCAST RUNNING MULTICAST  MTU:1500  Metric:1
     RX packets:22548 errors:0 dropped:0 overruns:0 frame:0
     TX packets:24780 errors:0 dropped:0 overruns:0 carrier:0
     collisions:0 txqueuelen:1000
     RX bytes:2294916 (2.1 MiB)  TX bytes:18896789 (18.0 MiB)
     Interrupt:11 Base address:0xa000

lo   Link encap:Local Loopback
     inet addr:127.0.0.1  Mask:255.0.0.0
     inet6 addr: ::1/128 Scope:Host
     UP LOOPBACK RUNNING  MTU:16436  Metric:1
```

```
        RX packets:31198 errors:0 dropped:0 overruns:0 frame:0
        TX packets:31198 errors:0 dropped:0 overruns:0 carrier:0
        collisions:0 txqueuelen:0
        RX bytes:24317998 (23.1 MiB)  TX bytes:24317998 (23.1 MiB)

sit0 Link encap:IPv6-in-IPv4
        NOARP  MTU:1480  Metric:1
        RX packets:0 errors:0 dropped:0 overruns:0 frame:0
        TX packets:0 errors:0 dropped:0 overruns:0 carrier:0
        collisions:0 txqueuelen:0
        RX bytes:0 (0.0 b)  TX bytes:0 (0.0 b)

[kermit@swinetrek ~]$
```

The key line above is highlighted in bold: it lists the IP address of the `eth0` interface. If that line doesn't appear, the interface doesn't have an IP address. A quick solution is to restart networking with `service network restart`, and see if that brings the network interface back to life.

 Tip

Be Careful!

If you're working remotely on a machine that has two network cards, be aware that this action will briefly drop all the network connections to the machine. If you're connected by SSH, that SSH connection will be dropped, too. If you can, restart networking from the machine itself, rather than over a network connection.

Index

Symbols

! command, 96

\#

    introducing comments, 116

    root user prompt, 92

/ root directory symbol, 64

\ splitting long commands, 92

~ home directory prompt, 88

A

abstraction using symlinks, 74

access logs, Apache, 261, 264

accidental deletions, 94

acronyms, 27

Add new inbound rule dialog, Firestarter, 284, 286

Add/Remove Applications tool, 245

Additional Software screen, Fedora, 30

Administration Tools package group,
26

Administrator account (*see* root user
account)

alerts, 294

    adding, using Webmin, 213

    Snort IDS, 291

aliases file, 132

Allow connections options, Firestarter,
283

Allow lists, 179

AllowOverride directive, httpd.conf,
185

Anaconda installer, 6, 50

Anacron tool, 129

Apache configuration file (*see* httpd.conf
file)

Apache Group, history, 157

Apache Web Server, 157–196

access logs, 261, 264

configuring, 167–186

configuring for secure connections,
186–196

configuring graphically, 137

configuring with MySQL and PHP,
163–166

error logs, 166, 261

installing, 158–162

performance tuning, 181

starting and stopping, 162, 194, 196

starting automatically, 193

updates, 159

Apache Web Server module, Webmin
tool, 205

apachectl command, 162, 195, 299

Applications menu, GNOME, 58

Archive Manager, 146

at command, 131, 203, 300

auditing security, 268

authorization badge icon, 105

automatic execution with .bashrc, 111

automatic mounting, 116, 118

automatic partitioning, 11, 36

automatic starting

    Apache, 193

    services, 123, 286

automating routine tasks, 124–132

    backups, 253–260

B

background applications (*see* daemons)

backslash escaping, 91

backticks, 127

backup.sh example script, 127

backups, 253–260

    dump utility and, 117

    enterprise level tools, 260

    removing old, 85, 126

firewalls
(*see also* Security Level Configuration tool)
enabling Webmin access, 198
Fedora Core default, 20
layered security and, 268
remote configuration, 284
text-based installation, 45
Webmin Network Module and, 209
floppy disks, mounting, 112
Floppy Formatter tool, 149
forcing file deletions, 94, 307
forcing overwriting, 301
fsck utility, 117
fstab file, 114
FTP (File Transfer Protocol), 21, 207

G

gateway machines, 280
GDM (GNOME Display Manager), 60
gedit text editor, 72, 76
GNOME desktop, 55–60
(*see also* Nautilus)
bottom panel, 56
customizing the GNOME terminal, 84
gedit text editor, 72, 76
GUI naming conventions, 78
installation, 24
root password prompt, 104
top panel, 57
VNC startup and, 250
window display, 60
GNOME Display Manager (GDM), 60
GNOME Terminal application, 84
GNU Privacy Guard (GPG), 161
graphical installation, 5–31
grep command, 304, 311
group permissions, 71
groupadd command, 110, 304
groupdel command, 112, 304

groups, software (*see* package groups)
groups, users (*see* user groups)
GRUB boot loader, 16, 39
Boot Configuration tool and, 139
boot loader location, 43
Webmin and, 210
GUI based editors, 76

H

Hardware Browser, Fedora, 150
hardware compatibility lists, 2–3
Hardware Group Modules, Webmin, 210–211
hello_world.sh example, 97
help, online, 26, 94, 299
hidden files, 89, 111
history command, 95
/home directory, 65
home directory, returning to, 90
Home icon, filesystem view, 70
host keys, SSH, 231
.htaccess file, 183–184
htpasswd tool, 184, 304
HTTP
Apache server default ports, 169
graphical configuration tool, 137
HTTP configuration tool, Fedora, 167–183
HTTP daemon, 119, 158
httpd.conf file, 167
apachectl tool and, 163
configuring Apache to use certificates, 195
editing with Webmin, 205
gedit example using, 77
.htaccess and, 183
HTTP configuration tool and, 167
Kate example using, 79
stopping the Apache daemon, 194
httpd.i386 package, 160

linking (*see* symlinks)
Linux distributions, ix–xi
  (*see also* Fedora Core distribution;
    Madriva Linux; SuSE Linux)
Linux Hardware Compatibility HOW-
    TO, 3
linux rescue command, 313
LinuxQuestions.org, 3
Live CD versions of Linux, x, 312
ll command, 89, 304
Lock File option, HTTP configuration
    tool, 180
log files, 260–263
  (*see also* error logs)
    analysis with Webalizer, 207, 264–
      266
    Apache access logs, 166, 261, 264
    disk usage and, 313
    failing services, 314
log levels, 174
log rotation, 263
logging into GDM, 60
logging modes, Snort IDS, 288
logging options, HTTP configuration
    tool, 174
logging out of GDM, 61
ls command, 88, 304

M

Mac OS X, 238, 244
mail server configuration, 207
Majordomo List Manager, 206
man command, 94, 299, 305
Mandriva Linux
    Drak Suite, 28, 167
    hardware compatibility lists, 3
memory
    installation requirements, 31
    usage, System Monitor, 155
menus, GNOME top panel, 58
mkisofs command, 257, 259, 305

mount command, 112, 305
    fstab file and, 117
mount points, 66
    filesystem assignment, 63
    fstab listings, 116
    naming conventions, 117
    selecting, 14
mouse, three-button, 256
mrtg package, 208
multi-user mode, 121
MultiViews option, virtual host, 178
mv command, 92, 306
MySQL daemon, 119
MySQL database server
    connection tools, 25
    installing, 163
    Webmin module, 206

N

name based virtual hosts, 171
naming conventions
    desktop environments and, 78
    mount points, 117
National Center for Supercomputing
    Applications (NCSA), 158
Nautilus, 68
    creating symlinks, 74
    trash function compared with rm
      command, 87
network card detection, 280, 315
Network Configuration page, Webmin,
    209
Network Configuration tool, 142
network devices, configuring, 150
Network File System (NFS), 136
    turning off nonessential services, 286
    Webmin Network Module and, 209
network invisibility, 314
network resources and runlevels, 121
Network Servers package group, 25
network settings, 142

Books for Web Developers from SitePoint

Visit http://www.sitepoint.com/books/
for sample chapters or to order!

3rd Edition
Covers PHP5, MySQL4
and Mac OS X

Build Your Own

Database Driven Website

Using PHP & MySQL

By Kevin Yank

A Practical Step-by-Step Guide

The PHP Anthology

Object Oriented PHP Solutions

Volume I

By Harry Fuecks

Practical Solutions to Common Problems

sitepoint

The PHP Anthology

Object Oriented PHP Solutions
Volume II

By Harry Fuecks

Practical Solutions to Common Problems

NO NONSENSE
XML WEB
DEVELOPMENT
WITH PHP

BY **THOMAS MYER**

MASTER PHP 5'S POWERFUL NEW XML FUNCTIONALITY

Build Your Own

ASP.NET Website

Using C# & VB.NET

By Zak Ruvalcaba

A Practical Step-by-Step Guide

HTML Utopia:

Designing Without Tables

Using CSS

By Dan Shafer

A Practical Step-by-Step Guide

THE CSS ANTHOLOGY

101 ESSENTIAL TIPS, TRICKS & HACKS

BY RACHEL ANDREW

THE MOST COMPLETE QUESTION AND ANSWER BOOK ON CSS

DHTML UTOPIA:
MODERN
WEB DESIGN
USING
JAVASCRIPT & DOM

BY **STUART LANGRIDGE**

PRACTICAL UNOBTRUSIVE JAVASCRIPT TECHNIQUES

BUILD YOUR OWN

STANDARDS COMPLIANT WEBSITE USING DREAMWEAVER 8

BY **RACHEL ANDREW**

A PRACTICAL STEP-BY-STEP GUIDE TO MASTERING DREAMWEAVER 8

Flash
MX 2004

The Flash Anthology

Cool Effects &
Practical ActionScript

By Steven Grosvenor

Practical Solutions to Common Problems

Kits for Web Professionals
from SitePoint

Available exclusively from
http://www.sitepoint.com/

Dreaming of running your own successful Web Design or Development business?

This kit contains everything you need to know!

The Web Design Business Kit

Whether you are thinking of establishing your own Web Design or Development business or are already running one, this kit will teach you everything you need to know to be successful...

Two ring-bound folders and a CD-ROM jam packed with expert advice and proven ready-to-use business documents that will help you establish yourself, gain clients, and grow a profitable freelance business!

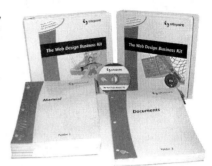

Folder 1:
Covers advice on every aspect of running your business:

- *How to sell yourself*
- *How to land bigger jobs*
- *What to charge*
- *How to keep clients for life*
- *How to manage budgets*
- *How to hire & fire employees*
- *And much more*

Folder 2:
Contains 64 essential, ready-to-use business documents:

- *Business Plan*
- *Sample Proposal & Contract*
- *Client Needs Analysis Form*
- *Marketing Surveys*
- *Employment Documents*
- *Financial Documents*
- *And much more*

CD-ROM:
Contains electronic copies of all the business documents in Folder 2, so you can apply them instantly to your business!

- *Ready to apply*
- *Easily customizable*
- *MS Word & Excel format*

The Web Design Business Kit is available exclusively through sitepoint.com. To order, get more information, or to download the free sample chapters, visit:

www.sitepoint.com/books/freelance1/

What our customers have to say about the Web Design Business Kit:

"The Web Design Business Kit (Documents & Manual) is the best marketing tool that I have found! It has changed my business strategies, and my income."

Barb Brown
www.barbbrown.com

"We've already closed 2 deals by following the suggested steps in the kit! I feel like I shouldn't pass the word about this kit to others or risk a lot of good competition!"

Jeneen McDonald
www.artpoststudios.com

"Of everything I have purchased on the Internet, related to business and not, this is (without question) the most value for the money spent. Thank you."

Thom Parkin
www.twice21.com